Law, Society, Policy series

Series Editor: **Rosie Harding**,
University of Birmingham

Law, Society, Policy offers an outlet for high quality, socio-legal research monographs and edited collections with the potential for policy impact.

Also available in the series

Intersex Embodiment
Legal Frameworks beyond Identity and Disorder
By **Fae Garland** and **Mitchell Travis**

Unsettling Apologies
Critical Writings on Apology from South Africa
Edited by **Melanie Judge** and **Dee Smythe**

Death, Family and the Law
The Contemporary Inquest in Context
By **Edward Kirton-Darling**

Deprivation of Liberty in the Shadows of the Institution
By **Lucy Series**

Women, Precarious Work and Care
The Failure of Family-friendly Rights
By **Emily Grabham**

Pandemic Legalities
Legal Responses to COVID-19 – Justice and Social Responsibility
Edited by **Dave Cowan** and **Ann Mumford**

Forthcoming

Fragile Rights
Disability, Public Policy and Social Change
By **Anne Revillard**

Find out more at

bristoluniversitypress.co.uk/law-society-policy

Forthcoming

Egalitarian Digital Privacy
Image Based Abuse and Beyond
By **Tsachi Keren-Paz**

Observing Justice
Digital Transparency, Openness and Accountability in Criminal Courts
By **Judith Townend** and **Lucy Welsh**

Children's Voices, Family Disputes and Child-Inclusive Mediation
The Right to Be Heard
By **Anne Barlow** and **Jan Ewing**

Adult Social Care Law and Policy
Lessons from the Pandemic
By **Jean McHale** and **Laura Noszlopy**

Find out more at
bristoluniversitypress.co.uk/law-society-policy

POLYGAMY, POLICY AND POSTCOLONIALISM IN ENGLISH MARRIAGE LAW

A Critical Feminist Analysis

Zainab Batul Naqvi

BRISTOL
UNIVERSITY
PRESS

First published in Great Britain in 2023 by

Bristol University Press
University of Bristol
1–9 Old Park Hill
Bristol
BS2 8BB
UK
t: +44 (0)117 374 6645
e: bup-info@bristol.ac.uk

Details of international sales and distribution partners are available at bristoluniversitypress.co.uk

British Library Cataloguing in Publication Data
A catalogue record for this book is available from the British Library

ISBN 978-1-5292-0969-3 hardcover
ISBN 978-1-5292-1081-1 ePub
ISBN 978-1-5292-1080-4 ePdf

Cover design: Andrew Corbett
Front cover image: Getty Images/Wenyi Liu
Bristol University Press use environmentally responsible print partners.
Printed and bound in Great Britain by CPI Group (UK) Ltd, Croydon, CR0 4YY

For You

Contents

Series Editor's Preface

The Law, Society, Policy series publishes high-quality, socio-legal research monographs and edited collections with the potential for policy impact. Cutting across the traditional divides of legal scholarship, Law, Society, Policy off ers an interdisciplinary, policy engaged approach to socio-legal research which explores law in its social and political contexts with a particular focus on the place of law in everyday life.

The series seeks to take an explicitly society-first view of socio-legal studies, with a focus on the ways that law shapes social life, and the constitutive nature of law and society. International in scope, engaging with domestic, international and global legal and regulatory frameworks, texts in the Law, Society, Policy series engage with the full range of socio-legal topics and themes.

List of Cases

Rye v Fuliambe (1602) Moo KB 683
Porter's case (1637) Cro Car 461
Middleton's case (1638) Kelyng 27
William's case (1641) March 101
Dodgson v Haswell (1730), PRO DEL/412
Andreas v Andreas (1737) 1 Hag Con (App) 10n; 161 ER 636
Vigevena and Silveira v Alvarez (1794) 1 Hag Con (App) 8n; 161 ER 636
Lady D'Aguilar v Baron D'Aguilar (1794) 1 Hag Ecc 773; 161 ER 748
Dalrymple v Dalrymple (1811) 2 Hag Con 54
Deane v Thomas (1829) Moo & Malk 361; 31 Rev Rep 738
R v Millis (1843–44) 10 Cl & F 534; 8 ER 844
Thelwell v Yelverton (1864) 16 CB NS 813; 143 ER 1346
Hyde v Hyde and Woodmansee [1866] LR1 P & D 130
In Re Bethell Bethell v Hildyard (1887) 38 Ch D 220
Choo Eng Choon v Neo Chan Neo (1908) SSLR 120
Chetti v Chetti [1909] P 67
Cheang Thye Phin and Others Appellants v Tan Ah Loy (Since Deceased) [1920] AC 369
Khoo Hooi Leong Appellant v Khoo Hean Kwee Respondent [1926] AC 529
Khoo Hooi Leong Appellant v Khoo Chong Yeok Respondent [1930] AC 346
The Sinha Peerage Claim HL Deb 12 December 1935 vol 99 cc 224–32
Srini Vasan v Srini Vasan [1946] P 67
Risk (Otherwise Yerburgh) v Risk [1951] P 50
Matthew Olajide Bamgbose v John Bankole Daniel 1952 14 WACA 111–15
Matthew Olajide Bamgbose, Appellant v John Bankole Daniel and Others, Respondents [1955] AC 107
Muhammad v Suna 1956 SC 366
Ohochuku v Ohochuku [1960] 1 WLR 183
Sowa v Sowa [1960] 3 WLR 733
Khan v Khan [1962] 3 FLR 496
Khan v Khan [1963] VR 203
Shahnaz v Rizwan [1964] 3 WLR 759
Imam Din v National Assistance Board [1967] 2 WLR 257

Crowe v Kader [1968] WAR 122
Indyka v Indyka [1969] 1 AC 33
Radwan v Radwan (No 2) [1972] 3 WLR 939; [1973] Fam 35
R v Sagoo (Mohinder Singh) (1975) 61 Cr App R 191
Nabi (Ghulam) v Heaton (Inspector of Taxes) [1981] 1 WLR 1052
Hussain v Hussain [1982] 3 WLR 679; [1983] Fam 26
Vervaeke v Smith (Messina and A-G Intervening) [1983] 1 AC 145
Lawrence v Lawrence [1985] FLR 1097
Re Spence, deceased [1990] 1 Ch 652
ECmHR Appl 19628/92, *Bibi v UK* (Dec) 29 June 1992
Zeenat Bibi v Secretary of State for the Home Department [1994] Imm AR 550
R v Immigration Appeal Tribunal Ex p Begum (Hasna) [1995] Imm AR 249
Khan v UK (1996) 21 EHRR CD67
R v Department of Health Ex p Misra [1996] 1 FLR 128
Gereis v Yagoub [1997] 1 FLR 854
Bibi v Chief Adjudication Officer [1998] 1 FLR 375
Azad v Entry Clearance Officer, Dhaka 2000 WL 1918688
Chief Adjudication Officer v Bath [2000] 1 FLR 8
A-M v A-M (Divorce: Jurisdiction: Validity of Marriage) [2001] 2 FLR 6
ECO New Delhi v SG [2012] UKUT 00265 (IAC)
Suzia Abdin v Entry Clearance Officer, Dhaka [2012] UKUT 00309 (IAC)
Akhter v Khan [2018] EWFC 54
NA v Secretary of State for Work and Pensions [2019] 1 WLR 6321
Her Majesty's Attorney General (Appellant) v Nasreen Akhter and Mohammed Shabaz Khan (Respondents) and Fatima Mohammed Hussain and Southall Black Sisters (Interveners) [2020] EWCA Civ 122

List of Legislation

Statutes

Marriage Act 1540

An Act to restrain all Persons from Marriage until their former Wives and former Husbands be dead 1604

An Act for granting to his Majesty certain rates and duties upon marriages, births and burials, and upon batchelors and widowers, for the term of five years for carrying on the war against France with vigour 1694 6 & 7 W 3 c 6

Clandestine Marriages Act 1753

Offences Against the Person Act 1828

Marriage Act 1836

Marriage and Registration Act 1856

Divorce and Matrimonial Causes Act 1857

Offences Against the Person Act 1861

Statute Law Revision Act 1892 (c 19)

Marriage Act 1949

Income and Corporation Taxes Act 1970

Matrimonial Proceedings (Polygamous Marriages) Act 1972

Matrimonial Causes Act 1973

National Health Service (Superannuation) Regulations 1980

Children Act 1989

Private International Law (Miscellaneous Provisions) Act 1995

Civil Partnership Act 2004

Marriage (Same Sex Couples) Act 2013

Anti-social Behaviour, Crime and Policing Act 2014

The Civil Partnership (Opposite-sex Couples) Regulations 2019

Divorce, Dissolution and Separation Act 2020

Domestic Abuse Act 2021

Bills

Arbitration and Mediation Services (Equality) Bill [HL] 2016–17

Acknowledgements

If someone asked me what my best advice is for writing a book during a pandemic, I would say don't do it. That being said, I did, and it took a village (or two!) to help this book to come into existence. There are so many people who have been on this journey with me, and I am grateful to all of them for their presence in my life. Doing a research project and writing a book are lonely ventures. I am increasingly aware of how much the academy and institutional pressures can take away the joy and pleasure of writing. I have never forgotten the wonderful Ambreena Manji's comment about being willing to go through the "pain of writing". We write because we have to, we write because we need to, and above all we write because it should be us doing the writing.

I started this project almost a decade ago with the support of the Economic and Social Research Council and am very fortunate to have received this funding. Moreover, I am indebted to my supervisors Rosie Harding, Sonia Harris-Short and Anastasia Vakulenko for their support and guidance while completing the doctoral research that this book is based on. To my colleagues at Birmingham, Coventry and De Montfort universities who provided me with the support and space to try out arguments and whinge about anything and everything – thank you for your patience and encouragement.

A number of people were extremely generous with their time as they read drafts of chapters: Farzana Azad (my accountability angel!), Kay Lalor, Sharon Thompson, Kate Cross, Máiréad Enright, Nadine El-Enany and Amina Easat-Daas. Thank you so much to you all for your encouragement, care and support. I also owe special thanks to Rebecca Probert for answering my technical questions about the law and for generously sharing her work with me.

When I completed my doctoral studies and threw myself into full-time academic life, it took time for me to find myself and regain my voice as a writer, and it was only with the help of my lovely friends and colleagues that this was possible: my fellow wenches on the board of *Feminist Legal Studies*, who surround me with love and humour; and mentors who have happily embraced me along the way – especially Ambreena Manji and

Rajnaara Akhtar, who welcomed me into their homes and families. I can never thank you enough.

My family have been my comfort and shelter throughout this experience. Thank you for everything. I love you.

Finally, to the strong, inspiring, gracious women who spoke with me, shared with me and trusted me for this project – you made me laugh and you made me cry; thank you for teaching me so many things and being so giving. This book only exists because of you.

Earlier versions of chapters in the book were adapted and published as the following:

Naqvi, Z. (2016) 'It's Women Who Suffer from a Lack of Recognition of Polygamous Marriage', *The Conversation*, [online] 11 May, Available from: https://theconversation.com/its-women-who-suffer-from-a-lack-of-recognition-of-polygamous-marriage-56406 [Accessed 26 January 2022].

Naqvi, Z.B. (2017) 'A Contextualised Historical Account of Changing Judicial Attitudes to Polygamous Marriage in the English Courts', *International Journal of Law in Context*, 13(3): 408–28.

Naqvi, Z. (2020) '*Nikah* Ceremonies in the UK: A Tool for Empowerment?', in R.C. Akhtar, P. Nash and R. Probert (eds) *Cohabitation and Religious Marriage: Status, Similarities and Solutions*, Bristol: Bristol University Press, pp 103–16.

1

Introduction: Polygamy, Law and Women's Lives

What do you think about when you hear the word 'polygamy'? When I think about this word, which refers to when someone is married to more than one person at the same time,[1] a childhood memory comes to mind. I am looking through some old photographs in the spare bedroom, and I come across the picture of a woman. She is standing in prayer, her eyes downcast with a serene expression on her face. I have never seen this woman before and take the picture to my dad to ask who she is. He tells me nonchalantly that the woman is his Bari Amma or elder mother. Bari Amma was my third grandmother (or maybe my first, since she was the eldest). She was married to my paternal grandfather, or dada, but she was unable to have children so she gave her husband permission to marry my biological grandmother, my Granny. My dad and his siblings harbour genuine affection for Bari Amma. Even now, something will trigger a memory of her in my dad and he will smile at the thought. Bari Amma never lived permanently with my dad's family, although she was especially attached to one of my uncles. Beyond this, I know little else about her. She and my grandfather passed away before I was born and so I never saw her or my Granny as actively polygamous wives. There was never any judgement of Bari Amma or of my grandparents' polygamy; they simply were, and are, a part of my rich family history.

This book is a response to my increasing curiosity about how women like Granny and Bari Amma are seen and treated in English law and policy.[2]

---

1 There are two main categories of polygamy: polygyny, where a man is married to multiple women, and polyandry, where a woman is married to multiple men. Polyandry is extremely rare, so I am generally referring to polygyny when I use the term 'polygamy' in the book.

2 The focus of this book is English law, so all references to law and policy, unless I state otherwise, relate to this framework which applies to England and Wales. I also refer to the UK context surrounding the women whose stories are shared in the book. In specific

I present the first exploration of the English legal framework on polygamous marriages, with an analysis of over 50 cases, drawing on critical postcolonial feminist perspectives.[3] I also share the stories of 26 women who spoke with me about their experiences and views around polygamy and marriage in law, society, culture and religion in the first empirical project of this kind in the UK. I situate English legal responses to polygamy in their wider context and disrupt the dominant narratives that have shaped them, arguing that the law in this area is severely outdated and remains heavily influenced by racist, sexist, imperialist and orientalist attitudes. These unacceptable attitudes are visible in wider social and cultural views of polygamy, which fail to reflect the wide spectrum of women's lived experiences and opinions in this area.

In recent times, the law has changed significantly to reflect expanding conceptions of marriage and the family in the UK. We have seen the formation of civil partnerships, an alternative legally recognised relationship that both same-sex and heterosexual couples can celebrate, as well as the recognition of same-sex marriage (see the Civil Partnership Act 2004, The Civil Partnership (Opposite-sex Couples) Regulations 2019 and the Marriage (Same Sex Couples) Act 2013). These reforms indicate a move in English law towards recognition of relationships that defy traditional understandings of marriage. Further, informal relationships like cohabitation have been attracting attention, with some scholars considering whether there should be some form of legal recognition and protection for participants (see, for example, Barlow, 2004; 2020).

Despite all this critical work around the family and marriage in law, polygamy remains on the margins. It tends to be examined within other scholarly debates around non-legally binding marriages, religious-only divorces, the regulation of informal religious arbitration forums (like shari'a councils) and more general work on cultural diversity and ethnic minority groups in English law (see, for example, Poulter, 1986; Jones and Gnanapala,

---

instances – around identity, citizenship and immigration, for example – the term 'British' is used. I use these various labels, but for clarity, it is English legal responses that are the subject of the book.

3 There is a lot of debate around the most appropriate terminology for exposing and challenging colonial legacies. The terms 'anti-colonial', 'decolonial' and 'critical postcolonial' have their own nuances, but they all reflect the same core mission: to resist colonialism in all its forms (Hiraide, 2021). After all, '[w]orking against colonialism, imperialism, and white heteropatriarchal supremacy takes many languages and vocabularies' (Lyons et al, 2017). I use 'critical postcolonial' in this book to signify that I challenge the idea of a 'post' colonial world while still recognising the decolonial and anti-colonial work that is being done around polygamy, so these terms may also appear in the book at times. The terms are not interchangeable, and I do not use one with the intention of erasing the relevance of the others. Rather, I am inspired by their common foundations to carry out my exploration of polygamy in English law.

2000; Shah and Menski, 2006; Parveen, 2018). This is mirrored in various policy papers, such as the Casey Review on opportunity and integration (Casey, 2016) and the Siddiqui Report on the application of 'shari'a law' (Home Office, 2018). These papers are not helpful. The Casey Review asserts that religious-only polygyny is more commonplace than we think, but bases the claim on 'accusations, anecdotes and assertions encountered throughout our engagement' (Casey, 2016: para 8.45). The Siddiqui Report adopts a more measured tone and merely talks about the need to consider polygamy as an issue in a deeper review of shari'a councils, but the report was commissioned by the Counter Extremism Unit so it reflects a particular agenda. The framing of polygamy and religious arbitration forums as issues for counter-extremism and integration policy is worrying. These reports have a political agenda that we also see manifested in Baroness Cox's Arbitration and Mediation Services (Equality) Bill [HL] 2016–17, which proposes legislation to limit the role and power of shari'a councils. These examples are all loosely linked to polygamous marriage but display wider anxieties about minoritised communities' lives and families and their compatibility with English law and society.

Amid these indirect moves against polygamy, there are a few notable works providing insight into English legal responses to it, such as Jones and Gnanapala's (2000) examination of broader judicial attitudes in case law towards the practice or Shah's (2003) exploration from a legal pluralist perspective of polygamy in relation to family reunion and immigration. There are also broader historical studies, such as Witte's (2015) exploration of polygamy in the West, that include a consideration of past English legal responses. These works highlight the usefulness of looking more deeply at the law to highlight the ways it can affect individuals, but they are not rooted in the real experiences of people practising polygamy. There is very little empirical research based on original data or information on the experiences of polygamous wives in England and Wales for me to draw on. Wing's (2001) examination of legal responses to polygamy in Southern Africa, Black Britain and Black America provides one of the rare examples of empirical, people-centred research on polygamy that includes the UK. Wing narrates the details of what seem to be informal personal interactions with polygamous families in the UK, but the research seems to be more of a scoping exercise on what in-depth research in this area could look like. More recently, in the largest study of Muslim marriage to date, carried out for a television programme that aired in 2017, just over 10 per cent of 903 women interviewed in the UK were in non-legally binding polygamous Muslim marriages (Akhtar, 2017). However, the prevalence of this type of polygamy is a tangential finding rather than the main subject of investigation, so it does not tell us much about this sort of relationship in a wider sense. A detailed exploration of non-legally binding ceremonies, which could include polygamy, was undertaken in England and Wales in 2022, but again this does not directly engage with polygamy or offer much detail (Probert et al, 2022).

Polygamous marriages in English law and policy

There is a very long history of polygamy in Britain. From accounts of polygamist kings in pre-Christian ancient Britain to records of the monk Augustine asking for guidance from Pope Gregory I about how to approach the polygamous Anglo-Saxons in AD 579 (Chapman, 2001). Polygamy is therefore not alien to Britain.

The appearance of this relationship before the courts is also well-documented, with the first recorded definition of marriage in English law being laid down in a judicial decision that was about polygamy. *Hyde v Hyde and Woodmansee* [1866] LR 1 P & D 130 (hereafter *Hyde*) was about John Hyde, who had left his Mormon Christian community and wife in Utah to return to England. After he left, in line with local custom, his wife had married another man, even though she and Hyde were still married. Hyde petitioned for a divorce in the English courts, and Lord Penzance decided that for matrimonial relief purposes, the relationship did not fall within the definition of marriage. The judge said: 'I conceive that marriage, as understood in Christendom, may for this purpose be defined as the voluntary union for life of one man and one woman to the exclusion of all others' (*Hyde* [1866]: 130).

Clearly, Hyde's marriage, which involved two men and one woman, did not fall within Lord Penzance's definition, although, even in 1866, there were many marriages that would have equally fallen foul of his statement – marriages where there was force or coercion so that the parties were not in a voluntary union or marriages where one party was unfaithful so there was more than one man and one woman in the relationship. And there was certainly no room for divorce once you were married. This definition is therefore more accurately understood as Lord Penzance's idealistic view of marriage in England, wherein parties should be voluntarily married, monogamous, heterosexual and faithful for life (Poulter, 1979; Probert, 2007). This definition may be based on wishful thinking, but legal perspectives on marriage remain influenced by this idealistic approach.

It has never been possible to enter into a legally recognised polygamous marriage in the UK, and any ceremony of this nature would be void (s 11(d) Matrimonial Causes Act 1973). If you are a British citizen or domiciled in the UK and celebrate a polygamous marriage inside or outside of the state, the marriage would be seen as void in the English courts (s 47 Matrimonial Causes Act 1973 as amended by s 5(1) Private International Law (Miscellaneous Provisions) Act 1995). For an individual who celebrates their first marriage abroad in a place that permits polygamy and then comes to the UK and adopts it as their home or domicile, their first marriage is converted to a legally recognised monogamous one.[4] If they try to celebrate another marriage in the UK while their first marriage subsists, they will have committed bigamy (see *R v Sagoo (Mohinder Singh)* (1975) 61 Cr App R 191). Bigamy is the criminal offence defined as occurring when a lawfully married person who is domiciled or resident in the UK enters into a second legally binding marriage while their first marriage subsists (s 57 Offences Against the Person Act 1861). Bigamy therefore criminalises situations where a person celebrates multiple marriage ceremonies that would be valid in English law. In this way, the offence criminalises any attempts to practise polygamy in a legal or formal sense in England and Wales.

So, even with recent legal developments around same-sex marriages, no-fault divorce and the prevention of forced marriages, Lord Penzance's idealised picture has not been fully dismantled.[5] Polygamy has been practised for millennia, and its existence has been documented in at least 80 per cent of societies around the world, including England, but this is hardly recognised in English law (İbiloğlu et al, 2018). Yet British citizens and domiciliaries continue to celebrate polygamous marriages in England and Wales. The form and substance of these marriages do not fit within the *Hyde* definition or within legal understandings of a valid marriage, but the parties still see themselves as married. These marriages can be celebrated in religious or customary ceremonies at a domestic level but are not legally binding. They could also be celebrated overseas, but again, while they may be valid in the place of celebration and in other states, they would not be seen as legally binding in English law.

In terms of law reform, polygamous marriages have not generally captivated law and policy makers, and changes to the framework have been few and far between. It was not until 1971 that the Law Commission examined and published a report on polygamous marriages, although in the intervening period, polygamous marriages were being recognised for certain legal purposes by the courts and authorities. The report recommended the abolishment of the rule laid down in *Hyde* in 1866 that a person in a polygamous marriage is automatically barred from matrimonial remedies and relief. It therefore took 105 years for reform to be recommended at a legislative level. The 1971 report was followed by a report in 1985 by the Law Commission and the Scottish Law Commission, which confirmed that

---

4 This first marriage abroad would be monogamous in law and fact.

5 Forced marriages were criminalised in the Anti-social Behaviour, Crime and Policing Act 2014. The Divorce, Dissolution and Separation Act 2020, which eliminated fault from the divorce process, came into force in April 2022.

because of increased immigration to the UK, the law needed to respond to the greater diversity in marriage practices. Ten years after the 1985 report was published, the recommendations were implemented into legislation, which means the last significant development to the law happened almost three decades ago. Polygamy has not been looked at by the Law Commission since. In 2015, in its review of the Offences Against the Person Act 1861, the Law Commission expressly stated that the offence of bigamy was outside the scope of the review (Law Commission, 2015b). In the Law Commission's review of weddings law, there is very little mention of polygamy, although emphasis has been placed on expanding the regulation of legally valid marriage ceremonies to include practices of minoritised groups (Law Commission, 2020; 2022).

From what it is to how we do it, its consequences and how we dissolve it, marriage attracts a lot of scrutiny and criticism (Davis, 2010). In the UK, this attention has led to broader and more inclusive understandings of marriage and who can be married, but polygamy remains overlooked in all of this. The conversation around polygamy has developed very little: the same arguments being made today to justify the current approach are ones that have been made for centuries. Why is this the case? There are greater forces at play here than lack of time and resources to spend on this. Polygamy has been ignored because it has been racialised and cast as inferior in the law, based on colonialist understandings of this relationship and the people who practise it.[6] For this reason, it is viewed with hostility and deemed unworthy of deeper consideration. These issues are not limited to the specific legal provisions and judicial decisions directed at polygamy, but are also relevant to legal understandings of marriage and family as a whole. The law imposes a specific definition of marriage on people which is not far off the wishful thinking of Lord Penzance in 1866 and is underpinned by colonial legacies. This is neither helpful nor realistic for many people, and we need to start having conversations around how to craft a legal framework that is responsive and suited to the needs of women in all relationships.

Key themes and arguments

Although polygamy in the UK has not attracted much attention, there is a lot of international research and literature across numerous disciplines looking at this type of marriage. Existing scholarship in this area addresses questions ranging from whether Muslim women need saving (Abu-Lughod,

[6] In recognition of the White colonialist privilege that underpins institutional processes and spaces in the UK, I use the terms 'racialised' and 'minoritised' to refer to when people and practices are marginalised, excluded or treated differently because they are not White or associated with Whiteness (see further El-Enany, 2020).

2013) to whether ethnic groups that practise polygamy engage more in civil wars (Gleditsch et al, 2011). As varied as these published works are, many of them implicitly orbit around a central question or problematic: should polygamy exist? I frame the implied question like this because by questioning its *existence*, the debate around polygamy is more extreme than merely asking whether it should be permitted. As we shall see, English law also reflects this approach by seeing polygamy as something that should or should not exist and legal responses are shaped by this paradigm. My approach in this book is not focussed on whether polygamy should exist. It has existed for a long time and is not going to disappear any time soon, regardless of how many people argue against or in favour of it. Instead, I urge us to move past this limited debate in the mainstream around polygamy's existence to think about the conditions that have shaped legal attitudes towards it and to consider how women live it and view it. From my analysis of the legal framework as well as the narratives of the women who spoke with me, I make several key arguments.

Context and disruption: the coloniality of responses to polygamy

I first argue that legal responses to polygamous marriage are embedded in and structured by coloniality. While in English domestic conceptions of marriage, the law adopts an approach of colonial indifference to polygamy, when it is encountered in the colonial or overseas context the law is openly hostile. In *Hyde*, Lord Penzance mentioned that his definition of marriage was one that was 'understood in Christendom' (*Hyde* [1866]: 130). This is an interesting choice of words for an English judge in an English court. Why was the definition not marriage as understood in England or English law? To answer this question, we need to think about the backdrop against which this case was heard. In 1866, England was at the head of an extremely large empire built by colonising other places and people around the world. In 1800 the British Empire comprised 1.5 million square miles and 20 million people; by 1900 it spanned 11 million square miles and encompassed 390 million people (Huntington, 1996). England was not just a small island in Europe; it had control, alongside other European empires, over a significant portion of the world. Therefore, we cannot make sense of Britain and its history without the empire, and the empire cannot be understood without Britain (Cannadine, 2002; Probert, 2017). The reference to Christendom alludes to this European imperial context – there was no space for polygamy in Christendom and the empire. This imperial context is hard to ignore, particularly if we think about how *Hyde* concerned a marriage conducted in the US – a former British colony.

Coloniality comprises the sexual, political, epistemic, economic, spiritual, linguistic and racial domination and exploitation of racialised groups by the dominant group. This happened in the past because of colonial rule and occurs today across the European/non-European divide (Grosfoguel, 2007). The ideology that underpinned these invasions is known as imperialism, and to justify it, colonisers orientalised the colonies by telling stories about them that were intended to make the natives[7] and their lands seem inferior and therefore in need of control (Said, 1978). Colonisers were not just interested in taking possession of physical land but also wanted to colonise the minds of natives, and this required them to destabilise native communities. To achieve this, they attacked the families, beliefs and knowledges of these communities using law and religion. Thus, the connection between marriage and religion in English law, which has always been strong, has wider implications.

A good indicator of how a people or community are seen in English law and society is to look at how their marriages are regulated. For example, historically, any legal questions concerning Jewish marriages were dealt with as a matter of foreign law because the Jewish community were seen as 'aliens' (Henriques, 1908: 406). By celebrating their marriages differently according to their different religion, a story is told in the law about about how this community deviates from the norm. By highlighting these differences, the community is orientalised and 'othered'. The legal regulation of marriage is therefore constructed around one religious ideal and how other communities fail to match it. This use of religion to determine what marriage and families should look like was heavily deployed in the imperialist civilising mission and enforced in law against colonised societies.

Colonial ideals of domesticity and the monogamous family structure were imposed on natives using imperial-approved laws and religion to strip away customary and polygamous marriages (McClintock, 1995). It follows that this strategy used in the colonies is also relevant to how marriage is constructed at a domestic level in the imperial centre. The colonial context surrounding polygamous marriages in English law is not something we can confine to the past; rather, we look back in history to better make sense of the current framework (Haggis, 2003). Moreover, coloniality is not just embedded in law but also affects social, cultural and religious practice, so we need to look at the effects of the law on women's lives in a more nuanced and holistic manner. Previous scholarship looking at polygamy confirms that these marriages have been viewed through a colonialist lens in most contexts. From polygamy in the Aztec empire (Hassig, 2016) to early American history (Pearsall, 2019), the attitudes of colonialist administrators and Christian missionaries were all affected by the idea that marriage should be as Lord Penzance described

---

7 The term 'native' is rightly contested. Throughout the book I use it critically to convey the problematic perspective of the coloniser.

it: heterosexual, exclusive and monogamous. Polygamous communities and societies were and continue to be separated out from this description: they are othered and treated as inferior to White Euro-American monogamy. In keeping with the White supremacist ideals of colonial authorities, despite there being traces of polygamy in most places around the world including Europe, it has become synonymous with racialised and colonised natives as well as a particular world religion: Islam (Zeitzen, 2018). Polygamy is not something that the civilised White person engages with – it is only for the uncivilised non-White native and their religious or cultural systems: an attitude that persists today.

The limitations of this colonial approach have been exposed by the White people practising religious polygamy in Mormon Christian communities. A wealth of literature challenges the colonial mindset through critique and commentary on these communities in North America.[8] The case of *Hyde* itself was a clear challenge to the monogamous marriage ideal because the parties were White Mormons, but Lord Penzance still managed to racialise polygamy as something that does not happen in Christendom even with Mormonism being a sect of Christianity. Ertman (2010) argues that a favoured strategy of colonial states is to racialise Mormon polygamists and brand them traitors to the White race because they practise polygamy. They cannot possibly be White, because polygamists are not White. According to Joffe (2016), the growing interest in polygamy has been prompted by news reports of child abuse and grooming in these communities and increasing immigration to North America from Muslim-majority countries that allow polygamy. This demonstrates how heavily associated polygamy is with outsiders and criminal activity, leading to this question of whether it should exist.

To ask whether something that has been around for millennia should even exist is an extreme question, but views against polygamy are this extreme, and legal responses confirm this. In English law, and in the arguments against polygamy, the goal is not to prevent polygamy from happening but to eradicate it. Colonisation was a project to erase the existence of the colonised and replace them with the coloniser. This was also true of their ways of life, including their marriages. In English law, the lack of detailed or meaningful engagement with polygamy indicates that the law chooses to ignore polygamy's existence and practice in the UK. There is no

[8] This covers the Canada and the US, which are typically seen as part of the West. See, for example, Bennion (1998), Denike (2010), Ertman (2010), Chan (2011), Jacobson and Burton (2011), Campbell (2013), Sweet (2013), Calder and Beaman (2014), Johnson (2014) and Song (2016). Following Bonnett (2004), I use 'the West' to describe predominantly White nations with Christian-influenced values and institutions.

polygamy, and so there is no need for a legal approach that acknowledges it. There are various legal tactics to realise this, from what I term 'colonial indifference' towards polygamy celebrated in the UK through to outright hostility against polygamous wives and children because their presence in the UK fails to uphold the public good. These tactics focus on preserving and foregrounding monogamy as the ideal, which enjoys the privilege of being practised without question. The question of whether monogamy should exist is not asked; it is just accepted that because people are in such relationships, it should exist. As Vasallo (2019) states, monogamy is a system and compulsory form of relationship in the Western world. Marriage is subjected to a more critical view, but again, there is less emphasis on questioning whether marriage should exist (because there is no denying that it already does) and more on its forms, rights and responsibilities, and underlying aims (see, for example, Barker, 2012; Brake, 2012). The different treatment of polygamy is further demonstrated in the way 'slippery slope' arguments for same-sex marriage are tackled. For example, some argue that allowing same-sex marriage will push legal recognition down a slippery slope towards allowing polygamy, incest and bestiality (see further Macedo, 2015). Polygamy is associated with incest and bestiality despite having been a recognised form of marriage in many places for so long. Incest and bestiality are practices whose existence are rightly questioned, but should polygamy be in the same category? I argue that this perspective is racist and reflects colonial strategies to destabilise, control and erase family structures that do not fit within the compulsory monogamy ideal. Legal and policy debates therefore need to be redirected away from the question of whether polygamy should exist and instead address how to best serve the needs of its practitioners.

Another important point is that coloniality poses an additional problem for women: the 'White saviour' narrative. Racialised women are repeatedly told that they need to be saved from racialised men and that the White male coloniser is their saviour (Spivak, 1999). This dominant discourse needs disrupting. The question of whether (Muslim/racialised) women need saving is constantly reproduced in debates around minoritised practices and lives. For example, the coloniser has been desperately trying to save Muslim women from their veiled existence when really, the issue is not the veil but who they are veiled from. By being hidden from the coloniser's gaze and therefore inaccessible, the only way to expose them is to save them from themselves and their male relatives, who must be forcing them to stay hidden. This has been disrupted by critical postcolonial feminist scholars, who show how the veil is used by Muslim women to resist the colonial gaze and control (see, for example, Woodhull, 2003; Yeğenoğlu, 1998). In addition to producing a more contextualised account of English legal responses to polygamy, I disrupt the colonialist stories and narratives that dominate the legal imagination around this relationship and the perception that women need to be saved from it. I draw on women's stories of disruption around their religious and cultural practice, their experiences of equality and harm, and their views on legal recognition to complicate the stories we are told about polygamy in English law and society. This builds on the existing story-led research that has been undertaken in other contexts with an African American Muslim community (Majeed, 2015) and Canadian Mormon communities (Bennion, 1998; Campbell, 2013), to share alternative accounts of minoritised women in marriage and polygamy today.

Disrupting religion and culture: orientalist hierarchies of marriage

My second key argument is that religion and culture are highly influential in understandings and experiences of polygamous marriage but there is a tendency to collapse these two identity markers into a religio-cultural identity which is unrealistic. Instead, I frame religion and culture as dual and alternative sources of identity. They are linked but sometimes they conflict, so we need to make space for this close but complex relationship. The reference to Christendom in *Hyde* reinforces the source of Lord Penzance's ideals: religion. Even the early responses to marriage and polygamy were governed by religious authorities. Whether it was the Anglo-Saxon King Ethelred II declaring polygamy a violation of divine law in AD 994 or the debate on whether it would be preferable for Henry VIII to remain married to Catherine of Aragon and take Anne Boleyn as a second wife, we see that religion takes a central role in this area (Chapman, 2001). As Christianity became the dominant faith in England, marriage matters were ruled over by the ecclesiastical or religious courts. Eventually, the monarch and then the state took over from the religious authorities, but this does not mean that the Christian influences and rulings disappeared. Instead, Christian perspectives on marriage continue to dominate marriage law in the UK which emphasises the preference for monogamy. This leaves very little room for the alternative forms of marriage that are practised by minoritised communities. Moreover, the Christian underpinnings of marriage feed into imperialist behaviour and ideals. Religion and law were tools to colonise the minds of racialised natives and save them from themselves and their communities. The orientalised natives were not only inferior but also needed to become civilised, and by following the true Christian faith, they would be better. English law has historically been used as a tool to coerce Christian belief and practice in direct ways, and marriage law is heavily influenced by Christian ethics (Rivers, 2012). In addition, there is no separation between church and state in England – the monarch is head of both, displaying the elevated position of Christianity. The use of Christianity and law to control and oppress racialised people tells us that we need to be wary of the religious coloniality present in today's laws around marriage and the family.

This caution is also important because religion and culture are very influential for women in polygamous marriages. For example, Majeed (2015) shows us that African American Muslims who practise polygamy do so because of their religious beliefs. The same is true of Mormon women in polygamous communities in Canada and the US (Campbell, 2013; Johnson, 2014). Kaganas and Murray (1991) show that women in South Africa practise customary polygamy as part of their culture. Moreover, the concept of race treason in this context – that White polygamists are traitors to their race and therefore cannot be seen as White – shows how ethnic origin and cultural values also impact on views of polygamous women (Ertman, 2010). What is worrying is the deployment of cultural difference in law as a substitute for racial difference. Instead of race, minoritised cultures are measured against the dominant White culture and found wanting (Balibar, 1991). In private international law, which considers conflicts between the laws of different states, the assessment is not of law but of culture and society. The question being asked in conflict cases is whether the culture and society of a place are similar enough to the colonising power's domestic system. If they are, their laws might be acceptable and can therefore be considered during the proceedings. Again, the ideal is English law and the culture and society that have formed it – any system deemed inferior in the past is likely to remain that way today. This is important when thinking about legal attitudes towards polygamous marriages celebrated overseas. If the rules of private international law apply, this perception of minoritised cultures where polygamy is a norm leads to them being subjected to colonial-inspired cultural racism.

It is therefore difficult to untangle religion, culture and polygamy in the postcolonial context, and this confusion is manifested in the law and scholarship. There is a trend in research for religious and cultural identities to be combined into a singular religio-cultural identity (see, for example, Basit, 1997; Abbas, 2003; Abbas, 2010; Olds, 2010). This combination is problematic because collapsing these two markers into each other affects minoritised women more since they generally view them as distinct but linked. Another implication of having a combined religio-cultural marker is that it suggests religion and culture work together in harmony leaving no space for them to oppose and disrupt each other. In the first instance, religion is viewed through the dominant lens of Christianity in English law so the default definition of religion is tied to one faith. This means that there is a hierarchy of religions with Anglican Christianity at the top of the pyramid and everything else is either below or does not even feature. This is evidenced in the courts as well where minoritised religious beliefs are equated to cultural values which downgrades and limits them (Jivraj and Herman, 2009). The hierarchy tells the story that non-Christian religions and marriages are inferior thereby orientalising them. This conflation needs to be disrupted and so I position religion and culture as dual and alternative sources of identity which better matches minoritised people's conceptions of them (Jacobson, 1997; 1998). We need to be critical of the legal stance on minoritised religions and cultures and the complex ways they interact and impact on views and experiences of polygamy.

Disrupting harm and equality in marriage

Over the centuries, two main charges have been made against polygamy to prove that it should not exist: that it causes harm and that it leads to inequality. Countering this, my next key argument is that harm and inequalities in polygamous, and indeed all, marriages are a result of patriarchal power relations. To be clear, I am not defending polygamy as a relationship, because that would feed into the tired debate of whether polygamy should exist and we need to move beyond that. Instead, I advocate for a more nuanced and realistic engagement with polygamy and the range of experiences that women have around this practice. There is a lot of literature that supports the charges that polygamy is harmful and unequal. For example, McDermott and Monroe (2018) examined 170 countries, finding that polygynous structures increase violence against women and children, decrease rights and liberties in the state, and lead to an increase in resources being allocated to buying weapons. Speaking from a similar context, Bailey and Kaufman (2010) find that in the places it is practised, polygamy is generally part of a package of laws and policies that maintain gender inequality that also includes one-sided divorce and unequal access to education and economic opportunities. Looking at this in more depth, polygamy is viewed as harmful because it is structurally inegalitarian in both practice and theory (Brooks, 2009). It is inegalitarian in practice because it almost always involves men with multiple wives rather than the other way round, so women are not able to practise it in the same ways as men. It is inegalitarian in theory because a man can divorce any of his wives at will, but the wives can only divorce him and not each other. As a result, polygamy is harmful and can make spouses feel dispensable, whereas monogamy offers a better chance of enjoying equality (Parekh, 2010).

At first glance, these arguments do not seem surprising, but there is a serious problem with this line of reasoning in that these arguments position monogamy as the ideal harmless and equal option. Taking the scholarship mentioned earlier for example, McDermott and Monroe state that their study was triggered by the events of 9/11 and the question 'why does the Muslim world hate us?' (2018: 10). This reactionary question is not only offensive but uses polygamy, which is a minority practice that is not exclusive to Muslims, as the case study to examine the unrelated issue of buying weapons. It is not clear how this can be blamed on the ways families are structured. This is just one example of the problematic material being shared about polygamy. Along the same line, Bailey and Kaufman (2010) conclude that polygamy generally exists in systems where women are treated as inferior, and it is implied that these systems are outside of the West. But can we really blame polygamy alone for poverty and abuses of power in divorce proceedings? These studies take an orientalist approach that others and demeans certain groups associated with polygamy. The implication is that polygamy is the root of a range of harms and hatred against 'us'. But we should question whether these attributes are solely found in places where polygamy is a socially and legally recognised norm and remember that polygamy is practised in the West too.

There is something that is causing women to suffer harm and inequality: the patriarchy. The patriarchy, or the systems and processes which distribute and concentrate power in ways that disadvantage and oppress women, is the real culprit here. As Calder (2009) argues, the patriarchy transcends family structure: it would be naïve to assume otherwise. Based on the assumptions about polygamy giving rise to harm and inequality, women in these marriages are repeatedly portrayed as victims in need of saving by the colonial saviour since monogamy and the West are free from problems. This not only dismisses the agency of women in polygamous marriages, but also downplays the harm and inequalities that women in monogamous relationships experience (see also Brake, 2012; Sweet, 2013). The link between harm and polygamy is therefore more complicated. It is true that polygamy can be imposed on women and used as a tool for harm, but does this justify our rejecting polygamy and refusing to engage with it? The accusation that polygamy is a source of inequality is similarly used to reject it. Equality has traditionally been taken to mean people should be treated the same, and this is the approach in law; but that does not help here. It reduces the assessment of equality in relationships to a numbers game. In monogamy, a person is equal to their partner, whereas in polygamy, one person (usually a man) represents one whole while several partners represent a fraction of that person's value. This approach does not help to make sense of inequality and polygamy because patriarchal stereotypes have created this structure of a wife representing a fraction of her husband.

Inspired by Cooper's (2004) equality of power framework, I look at how organising principles of inequality – like race, gender and class – are sustained by normative principles. I argue that gender equality itself is one of these normative principles, because it has been developed with the West in mind. We therefore need to think about whether it is appropriate to base the rejection of polygamy on gender equality and measure women's experiences against it. Some scholars like Mahmood (2005) argue that we need to look to agency rather than equality to make sense of women's decisions to behave in ways that seem to undermine conventions around gender equality. The idea is to challenge the narrative that polygamous wives are always victims. By rejecting polygamy because it is harmful and unequal, and ending our engagement there, we silence women's voices and the potential for learning about their range of experiences and stories around this relationship.

Disrupting marriage recognition

My final key argument is that wholesale recognition for polygamous marriages in English law is not an appropriate response to women's needs because it is impossible to construct a legal framework around marriage that is free from coloniality. The question of whether polygamy should be legally recognised is linked to the overarching question of whether it should exist since legal recognition gives a practice legitimacy and validation. Evaluating the arguments for and against legal recognition seems to be a simple enough exercise to begin with, and this has been done effectively in North America from constitutional and doctrinal perspectives (for example, Otter, 2015; Bennion and Fishbayne Joffe, 2016; Goldfeder, 2017). Legal recognition for a marriage gives the parties certain rights and responsibilities. It is also tied to public processes and systems, because being married has consequences for your finances, property and parental status among other things (O'Sullivan and Jackson, 2017). This was acknowledged by the Law Commission (2015a) in their scoping paper on weddings law, as they noted that certain groups are being excluded from marriage recognition and the associated benefits because their wedding ceremonies are too different from the Anglican Church wedding. The practical results of being a legally recognised wife are important because they can affect women's lives and residence, but there is less emphasis on the wider social and symbolic implications. This highlights recognition as a force that impacts on identity formation and self-worth, which has led to its prominent positioning in social justice struggles (Hines, 2013). In this interpretation, recognition is a way to be accepted by the dominant majority and achieve equal social standing. We therefore need to think about recognition as something that confers more than practical benefits for women and their marriages.

Research around polygamous marriages is focussed on answering the question of whether it should be recognised and therefore whether it should exist, but we need to take a step back and think about what recognition is in the first place, not just whether it is the way to achieve justice. Recognition has a troubled history where minoritised groups are concerned, and we can also see this clearly in the marriage equality mission. For example, legal recognition for marriage was used to enact racist violence against newly emancipated enslaved people in 19th-century America (Franke, 2015). With legal responses to polygamy being so enmeshed in imperialist and racist attitudes, we cannot ignore the use of recognition as a tool for oppression that forces communities to conform to colonialist ideals of what a marriage should look like. I argue that the current legal recognition for marriage is not designed to serve the needs of polygamous wives because it remains trapped in these ideals and is indifferent to them and their humanity. Drawing on critical postcolonial theorists like Fanon (2008) and Bhabha (1994), I argue we should shift our focus away from achieving recognition to first building a universal category of humanity that includes the marginalised and excluded. Building on this, I show that women are already engaging in a disruptive politics of recognition by choosing to marry outside of state and legal recognition, thereby creating a third space. In doing so, they reimagine recognition for themselves outside of state validation. They write their own stories of recognition and ensure that they are fully included in the universal category of humanity the law excludes them from.

As a result, I cannot argue in favour of recognition for polygamous marriages in English law. The fundamental changes required to develop a sensitive, nuanced and inclusive framework are beyond the scope of the current legal framework and this is not going to change any time soon. Moreover, polygamy is a form of marriage: for the women who practise it, there is no alternative which does not involve a marriage ceremony as in cohabitation for monogamy. This means that if we had universal recognition for polygamy in the UK it would be difficult to ensure that women who do not want legal recognition can evade it. However, this does not solve the immediate issues of women who believe they are legally married in the UK but later discover they are not. To support them, I propose a sticking plaster reform that gives legal recognition for non-legally binding marriages under certain circumstances. This is intended to address the immediate needs and concerns of these vulnerable women while respecting the rights of those wives who wish to remain unrecognised so that they can continue to be disruptive and inhabit the third space they have created.

Notes on methodology: voice and storytelling

This book is not just about theory, but the voices and stories of women living in the UK. In this way, my analysis of the law is informed by both the theoretical and the empirical. In Chapters 3 and 4, I focus on showing the problems around polygamous marriage in the English legal framework in light of its colonialist and sexist foundations. My broad analysis in Chapter 3 of domestic polygamy celebrated in England was limited by the availability of source materials. I relied mostly on existing writings to build a picture of legal responses to polygamy in England. In my examination of legal responses to overseas polygamy in Chapter 4, I was able to obtain over 50 legal judgments which make up the first primary source I analysed to evaluate legal and judicial responses to polygamy. I carried out a judicial discourse analysis of the case law to show how judicial language is formed and constructed around polygamy and marriage. We already have some interesting accounts of certain themes in the case law around contemporary human rights and immigration issues (see for example, Shah, 2003), but my interest stretches beyond this. I want to look beyond what the law is saying to us in the here and now. I therefore consider judicial discourse as part of a continuum and investigate historical constructions of polygamy to see what they tell us about how the relationship is viewed today. My critical discourse analysis approach is inspired by Herman's (2011) arguments on judicial agency. While investigating attitudes to Jews and Jewishness in English law, Herman argues that '[j]udges articulate, reflect, and, importantly, represent ubiquitous understandings' (2011: 20). Judges hold an important position in the legal system because they interpret and narrate common law into existence and this work is influenced by their understandings as (mostly) members of the dominant cultural majority (Rackley, 2013). By taking this approach, I look at the wider embeddedness of social, cultural and religious conceptions of polygamy to see how they are reflected in judicial discourse as part of ubiquitous understandings of the practice. One of the key insights from this analysis is that the law has been formed without women in mind. Polygamous wives and their humanity are ignored and treated with indifference and hostility.

In Chapters 5, 6 and 7, I address the dismissal of polygamous wives in mainstream legal processes by sharing the stories and views of women in the UK. There have been several empirical studies involving interviews and focus groups in other countries. However, existing research and literature focus mostly on women's experiences, with less emphasis on men's stories.[9] I have chosen to centre women's lived realities, voices and experiences, for two main reasons. First, discussions around polygamy tend to be localised around the 'woman as victim' paradigm wherein polygamy is harmful and problematic for women. This has been challenged in existing feminist literature,[10] but there needs to be a deeper interrogation of this paradigm in a critical postcolonial context to look at the law's capacity to be harmful. Second, there is not enough space in this book to do justice to the different experiences and considerations around polygamy for men compared to women, so I concentrate on interviews with 26 women in the UK. Their

[9] Majeed's (2015) study on polygyny practised in African American Muslim communities shares the experiences of both men and women, but most scholarship looks at polygamous wives. See, for example, Campbell (2013) and Calder and Beaman (2014). These works are based on the Canadian and US contexts – there have been no in-depth empirical studies of polygamy in the UK.

[10] See, for example, Kaganas and Murray (1991) and Beaman (2014).

ages ranged from 21 to 53, and they identified as either single, married, divorced, widowed or in a relationship. Seventeen identified as British women of colour, five were White British, and four did not consider themselves British at all. Only three of the women identified as having direct experience of polygamous marriage.

I undertook in-depth semi-structured interviews with these women, so although I had a schedule of questions to ask, the conversations would at times go in a unique direction according to what was being narrated. They would tell me something interesting while answering a preset question, causing me to ask follow-up questions. They told me about themselves, their families and their relationships. They described marriage and what it means to them, and they commented on whether they think it is good for people. The women shared their thoughts on whether marriage is more of a religious, cultural, social or legal institution, and its benefits and advantages. I asked them for their definitions and views of polygamy, its acceptance in Islam, and their thoughts on its legal recognition. In designing and carrying out the study, I adapted a critical race feminist-based methodology, which centres women's voices. Critical race feminism is a school of thought that encourages us to look at the ways a woman's multiple and competing identities intersect so that we foreground their experiences and privileged knowledge (see for example, Wing, 2000). It is a type of standpoint feminism with a narrative methodology for seeking out and highlighting the experiences of women of colour. It harmonises well with critical postcolonial perspectives because they both recognise the importance of stories. Telling and sharing stories and memories is a rich part of many cultures and traditions around the world (Coughlin, 1995). Stories are one of the most fascinating methods of sharing and preserving history. Whether passed on between an elder and child, two friends or even complete strangers, stories bring places, events and the past to life. Relationships are personal and intimate and so are stories about them. When you talk with someone, you can get a deep insight into that person, their thoughts and their context.

However, with this methodology there are concerns around representation and whose voice is being heard. In critical race feminism, the issue of whether women's experiences can be falsely homogenised has been raised (Brooks, 2007). That is, by hearing and sharing the experiences of one woman or a small group of women, we risk them being taken as representative of all women of colour, though each woman and her story is individual to her. There is a need therefore, to avoid making sweeping claims about a large group of people based on too little evidence. It is nearly, or perhaps completely impossible to find a representative sample of views and experiences around a niche and minoritised practice like polygamy (Majeed, 2015). The stories that I share in the book are therefore not generalisable – they cannot tell us what every woman thinks and experiences around polygamy in the UK.

For this reason, it is the spirit of narrative methodology that governs my approach. My aims are to show the weaknesses in the law because of the way history and colonial governance have affected it, and to share the patterns of thought and experiences that the women who spoke with me identified. I do not intend to make any grand proclamations about the way law affects society; rather, I aim to foster a better understanding of the law in this area and its context, along with the potential impacts on those affected by it. This book is the start of a conversation about how marriage is constructed in English law and whether it can meet the needs of the minoritised women in the UK it has previously not thought about.

Another concern is my position as a researcher and the possibility that the project and this book are affected by my views. At the start of this chapter, I openly shared my personal stake in the conversations around polygamy. I do not claim that I am an objective, dispassionate observer in this process. I have the privileges of being an insider (Brown, 2012). Moreover, being a visibly Muslim woman helped in attracting other Muslim women to the project and, as a consequence, many of the experiences and views expressed in the later chapters of the book are from the Muslim perspective. However, perspectives from other religious and customary belief systems are also included, so I cannot say that the stories shared here are exclusively about Islamic polygyny and limit the scope of the book in this way. As a critical scholar, I contest the idea that we can be objective and dispassionate about our research and ideas. My insider status is a strength rather than a weakness: it led to many women opening up to me during this project, and some women even approached me afterwards, once they found out that I was looking at polygamy to share their stories on the topic. I believe that this openness would not have been possible in the same way had the researcher been an outsider. The challenge though, was to ensure that my voice did not drown out theirs – my job was to listen and document rather than to speak for them. To ensure this, I reflected on my rightful place and reminded myself of this throughout. With the same aim of centring women's voices, I intersperse my discussions of the interviews with the unfiltered stories of three women: Noreen, Jamilah and Karimah – three different women from different backgrounds, in different age groups and in different locations. However, they are connected by their direct experience of polygamous marriage. I lightly edited their stories for clarity, but their voices are undiluted and strong as they speak about their lived realities.

I used a form of thematic analysis on the interview data to look for patterns of thought and experience in the women's narratives (see Braun and Clarke, 2013). Thematic analysis is useful because it is flexible: it did not require me to conduct the interviews in a specific way or use a particular theoretical or methodological approach. Again, the themes that emerged are not meant to tell us what every woman thinks or has experienced around polygamy, but they give us food for thought. If several women narrate a similar attitude or experience, it would be foolish to ignore this even while we acknowledge that each woman and her story is unique. There is another benefit to this approach. While looking for patterns in behaviour and perspectives, we can also see where accounts do not fit within the patterns or even reject the accounts of others. One of the benefits of critical race and postcolonial feminisms is their emphasis on counter/disruptive narratives. For the minoritised and marginalised, the ability to tell their own stories has been taken away from them throughout history. Instead, orientalist stories have been told about them and then fed back to them and to the rest of the world. By centring the disruptive and counter-stories of women, we can build a more realistic picture of the law and its effects on minoritised women's lives and marriages. These disruptive voices are key to critiquing English legal understandings of marriage and polygamy.

Overview of the book

In Chapter 2, I set out and explain the critical postcolonial feminist conceptual framework that underpins the book. Critical postcolonial feminism promotes consciousness of the historical context around the law and calls for us to disrupt dominant discourses that orientalise and diminish racialised and minoritised people. I develop this to argue that we need to look more widely at the context surrounding polygamy and the law since the colonial attitudes that underpin this area are not consigned to the past, but are live and influential today. The law needs to be viewed critically with a view to thinking through the consequences for women. The best way to learn about the potential impacts for women is to foreground their voices and stories so that the individual behind the words is seen. By exploring contexts and calling attention to disruptive voices, we can then start to construct alternative accounts of orientalism and imperialism in order to situate conceptions of polygamy and law in the present day.

In Chapter 3, I start to build a more contextualised account of the legal framework around polygamous marriages celebrated in England. I trace historical religious and legal responses to first argue that Christianity has dominated legal understandings of marriage from before the ninth century and continues to do so today. I further argue that the law in this area is underscored by colonial indifference; on the surface this sends the message that the law does not know about polygamy and so does not want to engage with it, but the law's real message is that it does not care. This is evidenced by the extremely sparse legal and policy engagement with domestic polygamy, an approach which has expanded to include other minoritised marriage practices like religious-only marriages.

In Chapter 4, I continue to develop my contextualised account with a critical discourse analysis of the case law around polygamous marriages celebrated overseas. I show how the private international law that governs this type of polygamy is rooted in coloniality and I set out three of the strategic moves made by the courts in relation to this. The first and earliest response is denigration of polygamy – it is not a form of marriage and was criminalised. Here, judgments contain racist, sexist and orientalist statements against polygamy and polygamous wives. The second strategy is mutation. Before the 1970s, even monogamous marriages celebrated in places that allowed polygamy were labelled potentially polygamous and were not recognised. As time passed, the courts started to mutate or convert these potentially polygamous marriages into monogamous ones and then permit parties to access remedies in the English courts. This forced non-Christian marriages into the imperialist-approved format which was demeaning and reminiscent of the civilising mission to convert colonial natives to the Christian way of life. Closer to the present day, the courts are no longer explicitly racist or orientalist, but employ a subtler strategy to differentiate polygamy from English marriage. This is done to protect state resources and uphold monogamy as the ideal – both of which were priorities of colonial administrators when they ruled over colonies.

Chapters 5, 6 and 7 are where women's voices take centre stage. Each chapter is preceded by a short story adapted from one of the interviews I carried out. Noreen's story offers insight for Chapter 5. She talks about the role of religion and culture in her life and decision to become a polygamous wife. I argue that the law treats minoritised religions and cultures as inferior to those of the dominant cultural majority. One of the ways it does this is by collapsing religion and culture into a single identity even though this does not always reflect women's lived experiences. Religion and culture need to be seen as dual and alternative so that they can be linked but also disrupt and oppose each other.

In Chapter 6, I take insights from Jamilah's story to tackle the two main charges against polygamy: that it is harmful and that it promotes inequalities for women. My intention is not to defend polygamy; to do so would legitimise the debate on whether it should exist which is orientalising considering monogamy's existence is never questioned. I instead disrupt the use of these arguments around harm and equality to reject polygamy. Relying on these arguments in this way without deeper engagement obscures their patriarchal and Eurocentric foundations. It also cuts off women's voices and the potential for hearing a wider range of experiences and stories around polygamy wherein they exercise their agency and act disruptively.

Finally, in Chapter 7 I draw from Karimah's experiences of marriage, polygamy and immigration to look at the implications of being a legally recognised wife in the UK. I show that recognition is often looked at uncritically and seen as something for marginalised groups to aspire to when seeking acceptance from society. After exploring its dark past in relation to marriage, I question how desirable legal recognition is and argue that we need to keep its limitations in mind. This is reinforced by the fact that some women are living a disruptive politics of recognition where they actively choose to be in non-legally binding marriages. I conclude by thinking through options for reform and suggest that though there is currently little appetite for this, more work needs to be done to address the issues with the law uncovered in the book.

2

Consciousness and Disruption in Critical Postcolonial Feminism

This chapter sets out the foundation for my analysis of responses to polygamous marriages in English law and the courts. I draw from the insights provided by critical postcolonial feminist literature and the critiques of orientalism and imperialism to shed light on the law and women's experiences and attitudes concerning polygamous marriages. After providing a brief overview of the relevance of critical postcolonial theory and feminist thought, I employ two tools from this approach to advance understandings of polygamous marriage regulation in English law. The first of these tools, historical consciousness, is especially useful for a relationship practice that has been around for thousands of years, like polygamous marriage. Based on this historically conscious approach, I show that current legal and judicial attitudes and approaches to polygamous marriage remain influenced by and entrenched in colonialist attitudes towards this relationship and the women who practise it. The law is outdated and needs to be reconsidered for the present day.

The second tool pertains to the challenging or disruption of dominant narratives and discourses. Using this tool, I examine the key concepts of orientalism and imperialism and show that progress has been made in the literature to define these in a more sophisticated manner. However, we need to do more to understand how they manifest and operate in the contemporary context so that we can see how they influence the ways polygamous marriage is framed in law and in real women's lives. Critical postcolonial studies, in its historically conscious way, has exposed orientalism and imperialism very clearly as powerful historical discourses, but less has been done to construct alternative accounts of these concepts which speak from the perspective of the colonised or those subjected to these discourses. Critical perspectives on the colonial demonstrate the potential to build these alternative accounts by challenging the dominant narratives of what these concepts mean and do to real women. I draw on this to complicate the current legal approaches to polygamy, which are rooted in colonialist orientalism and imperialism.

Postcolonial feminism is a critical movement disrupting dominant discourses and narratives that oppress those subjected to and by the 'colonial'. Taking this historically conscious and disruptive path, it is these voices of the marginalised and the ignored that I seek to centre in this work. I undertake disruptive and historically contextualised work by uplifting the alternative, disruptive histories of those with non-Eurocentric perspectives and experiences concerning polygamous marriages. In doing so, I contribute to existing work of scholars in this area to combat the notion that people who are stereotypically associated with or located in the colonial native position should be consigned to the margins and spoken for rather than speaking for themselves (see, for example, Gopal, 2019; Narayan, 2019). I reinforce this by emphasising the position of those in polygamous marriages and sharing the views and experiences of the women who spoke with me for this project. The most effective way to disrupt dominant legal and judicial attitudes to polygamy is to foreground the experiences of those who practise it and to do so in such a way that their voices are heard.

Critical postcolonial theory and feminism: introduction and relevance

The purpose of this section is to explain what I mean by postcolonial approaches and to introduce the main intellectual themes that I take from this field to build my critical lens which I then expand on in the sections that follow. Postcolonial theory is concerned with exposing and critiquing the 'cultural, political, economic and literary impact of imperial expansion by European states across much of the globe', so it is tied up with questions surrounding European empires and the effects of colonisation (Festa and Carey, 2013: 1). Carey and Festa further argue that the inclusion of postcolonial theory in 18th-century studies has shed light on the 'resistant practices of indigenous populations and uneven development of early modern categories of gender, race, and nation' (2013: 1). This description of the contribution of postcolonial theory is not limited to 18th-century studies and is helpful for thinking through the effects of empire on legal responses to polygamous marriage. As a non-normative form of marriage, polygamy is a 'resistant practice' because it refuses to conform to the empire-approved monogamous Christian marriage, demonstrating the usefulness of postcolonial theory for analysing this practice. Additionally, in later chapters it will become clear how connected to colonial encounters legal perceptions of polygamy are, displaying the relevance of a critical postcolonial lens for this area. Seth states that postcolonial theory allows us to question 'the universality accorded to moral and legal perspectives which reflect and reproduce the power relations characteristic of the colonial encounter' (2013: 15). A critical postcolonial perspective exposes the attitudes underlying morality and law which have been shaped by imperialists during the process of colonisation. This insight is particularly important for an analysis of polygamous marriage because it encourages us to look beneath the surface of the law to examine how and why its current form has taken shape through the ongoing colonial encounters between the law and polygamy.

Despite this helpful start provided by mainstream postcolonial theory to further understandings of polygamous marriage, it does little to include the concerns, experiences and contributions of women around the processes of imperial expansion and colonisation. For this reason, I add a feminist angle to my critical lens. Postcolonial feminist theory works at the intersection of gender and colonial critiques by considering the presence and effects of colonisation on women. This creates a two-pronged focus for my analysis: on one hand, I apply a postcolonial feminist lens to the legal framework while on the other, I apply the same lens to the experiences and attitudes of women. Lewis and Mills state that postcolonial feminism places pressure on traditional postcolonial theory to include gender issues and provide more dynamism for the development of studies in 'colonialism, imperialism, race and power' (2003: 1–2).

Further, this critical branch of feminism has two aims: 'to racialise mainstream postcolonial theory and to insert feminist concerns into conceptualisations of colonialism and postcolonialism' (Lewis and Mills, 2003: 5). My tools of historical consciousness and disruption enable me to meet these aims. To meet the first aim, the racialised impacts of the law are highlighted in my analysis, because polygamy is bound up in colonialist constructions of race. To meet the second aim, I unpack the notion of feminist concerns by first asking: how does the project of gendering postcolonial theory add or contribute to understanding the effects of colonisation? Gender is 'both a relation of power and a way of signifying relationships of power that produced and orchestrated the changing meanings of sexual difference in time, shaping social institutions, privileges, expectations and experience' (Wilson, 2004: 14; see also Scott, 1999). This statement demonstrates that the interaction of gender with power has broader consequences for wider social constructions of identity and institutions like marriage, based on 'sexual, national, and racial difference' (Wilson, 2004: 15). The reference to difference is notable here because it shows how the focus on gender, racial and relationship identities during colonialism was configured according to the differences in gender relations and identities between colonised natives and colonising forces.

By inserting gender questions into conceptions of colonialism and postcolonialism, postcolonial feminist theorists have shown that the emphasis on sexual difference gave rise to gendered constructions of the colonising society and its differences from the colonised society. Thus, the role of women, the form and purpose of marriage, and the position of a wife were used as indicators of the social advancement of a particular society (Hall, 2004: 50–1). In this way, women and marriage played a crucial part in underscoring the imperial expansion mission. The ideals and treatment of women dictated by the empire were vital for defining and policing the borders of national identity (Bush, 2004: 90, 109). The civility and respectability of a nation was measured by how its women were treated and married, and this was determined by imperial societal standards on domesticity and marriage.

Labelling this the 'cult of domesticity', McClintock (1995) delves into this domestic realm of the family to argue that Victorian morality and empire were co-constitutive. This emphasis on Victorian interpretations and ideals of morality reflects the period in which colonial expansion rapidly occurred. British imperial society was Victorian, and its moral codes and structures were imposed on colonised peoples. The Victorian middle-class household provided the moral and physical ideal for how homes and families should behave and be organised. More pertinently, the verb 'domesticate', which is concerned with becoming good at fulfilling the responsibilities and duties of a good home life, has close linguistic roots to 'dominate' – a verb that is itself derived from the Latin *dominus*, meaning lord of the *domus*, or home (McClintock, 1995). Connected to this notion of domesticating and building a good (imperialist Victorian) life is that of civilising – a vital function of the imperialist mission that saw domesticating the colonised natives and their homes and families as civilising them. This function is the backbone of the imperialist mission – to civilise and bring improvement to the natives and their way of life – justifying colonial expansion by upholding Victorian moral values. Without this, the natives would remain uncivilised and savage.

In his discussion of imperialism and international law, Anghie (2005) demonstrates how imperial authorities relied heavily on civilising discourses and morality to create distinctions between the superior colonisers and the inferior natives in terms of law and lifestyle. The natives' failure to meet the Victorian standards maintained by the colonisers, particularly in the home, led to the need for them to become civilised. This imposition of domestic and legal standards confirmed that in the private and public realms of society, the natives needed to be shown how to be better. Anghie shows that this was not straightforward in practice. When colonisers measured colonies' legal frameworks against their imperialist standards of sovereignty and control over a territory, it was clear that native systems were able to meet the imperialist standards. This led to complex mental and theoretical gymnastics by colonisers to distort their own standards and dismiss their own findings in order to maintain that the colonised natives were not capable of forming civilised legal doctrines. The colonies' systems were perceived as too alien in character because even though the countries they belonged to were formally sovereign, those countries failed to meet the standards for a 'civilised international society' (Anghie, 2005: 58). Here, there was a deliberate attempt to carve out differences between the civilised imperialist and the uncivilised native. When it was not possible to do this based on law, the coloniser broadened out the comparison by looking at the societies of these states. This is an example of an 'othering' process: colonised states were marked out according to their differences and designated as 'other', because they could not be 'one of us'. The domestic sphere and the family are encompassed in this use of society as a measure of the ideal. Domesticity and family then, are central to the formation of British imperial identity. The colony became a Victorian domesticated space, only civilized when the home and family conformed to British imperial Victorian ideals. These insights encourage a deeper consideration of the colonial context which I draw out in the remainder of this chapter.

One aim of inserting feminist concerns into the conversation is to expose the 'colonial saviour' narrative that was imposed on women in polygamous marriages. This is yet another way that the empire undertook its civilising mission. Spivak (1989; 1999) finds that colonised women are portrayed as Brown women that need White men to save them from Brown men.[1] She observes that for colonised women, gendered power relations have a further dimension as they are subordinated by colonised men, who are in turn subjugated by the White coloniser. These women are in a far more vulnerable position than White women, as they are subject to the oppression of both the colonising and the colonised man. This is linked to my comments earlier that gender relations and the treatment of women are heavily relied on to indicate the quality and nature of a nation. By characterising Brown women in this way, the element of harm is introduced into the postcolonial critique. It is not just how women are treated and married that tells us how 'respectable' or 'good' a nation is, but how much harm they are subjected to and what or who causes those harms. The imperialist civilising mission always positions the Brown woman as the victim of the Brown man. This obscures the harms caused by the White man who, to escape criticism and censure for his own actions, portrays himself as a saviour. We see later that these themes of salvation and harm are reproduced by legal approaches to polygamy as well as in women's lived experiences.

1 Spivak frames her theory in relation to the Brown woman, but I interpret it as applying to all racialised women.

Polygamy and history: a more contextualised approach

In the previous chapter, I noted the wide range studies of polygamous marriage in law to show how much interest this form of relationship has attracted. In Canada and the US – both colonial societies – there are some fascinating insights into the effects of historical colonial attitudes on the law, but the same is not readily available for the UK. To address this, I apply my postcolonial feminist lens by using the tool of historical consciousness to scrutinise polygamous marriage and its legal regulation in the UK. By centring the historical colonial context and its continuing impact, I argue that the law remains entrenched in understandings of polygamy which were constructed in a historical colonial context. Haggis (2003) persuasively refers to postcolonial feminism as a 'feminist historical project' in which scholars use the past to better understand the present so that they can then question whether a present situation or attitude is appropriate. By looking at how opinions of a concept or practice have formed during colonial times, theorists can then examine whether, even after formal decolonisation has occurred, present-day opinion is still being influenced by colonialism. For example, Lilith (2000–01) casts a postcolonial feminist eye over mail-order brides and inter-country adoptions; though seemingly very different, parallels can be drawn between them based on historical context. They are both examples of how the (female and child) populations of former colonies are being 'purchased' to complete the families of those in the former empire (Lilith, 2000–01; see also Perez, 2003). In both practices, there is a saviour who can provide a better life. Lilith's analysis demonstrates that narratives of the colonialist saviour are still being reproduced through the purchase of women and children from former colonies.

My argument that the law remains entrenched in colonialist understandings of polygamous marriages is rooted in the broader claim that the legal system overall is still underpinned by colonialist attitudes. This is well established in the scholarship, but it is worth unpacking how and why these attitudes are so deeply ingrained in the law. Benton and Ford (2016) argue that in the early 19th century, a 'rage for order' overtook British subjects, referring to a reordering of places and people all over the world in the context of Britain's newly acquired status as a global power. This reordering was accomplished via the reconfiguration of British imperial law and its expanded use in the empire and even beyond. This provides an initial indication of the significant role that imperial legal order played in Britain's development into a global power at that time. Continuing into the peak of colonial expansion, the law was a prominent aspect of the colonial mission, a key tool or technology to establish and maintain the empire's dominance over the colonies.

Colonialism was not only about money, land and technology but also sought total ideological and racial domination (Roy, 2008). Success depended on the imposition of colonial order which was operationalised using the law. For this reason, legal order and origin coheres with the colonial; the colonial mission was bound up in the legal from the start. When the power of a nation increased, the family of law it created or used was imposed on its subject nations (Schmidhauser, 1992). This legal imperialism was designed to prevent the threat of 'native' laws being invoked to challenge colonial powers and their mission. If the law, which is rational and represents what is right and good for all, said that colonial authority and operations should be imposed, this must be true. The violence of colonisation and the identity of the colonial power was therefore 'legitimised' because it was exercised by and through law (Fitzpatrick, 2001). Without law, colonial power would not exist then or today (Klerman et al, 2011).

This deployment of law as a colonising tool was complicated, messy and fractious, leading to inconsistencies, such as the codification of Hindu law and the retention of some Muslim personal laws during the British colonial administration of India, rather than their complete erasure. At first this seems unusual and even nuanced, but it was in fact pragmatic. This approach was taken by British colonial authorities to maintain the stability of colonial rule, which would have been threatened by cultural and religious confrontations arising out of the dismissal of such laws. Moreover, these codifying and stabilising processes were another form of legal colonisation, in the form of organising and translating these indigenous laws into a form which was understandable and palatable to the coloniser (Spivak, 1988; Schmidhauser, 1992).

This did not end with the formal breakdown of the empire. The deployment of law as a tool to colonise, dominate and subjugate those who are associated with the colonial persists today. European laws imbued with European values are still embedded into legal systems all around the world (Roy, 2008; Kapur, 2019). Colonial approaches and attitudes in and around law are an instrument of control portrayed as superior and constitutive of real, legitimate law and order, even in the 'postcolonial' age. While critically examining legal orientalism and Chinese law, Ruskola (2013) argues that the role of law in informal imperialism and practices which fall short of formal territorial colonialism are underexplored in existing scholarship. To address this, it is necessary to trace contemporary forms of harm and domination in the law to challenge such an unrelenting imperial legal order.

The subject of this book is the English legal framework around polygamous marriages which seems less directly affected by colonial encounters because the relevant laws operate in the imperial centre rather than the colonies. The ongoing legacies of imperial order tell us that the colonial is still relevant and indeed dominant in approaches to polygamous marriage. Polygamy is a racialised relationship: one which is associated with those who are not as connected with the British imperial centre because they are different, other and linked to the colonies. In the critical examination of the law in the following chapters, I show how this association is relied on today by the courts to make sense of this form of marriage and deal with legal issues that arise from it. Much like the approach of translating personal religious laws into a palatable form for the colonial administration in India, polygamous marriage laws have been formed to make sense to authorities rather than to serve the women affected by them.

Previous research supports the relevance of my approach. For example, Kaganas and Murray (1991) illustrate the effectiveness of historical consciousness for examining polygamous marriage by grounding their analysis of South African polygyny in colonial history so that prevailing attitudes can be problematised. Because legal responses towards marriage are shaped by prevailing social attitudes, the use of history to contextualise the development and presence of colonial discourse is effective in furthering contemporary understandings of the law. Another example of this is found in Probert's (2012) study into how societal views of cohabitation have impacted on legal developments relating to it. Doing the same for polygamy will provide a clearer picture of how the current legal situation has developed and allow progress to be made towards interrogating contemporary attitudes towards polygamy in English law.

There is a disconnect between the law and contemporary polygamy. The law, which is stuck in the colonial past, is being applied to a relationship that like other relationships, including monogamous marriage, has developed and changed over time. Here, we can see that polygamy is being considered, judged and regulated out of context, and it is by using history as the starting point that we can start to unpick this. Once the historical background to colonising and the underpinnings for this are made visible, the ideas and judgements which led to colonising can be uncovered to build a more situated account of polygamy and marriage for the past and today. By undertaking this situated analysis of the practice and its legal regulation, we can also see how it is dealt with in a relational sense to other forms of marriage. For example, there is an overwhelming trend in existing critiques for monogamy in its modern form to be compared almost exclusively to polygamy's dominant historical form (Zalesne and Dexter, 2018). Polygamy is portrayed as static and the same throughout time, but monogamy is not. This is rooted in notions of colonialist authoritative superiority where assessments are made of different ways of living to dismiss and diminish their legitimacy purely because they are different.

As a result of this historical versus contemporary binary, it is important to note that there are limitations to being historically conscious in the colonial context. When we look at history, we need to deal with the realities of what history and time mean. This starts with thinking about the 'postcolonial' in critical postcolonial approaches. What does this signify? And how should we address its inconsistencies? The term 'postcolonial' is conflicted; for some, it relates to the specific period which followed decolonisation (John, 1996: 1). The temporal character of this definition is problematic as it implies that there is a definite start point and end point to the postcolonial era. It fails to account for the current impacts on former colonies and the 'diverse genealogies and histories that emerge from multiple locations' affected by these colonisations (Asher, 2017: 516). This definition of postcolonial is incomplete and must be broadened to provide for the continuing effect of colonisation. Lee draws attention to the naivety of the assumption that five centuries of colonisation and its after-effects can be undone with a mere half-century of 'counter-discursive practice' (1997: 114). To reinforce the notion that the postcolonial era is timeless and dynamic, I approach postcolonial in a way which highlights Britain's presence, power and continuing influence on former colonies (Chrisman, 2003; Sinha, 2004). This then provokes the question of how best to use the idea of a postcolonial context to frame a contemporary analysis of polygamous marriage in English law – how do I delve into the history of the law in a way which is useful in the present?

The concept of coloniality helps with this. Coloniality is the result of critical engagement with defining the colonial and postcolonial (Grosfoguel, 2007). Drawing from Quijano (1992), Grosfoguel (2007) argues that colonialism refers to 'colonial situations' imposed by the presence of colonial authorities or administration. Colonialism therefore denotes the classical colonial encounter and better describes past processes and events around colonisation. Coloniality, on the other hand concerns colonial situations in the present where colonial authorities have almost been (formally) eradicated. Colonial situations include the oppression and exploitation of subordinate racialised groups with or without the existence of colonial authorities. It is not necessary that these authorities officially exist for a situation to be colonial, because as stated earlier, five centuries of European colonial domination did not simply end. Colonial domination is being produced and reproduced in different forms even today.

Moreover, Sara Ahmed argues that because there were so many unique colonial encounters, 'post-coloniality is impossible to grasp in the present' and is a 'failed historicity' that cannot adequately address the multiplicity of histories, experiences and realities that have arisen in a colonial context (2000: 1). Not only is coloniality pervasive today, but so are its essentialising techniques that create the image of a single colonialism, rather than colonialisms in their many diverse forms. This exposes a major issue with the legal framework for polygamous marriage: it is based on colonial attitudes, but this is complicated because those attitudes essentialise and universalise the colonial experience and context. The colonialist mentality reduces colonialism to the same form in every time and every place, which in turn reduces polygamy to something that is practised in the same way over time causing the same issues to reappear. This is because the colonial mindset has an oversimplified view of the world which reduces it to the binary of superior colonial/inferior colonised erasing the multiplicity of colonial histories. There is no nuance displayed in English law towards the multiplicity of experiences and understandings of polygamous marriage. Yeğenoğlu (1998) states that through a rhetorical strategy, non-Western societies are pushed back in time to be constructed as backward and the law does the same to polygamy. It pushes polygamy into the past, dismissing it as irrelevant to English law today on the basis that it fails to compare to modern-day monogamy.

Due to these limitations of applying a historically conscious approach, more engagement is needed with the cultural, social and religious embeddedness[2] of polygamous marriage in women's lives. By broadening these contextual parameters, I can develop my analysis and the focus on postcolonialism as a marker of timelessness by speaking to real women and situating my exploration of polygamy in the specific time and space of present-day England. In doing so, I aim to complicate the historical insider colonialist/outsider colonised boundary which creates an unrealistic division between British identity and the identity of those who practise polygamy because the current legal framework assumes that polygamy is only practised by those have come from outside the UK. This is not always the case. The notion of embeddedness is vital in a broader sense because it leads to a more contextualised analysis of the feminist approach itself. Dixon notes that feminist analyses typically take 'Greco-Roman and European-American forms of patriarchy' as their basis (2009: xxxi). This ensures not only that 'the social structures and practices of peoples in other cultures throughout the world are often inadequately examined' but also that such analyses 'divert attention from the majority culture's own inequalities' through their lopsided view which can lead to the dominant majority culture fostering ideas of superiority (Dixon, 2009: xxxi; Song, 2016).

The condition of those who are oppressed is an important central feature of the analysis, but what about the forms that oppression takes? Patriarchy – the label for the ways that systems, structures and power are organised to facilitate male privilege – is relevant around the world, but that does not make it static or universally understood and experienced. By relying on the

---

2 The idea of thinking about the embeddedness of polygamy in culture, society and religion today has been inspired by Mama's (1995) attention to the embeddedness of the institutions of slavery, colonialism and racism along with their discourses and practices.

assumption that there is a 'universal' way to experience and express patriarchy everywhere, we do women outside of the hegemonic Euro-American and Greco-Roman context a disservice. They are subjected again to the imposition of a standard of what oppression means which is not meaningful to them or their lives. Their oppression must be of the right kind – translated into the context that is understood by the scholarly observer – or it is not oppression but something different. When their choices or experiences are measured by the Euro-American standard of patriarchy to be oppressive, this is accepted without question. This standard setting, judging and measuring is a major feature of colonialist ideological thought which I explore through the concepts of orientalism and imperialism.

Alternative accounts: orientalism and imperialism

I now drill down into the ideological influences and process of orientalism and imperialism that make up colonial encounters and shape the legal framework around polygamy. I expose the manifestations of these two concepts for this practice and using my second tool, disruption, show how they need to be disrupted for the present day. Starting with orientalism, this was originally perceived as a research discipline dedicated to the study of the Orient (Dvornik, 1961; Southern, 1962; Little, 1979; Hallaq, 2011). It was therefore established in the West by a church council centred on the study of oriental languages. With time, orientalism has been broadened as scholars have become more critical and cynical about a field of study in which Western scholars observe and then report on the Orient. Much of the work expressing criticism of this early discipline concerned the definition of 'Orient' and the negative discourses tied up with this. Simply put, orientalism created a divide between the West and the Orient so the latter signified non-Western nations (Said, 1978). Defining the 'West' is also plagued with difficulties. Bonnett (2004) argues that there are strong links between the desire to find a non-contentious alternative to what was once called 'Christendom' and the rise of the idea of the West.

Said's *Orientalism* (1978) is instrumental in this expansion because he unpicked the study of the Orient, concluding that orientalism is a discourse which encompasses dealing with the Orient, stating facts about it and authorising views of it. Due to its exotic and different nature, the West needed a way to deal with the Orient, and orientalism provided just that: a coping mechanism for the civilised West to understand the unfamiliar Orient. Said (1978) proceeded to add the dimension of control to orientalism because the Orient was being studied and defined in accordance with Western standards and biases. This definition suggested that Western scholars were not genuinely interested in understanding the Orient as a stand-alone 'place', only as a comparator to the West. Orientalists tried to force the Orient into a Western paradigmatic model it could never fit into, because it was different (Said, 1978; Elmarsafy and Bernard, 2013). This difference was held as evidence of the Orient's inferiority and supported the aims of imperialism because colonies needed colonising so that they could be improved. A leading thinker on the anti-colonial, Fanon writes that the inferiority of the colonised correlates with the European's feeling of superiority: 'the racist creates his inferior' (2008: 69). This is achieved through the creation of stereotypes: 'a major discursive strategy' and 'apparatus of power' for colonialism wherein the coloniser and colonised are slotted into stereotypical constructions of their imagined or idealised roles to characterise them as superior and inferior respectively (Bhabha, 1983: 18, 23).

Inherent in representations of the Orient and their use as a comparator are othering processes. Long before Said (1978) established this in relation to orientalism, explorations into the 'other' were well underway in the writings of philosophers such as Jean-Paul Sartre (1968) and Georg Hegel (1976). In these earlier works, discussions centred on the need for the other to define the self, because the self is defined by its difference to the other. Later, Simone de Beauvoir (1997) applied this to the male–female relationship to show that the female is other – she is defined by what she is not: the male. This process of defining the other by what they are not constitutes an 'othering' process and has been observed in many contexts.

For example, in his work on antisemitism, Sartre (1968) divides Jewish people into two categories based on their responses and behaviours towards antisemitism: 'inauthentic' and 'authentic'. The inauthentic Jew evaded and fled from their Jewish identity when faced with the pain of living in an antisemitic environment. This can be viewed as an assimilationist response in order to blend into mainstream society, rejecting the particularity of being a Jew because they suffered from an 'inferiority complex'. Sartre is quick to add that there is no 'moral blame' on inauthentic Jews, but they served to reinforce antisemitic propaganda through their behaviour. The authentic Jew behaved in the opposite way, affirming their Jewish identity regardless of the consequences. Authentic Jews refused to hide their identity, openly declaring it in the face of the objectifying and vilifying gaze of the antisemite. The actions of the both the inauthentic and authentic Jew are responses to being othered by the antisemite, who defines them according to their differences from non-Jews. Such differences have specifically negative connotations, and they intend to show how the Jewish person is 'inferior' to the non-Jew (according to the antisemite) which then gives rise to either Jewish assimilation or defiance.

In later work, Sartre (1968) distinguishes the situation of the Jew from that of a Black person. A Black person cannot flee from their identity the same way that the inauthentic Jew can. Hiding one's religious identity is possible, but the same cannot be said of skin colour. Fanon (2008) builds on this arguing that colonised Black people are defined and recognised according to colonialist understandings of them. These defining processes are bound up with racist, orientalist and imperialist discourses of indigenous peoples' inferiority, which again focus on how the colonised natives differ in a negative way. With time, colonised people start to internalise these colonising recognitions and definitions which is damaging at individual and collective levels. This leads to self-objectification whereby the Black person starts to see themselves through the colonialist gaze and believe the definitions ascribed to them. Feminist scholars have also noted this internalisation of dominant, colonising recognitions. In her recognition framework, Young (1990) labels this mechanism 'cultural imperialism' and notes that it constitutes one of five faces of oppression. The impact of being recognised, defined and labelled by someone other than oneself is pervasive, damaging and, as Young shows, a manifestation of imperialism which is perpetuated by orientalist 'knowledge'.

Said (1978) demonstrates that colonialist othering stemmed from the use of the West to define the Orient. In this way, the knowledge generated by the study of the Orient subjected oriental and colonised peoples to othering processes – they were not in the West and so they were characterised by how they differed from those in the West. Thus, orientalism gave rise to a specific type of othering which pitted the West against the Orient and was used as the authority for treating the Orient and those associated with it as inferior. Orientalists provided imperialist colonisers with knowledge which they would then use as a source of power to exercise over the backward colonial natives, showing how orientalism and imperialism are linked (Lewis, 1982).

Imperialism provided the ideological foundation for the colonial expansion of a nation-state which in turn expanded its resources. Colonisation is therefore a form of empire-building (Lichtheim, 1971; Young, 1995 Gathii, 2007; Roy, 2008) – for example, Bryce views ancient Rome and Britain as part of the 'European branch of mankind' who created a 'new sort of unity' in the World by 'annexing the rest of the Earth' (1914: 2). Imperial power was successfully used by Europeans to 'unite mankind', effecting a positive change in the annexed states. Bryce argues that non-European empires, including those of ancient Egypt, Assyria and the 'Mogul monarchy', were not comparable to Britain because they did not represent or come close to a 'modern, civilized state' (Bryce, 1914: 6). By positioning European empires as superior to those of the Orient, Bryce implies the West's superiority – unsurprising considering he was writing at the height of imperial rule. Emphasis was primarily put on imperialism's physical expansion process.

Later, in the 1970s, when the breakdown of the British Empire had been underway for some time, writers such as Curtin (1972) and Mommsen (1981) interpret imperialism as European ideas which related to the conquest and administration of non-Western countries. Mommsen additionally writes that White supremacy stems from 'biological and racial variants of national imperialism' and should be included in understandings of imperialism (1981: 8). Inclusion of biological and racial characteristics displays the close connection between imperialism, racism and White supremacy. Fryer persuasively shows that '[f]rom the 1840s to the 1940s Britain's 'native policy' was dominated by racism. The golden age of British Empire was the golden age of British racism too' (1984: 165). It was racist policy on native people which underscored the imperialist project and White supremacy was advanced by the imperialist notion that the races of colonised peoples were inferior. Mommsen (1981) states that imperialism may also be an objective process which results in the civilised coloniser saving a backward society. The nations that were being colonised were so uncivilised they needed fixing and this links to the civilising dimension of imperialism.

Although observations on the civilising mission are found in older work in this area, they have become increasingly exposed by decolonising discourses and contemporary understandings of imperialism (Curtin, 1972; Aristides, 1981; Duidam et al, 2013). Colonisation is the most recent form of empire-building justified by imperialist thought. When physical decolonisation started, imperialism was no longer explicitly defensible; however, it did not disappear. As with our awareness of the postcolonial, there is still a need to account for the long-lasting impact of the empire and its ideology. Among others, Thornton (1961–62) and Kaye (1995) observe that colonialists never saw themselves as exploiting colonies; they mainly viewed themselves as saviours and trustees of civilisation. Colonisation and empire-building was for the benefit of colonised nations and peoples. This civilising of the 'barbarian' natives was achieved through religious, legal and educational institutional changes, and a sense of religious conversionism was fundamental (Curtin, 1972). For natives to become fully civilised, they had to follow the most civilised religion: Christianity. Christianity was an essential facet of life in the West, and colonial natives would never be truly civilised until they were Christian.[3] The orientalist narratives of superiority spread by imperialist White and Christian supremacy persist today: the aftermath of the breakdown of the empire and the decolonisation process have not yet concluded. This is why 'postcolonial' cannot be a temporal marker. There needs to be a more sophisticated understanding of how orientalism and imperialism arise and operate in a contemporary legal context when the question of polygamous marriages arises.

As mentioned before, rather than 'postcolonial' being concerned with what happens after decolonisation, it really involves working towards the reconfiguration of colonialism within the now decolonised state (Ahmed,

3 The irony of Jesus and Christianity originating in Palestine are worth keeping in mind here (see Ash et al, 2018).

1996). The same can be said of orientalism and imperialism: it is not enough to think about these two concepts in the aftermath of decolonisation – they need to be reconfigured for the present day. This is reinforced by the observation of some scholars that although postcolonial theory has deconstructed and exposed imperialist 'knowledge' as a 'powerful form of historical discourse', there are few tools for 'reconstructing alternative histories of imperialism' from a non-Eurocentric perspective (Mackenzie, 1994; Kennedy, 1996; Midgley, 1998). This applies to orientalist 'knowledge' as well. Said's *Orientalism* (1978) made sweeping changes to this area, not least by changing orientalism into a discursive 'ism', like racism or sexism, and therefore liable to critique. However, this process of exposing the powerful historical nature of orientalism and imperialism needs to go further. The notion of hybridity is helpful for making sense of this.

Hybridity denotes the forcing together of things which are unalike causing a disruption (Young, 1995: 24). For those writing on the colonial context like Bhabha (1998) it occurs in conditions of inequality when the colonialist attempts to impose their culturally hegemonic practices (see also Grabham, 2006). Hybridity also represents the 'transgressive potential of the colonial subject' when faced with such impositions (Grabham, 2006: 18). The characterisation of orientalism and imperialism as the historical underpinnings of colonial power are useful, but hybridity shows us that there is a need to reconstruct alternative histories and accounts of them to account for the transgressive nature of the colonised. Colonial encounters comprised 'coexistent cultures and temporalities', meaning there was no singular, linear narrative as the imperialist would have us believe (Al-Saji, 2016: 6). Without recognising the hybridity of these encounters, we overlook the colonised as the key actors that they were. Building on this, even prominent critical postcolonial thinkers like Fanon, Bhabha and Said do not examine the intersections of gender with empire to a great degree (Moore-Gilbert, 2000). This is unsurprising given their male perspective, and while Fanon does pay more attention to women in his later works, such as *A Dying Colonialism* (1994), suffice to say there are limitations to his explorations of the gendered dimensions of empire. It is a start to unearth and deconstruct the historical discourses underpinning legal responses to polygamous marriage, but this is insufficient when thinking about the contemporary legal framework and the gendered dimensions as there is still Eurocentric dominance over the narratives. A historical lens alone will not effectively uncover and challenge modern manifestations of orientalist and imperialist thought in the legal discourse or even the challenges and transgressions performed against them by the colonised. I turn to postcolonial feminism to address this.

Postcolonial feminist scholars situate practices like veiling within their colonial context to show how modern-day incarnations of orientalist and imperialist thought impact on women today. They then proceed to disrupt these discourses, challenging the problematic attitudes which dominate society and law (see for example, Lewis, 2003, Woodhull, 2003; Yeğenoğlu, 1998). Postcolonial feminist writers present the hijab as a form of resistance to the Western gaze. The hijab is seen as key in symbolising the oppression of Muslim women in formerly colonised nations. For this reason, after decolonisation many women have used the hijab to make a political statement and declare their resistance to colonialist narratives which portray them as oppressed and forced to hide themselves and their bodies from the public gaze.

These women use the veil to disrupt colonialist discourses 'bestowing' a White male saviour on them. In doing so, they provide a historical and contemporary alternative to orientalist and imperialist accounts of veiling and the predatory approach to their bodies (West, 2010). The hijab was not inherently oppressive in colonial times and it is not inherently oppressive today. This demonstrates the potential to provide an alternative historical and modern-day account of veiling which is rendered possible when the development of orientalist and imperialist influences are traced into the present. Orientalism and imperialism are not merely remnants of the past; they permeate understandings of veiling and polygamy today albeit in an altered form (Narayan, 1997).

Applying this need for alternative constructions to polygamy in English law, given the formal breakdown of the empire, it is unlikely that legal responses to polygamous marriage are going to be overtly orientalist and imperialist. The law does not justify its approach to polygamy by baldly stating that it is inferior to monogamy, but that does not mean these concepts have lost their relevance. Colonialist othering and civilising discourses still permeate contemporary understandings of polygamous marriage but in a far subtler manner. Beaman (2014) notes that attitudes towards polygamy are constructed around an 'us' (monogamists) versus 'them' (polygamists) approach and this manifests in the lack of legal recognition for polygamous marriage. This divisive characterisation of polygamists is a form of orientalist othering and civilising discourse which places 'them' into a category 'over there' because they are not behaving in a civilised enough manner to inhabit the same space.

Although the monogamy versus polygamy model does not refer explicitly to the West, the creation of this dichotomy is bound up with imperialist and colonialist understandings of marriage. Earlier, I explained how domesticity and ideals of marriage were markers of imperialist societal advancement. The monogamous 'us' definition has been constructed according to the way that it differs from the polygamous 'them' within orientalist and imperialist understandings of marriage. In fact, Pearsall (2019) argues polygamy gave Europeans an excellent litmus test to apply to different cultures in other worlds as well as within their own. Polygamy crops up repeatedly in the judgements European colonialists passed against other peoples, while Christianity, marriage, progress and civility were so tightly melded together by colonialist powers that they are yet to be unravelled. In this way, orientalism and imperialism are not only historically powerful, but remain a persuasive influence on the 'superiority' of monogamy over polygamy today in a subtler form. My postcolonial feminist lens enables me to expose and disrupt the undercurrents of these colonialist processes which operate to create a divide even today between monogamists and polygamists based on historical attitudes. A contemporary, contextualised examination of how polygamy is othered and decried based on its differences to monogamy is necessary because these othering and civilising influences are no longer declared so openly.

In studies around the aftermath of initial colonial encounters, the emergence of nation-building to replace empire-building is another example of how orientalist and imperialist ideals permeate modern state and policy making. At the height of imperial rule, Christian monogamy was reinforced by colonisers and used to underscore the civilising mission because it was seen as a matter for humanity and for the good of the community. Nation-building has since replaced empire-building with the same, though updated, mission to secure and uphold national interests. It is now a matter for the nation and the nation's people though these people are the settlers who benefit from imperialist ways. The notion of preserving monogamy for national security reasons has become more corporeal as the budding nation-state protects its borders and resources and all those worthy of being protected within.

Denike (2010) provides insight into this through her consideration of race and polygamous marriage in Canada and the US. She observes the historical connection between nationalist sentiments and marriage noting that 'anti-polygamy campaigns were deeply implicated in the alignment of normative sexual monogamy and racial Anglo-Saxonism within the imperial logic of the nation-state' (Denike, 2010: 868). In charting racist and imperialist patterns of thought in these campaigns, she interrogates the denial of recognition for polygamous marriages and the preservation of a national monogamous identity. As a result, polygamy has developed from being a threat to the empire based on its barbarity to being a threat to the nation-state and its continuing concerns of national interests and security. Sweet (2013) addresses these ideas in her critique of Canadian nation-building discourses concluding that the monogamous marriage ideal is still viewed as essential for upholding national values and women's equality (see also Burton, 1999). This demonstrates how public interests and policies relating to the legal regulation of polygamous marriages have been formulated with reference to powerful historical discourses. Without thinking about the continued presence of orientalism and imperialism and how they operate now, it is not possible to construct an alternative account of polygamous marriage along with its contemporary characterisation as an obstacle to national interests.

In addition to the need for alternative accounts of orientalism and imperialism to situate our conceptions of marriage and polygamy in the current climate, I emphasise the other key function of alternative perspectives. Just like the women who challenge and transgress narratives around the purpose and significance of the hijab, it is crucial to highlight the alternative accounts of those with a less or non-Eurocentric view. The tool I use here is disruption without which we cannot hear or see real, lived alternative and contextualised experiences.

Disruptive (hi)stories and voices

The implementation of a historically conscious anti-colonial lens gives rise to urgent questions about history and the knowledges that it comprises. What history am I being conscious of here? What knowledges and sources make up our understanding of that history? I have already discussed how the law in its current form is outdated and shaped by a limited cross section of historical experiences and colonialisms. This was in temporal terms. I develop this to posit that the law's regressive stance is additionally formed in substantive terms from the colonialist's view, leaving no room for the voices and stories of those who have lived and are 'living' polygamy. Instead, the law is situated in the colonial gaze.

Fanon provides deeper insight into the history and voices being represented in and around the colonial encounter. He starkly states that '[t]he settler makes history and is conscious of making it' (Fanon, 1961: 51). Moreover, 'it is the settler who has brought the native into existence and who perpetuates his existence' (Fanon, 1961: 36). This means that the 'native has always known that he need expect nothing from the other side' (Fanon, 1961: 93). These observations portray the dominance of the colonialist's knowledges and understandings in the history that they purposely make to justify their actions and behaviour in perpetuity. Implicit in this is the making of the native in the first place. Colonised people were not subjected to outsider categorisations before colonisation; they were the people of their land and had their own ways of being and living. The coloniser arrived and turned them into natives to dismiss them and their ways. The coloniser constructed and shared stories about them and silenced their voices, leading to the knowledge that expecting to be treated with any level of equanimity was futile. The history of these people and practices (like polygamy) which came to be associated with them was likewise subjected to the same processes of nativising, silencing and dismissal. It is another tool of colonialist expansion to erase and replace the histories and knowledges of the natives, committing epistemic violence against societies and cultures that date back thousands of years.

Epistemic violence represents the way that knowledges and histories of oppressed peoples and societies are destroyed and distorted by their oppressors. de Sousa Santos (2018) shows that epistemologies of the South encompass the knowledge and histories of colonised societies' struggle for validation and recognition compared with the dominating epistemologies of the oppressors. This is echoed in Connell's (2014) claim that there is an assumption the 'Global South' is a source of data and subject of study, but not a producer of theory or original intellectual insights. Colonised societies are to be looked at and studied, but seemingly fail to create the conditions to study and gaze for themselves. Epistemologies of the South are not simply about identifying or labelling ways of knowing, but about the valorisation of knowledges which both constitute and emerge as forms of resistance. Such knowledges are grounded not in thought but in real life.

I am conscious of these epistemologies, this history and these voices to expose colonial violence and disruption is instrumental here. My disruption manifests in two ways: centring and building on the disruptive stories in existing critical literature while also exposing the problematic narratives on polygamous marriages and showcasing the disruptive voices of the women who spoke with me about their experiences and views. This disruption is inspired by critical engagement with the works of scholars like Said, Fanon and Bhabha. Said's foundational *Orientalism* (1978) has been criticised for writing out the colonised and their agency. This is contrasted against Fanon (2008), who does create an account of the native and their agency with some substance, while Bhabha (1986) argues that the native and the coloniser are complex and depend on each other for their identity formation (see further Moore-Gilbert, 2000). With this, Bhabha destabilises the coloniser and the power dynamics around colonial encounters to show that although the coloniser dismissed, silenced and rendered the native inferior, the native still resisted and disrupted against colonisation in multiple ways.

How is this relevant to a study of women in polygamous marriages and the law? In her study of polygamy in 19th-century America, Pearsall eloquently explains that: '[i]n colonial and postcolonial contexts, to love, to marry, and to divorce have sometimes been revolutionary acts. … The nation-state grew stronger, but there was always pushback against it' (2019: 293). To marry in a way which differs from the oppressor's ideal is a form of revolution. Polygamous marriage is an act of disruption to dominant ideals and approval but it is only by looking from the perspective of those criticised for practising it that we realise this. Current scholarship provides a fascinating insight into how polygamy can defy stereotypes which situate it as an ignorant, backward practice belonging to the past and associated with a lack of education and class. For example, in works looking at polygamy in the Aztec empire (Hassig, 2016); 19th-century America (Pearsall, 2019), and present-day Malay communities (Zeitzen, 2018), there is a recurring theme of polygamy as an 'elite' form of marriage reserved by communities for those in the upper classes. Three very different contexts and yet polygamy was/is practised by those in power using it to facilitate marriage within their social circles and preserve their wealth. This disruptive theme shows us how perceptions in the coloniser's history of polygamy as backward and ignorant are challenged. Polygamy was not just a marital structure; 'it was a political and economic structure' and a 'symbol of resistance' against colonialist impositions of Christian monogamous orthodoxy practised in the past and today by those with power, influence and social standing in their communities (Pearsall, 2019: 117). What was the most effective way to overcome a society or community through oppressive means? Attacking the domestic foundations of the upper classes and most privileged was a tried-and-tested colonial method for subjecting the natives. Disruption to their families and marriages destabilised and weakened the more privileged natives making them more vulnerable to oppression and abuse, which trickled down to the remainder of their communities. We can see, therefore, that polygamy was perceived and treated as a threat throughout colonial encounters because it was synonymous with power. This perception and treatment continue today with fears in contemporary discourse of society being damaged and overrun by polygamists.

Another critical disruption in the polygamy literature is concerned with the agency of women in these marriages. In her work on Mormon polygamy and religion, Johnson observes that women are portrayed as lacking in agency when making the decision to enter a polygamous marriage as 'a powerful social narrative presumes [their] consent to have been coerced' (2014: 110–11). Women are subject to assumptions regarding their agency to make the right decision about their marriage rendering their decision-making abilities inferior to women in monogamous marriages. In this situation the presumption of coercion depicts women in these marriages as in need of saving from the parties that coerce them, so they are Brown women in need of saving from other Brown people. This colonial saviour narrative is disrupted by research with women in such relationships such as the women of Bountiful in Canada who Campbell (2013) spent time with or the African American polygynous wives who spoke with Majeed (2015). The experiences of these women are wide-ranging as they demonstrate their choice, agency and personal decision-making processes. Understandings of marriage have evolved in English law, yet this progress is limited to monogamous, legally recognised relationships which include same-sex marriage and civil partnerships. Polygamy is still treated as a foreign, historical practice and we need to disrupt the colonialist influences over the law's outdated responses which do not account for the possibility of a woman choosing this marital form.

The saviour narrative in this area also appears in the contemporary framing of polygamous marriage as undesirable because it is an obstacle to gender and spousal equality. Parekh (2010) argues that monogamy provides a better framework and environment for equality and this is echoed throughout the literature in debates about polygamy and harm (see also Brooks, 2009). While the gender equality framework has been responsible for achieving a more gender-equal society, in the context of polygamy regulation I argue that questions and concerns about gender equality are still bound up with colonialist understandings of this form of relationship. By assuming that women have no agency to enter polygamous marriages they are viewed as being in a subordinated position. This is set against the equally powerful assumption that women not in these relationships enjoy gender equality when that is not a given (Volpp, 2001; Chan, 2011). Legal responses to gender equality and polygamy are construed narrowly because they are still permeated with historical colonialist attitudes that posit the West as superior at achieving gender equality and the protection of women. Gender inequality is a harm, but it is important to think about what gender inequality and harm mean in this context in a way which does not rely on colonialist constructions of them. These themes around salvation, harm and inequality need to be disrupted and complicated to reflect the lives of women subjected to the coloniser's gaze in relation to polygamy.

It is apparent then that multiple themes reflected in the literature reveal a lack of nuance towards polygamy and its regulation. A critical examination of the law is not enough to expose and address these damaging discourses. A more impactful disruption is required to ensure that the multiplicity of women's experiences of polygamy are foregrounded, and the best way to achieve this is to ask women how they experience and view polygamy along with its legal regulation in the UK. Sharing women's lived stories and their voices is the second stream of disruption used to explore the law in this area. However, this sharing of voices is a significant responsibility for me as a researcher. I need to ensure that these disruptive voices are shared in as unfiltered and authentic a manner as possible so that the narrator comes first, not the researcher. It was not my intention to subject the women who spoke with me to my gaze, reminiscent of a colonising observer. This disruption is inspired by a rich vein of literature that considers how and whether the colonised or subaltern can speak for themselves (for example, Mohanty, 1984; Spivak, 1988; Asher, 2017).

In her work with people affected by the partition of India, Das observes that those she asked to share their stories about violence during this dark period 'had speech but not voice' (2007: 8). From a speech pathologist's perspective: '[s]peech is more of a mechanical act; it's the way you structure the placement and movement of your articulators – lips, teeth, tongue', while voice 'is your unique signature; it reflects your personality, your mood, and your auditory identity' (Sankin Speech Improvement, nd). In this way, speech is a physical act concerned with how you shape and form words, but voice is a facet of your identity. Voice tells a deeper story; it immerses the listener in the narrative and compels them to pay attention. Voice is more likely to provoke emotion and thought because it reflects the identity, personality and, most importantly, the context of the narrator. The personal historical and contemporary context promoted by uplifting the voices of polygamous wives is key. This approach advances an understanding of the impact of these women's personal context on their experiences and attitudes towards marriage and polygamy in society, religion, culture and law.

However, there is still a risk regarding my presence and role as a researcher in this data collection process. In critical feminist schools, like postcolonial feminism, Western feminism is often criticised for 'speaking for' the other (Ahmed, 2000; see also Yeatman, 1993). When collecting and sharing the experiences of others, there is a risk of assuming authority over the narrations that have been gathered; in doing so, we could dismiss the epistemologies of the South and their struggle for recognition. We could remain silent and refrain from asking women about their experiences (Landry and MacLean, 1996), but as Ahmed (2000) contends, such a stance would cause us to fail in our responsibilities as researchers. Silence assumes a distance and difference between the researcher and participants which is reinforced because by not trying to speak with real people, we refuse to take responsibility for and mitigate that distance and difference (Ahmed, 2000). I do not represent the women who sacrificed their time and energy to speak with me and trusted me with their stories. They are the disruptors, and this book shares their stories and journeys through marriage and law in the UK. Highlighting their unvarnished tales is the main way to do this, and this forms the backbone of the book. This is especially displayed as I introduce Chapters 5, 6 and 7 with the stories of women who directly experienced polygamy told in their own words. Their voices provide a springboard for my discussion of the themes that arose during my conversations with all the women who spoke with me for this project.

Concluding thoughts

This chapter explained the approach that I take throughout this book to underpin my analysis of the law, policy and women's experiences around polygamous marriages. Using insights and tools from critical postcolonial feminism, I highlighted the ways in which this school of thought paves the way for a more meaningful and nuanced exploration of this form of marriage in the UK today.

To begin with, we must pay attention to history. The law and social attitudes towards polygamy are bound up with the colonial. This form of marriage has been constructed by colonialist voices as something which came from a foreign land and is not compatible with life here. This does not reflect the variety of relationship and marital forms that exist today in the UK. Examining history is important, but it is not enough to think through how women are affected by polygamous marriages today; this is where my mission to disrupt comes to the fore.

I delved into the ideological underpinnings of orientalism and imperialism to show that they are powerful historical discourses which resonate today but have also adapted and mutated into subtler contemporary influences over the law, state and society. We need to uncover and engage with these concepts in a more sophisticated and nuanced manner which accounts for their contemporary manifestations. In addition, we need to look for alternative accounts of these orientalist and imperialist discourses to decentre the colonialist's gaze and voice of 'authority' over polygamous marriage and the women who practise it. To construct these alternative accounts, I take a two-pronged approach. First, I uplift the counter-narratives and disruptive stories in existing literature, such as the understanding of polygamy as an elite practice. Second, I share the disruptive voices and stories of the women who spoke with me and shared their experiences of polygamy and marriage in the UK. In colonial contexts, marriage and love were revolutionary forms of resistance and disruption, but the people behind them, the women who were undertaking these acts, were no less revolutionary. Their entire lives and being were a form of defiant disruption in the face of colonialist oppressions and violence. Laws around polygamous marriages are framed to perceive and treat this form of marriage as a threat because the people who practise it were, and are, a threat to colonial governance and dominance. The law is rooted in colonialist fear – a fear which has not abated in the present day, but is unjustified in the face of contemporary legal, policy and social developments.

3

Polygamy in England: Tracing Legal Developments

In Chapter 2, I argued that we need to be more conscious of the context that surrounds the development of legal responses towards polygamy in England and Wales to better understand how the current framework came about. I now build this contextualised account of the law to uncover the forces that shape and frame the law and its effects on people in these marriages. I start in this chapter with the law around polygamous marriages that are celebrated in England and Wales between individuals who are domiciled and/or living in these countries. If a polygamous marriage is celebrated between two people who are domiciled and/or living in England and Wales, regardless of where the ceremony takes place, it would be void. This is because a UK resident or domiciliary who is already in a marriage which is legally recognised in the UK does not have the capacity to contract another legally binding marriage.[1] This approach applies where the ceremony falls within the scope of the Marriage Act 1949 because it purports to be the kind of ceremony that would be legally valid or because the parties have tried to comply with some or all of the requirements in the 1949 Act. However, there are also ceremonies that do not fall within the 1949 Act, and these are seen as non-qualifying ceremonies which are non-existent in legal terms. These tend to be marriages that are valid in religion, such as the Muslim Nikah, but do not meet the requirements of the 1949 Act around giving notice, registration and location. Why does it matter whether it is a void marriage or a non-qualifying ceremony? When a marriage is void, the courts are still able to provide financial relief to the parties if the relationship

1 s 11(b) Matrimonial Causes Act 1973 provides for marriage ceremonies being void if either party was already lawfully married at the time and s 11(d) of the same Act provides that a polygamous marriage celebrated overseas when one or both of the parties is domiciled in England and Wales at the time of the ceremony is also void.

breaks down. The same is not true for a non-qualifying ceremony. As it is non-existent, there is no opportunity for the parties to seek relief from the courts. Polygamy celebrated informally in England and Wales is most likely to fall under this category.

It is difficult to produce a stable or linear narrative of how this framework has developed over the centuries, although there are some detailed explorations of its historical development that we can draw from (see for example, Witte, 2015). I add to this existing work by thinking through the wider contextual issues and dominant discourses around the law which need to be disrupted to better meet the needs of people in polygamous marriages. To achieve this, I organise the chapter around a series of key legal moments in English matrimonial law stretching back to before formal European colonising processes. I then look at the first English statute that criminalised polygamy which was introduced in 1604, as well as the Clandestine Marriages Act 1753 and the Marriage Act 1836, which provided for the civil marriage ceremonies we have today. From my analysis of these key moments and their context, I make three arguments. First, Christianity – more specifically, Anglican Christianity – dominates legal understandings and the structure of marriage in England and Wales which prioritises monogamy. Second, this Christian dominance is intertwined with coloniality to make English law indifferent to the context in which polygamy and other forms of non-Christian marriage are celebrated in England and Wales. It is also worth remembering here that Christianity played a significant role in the colonial civilising mission so this link between religion and marriage law is not surprising. Finally, due to these two forces of Christian dominance and colonial indifference, marriage ceremonies and relationships that do not conform to Christian monogamous ideals have been invisible or ignored in English law for centuries. Before delving into my discussion of the law, I explain what I mean by the law's indifference and why it is a problem as inspired by critical postcolonial understandings of this concept.

Law as indifferent

What does it mean when I argue that indifference underpins legal responses in this area? At first glance, this seems like an innocuous statement. Granzow (2020) observes through various Oxford Dictionary definitions that indifference amounts to having no particular interest. In its origins, a sense of being neither good nor bad was communicated through this term. To be indifferent is to be apathetic, to have no feelings, concern or sympathy towards something or someone. As Granzow declares, this word denotes an absence or a lack of care. To have neither positive nor negative feelings ensures that indifference is seemingly the epitome of neutrality. Indifference has been the subject of deeper contemplation by thinkers such as Locke who devoted attention to it in his posthumously published treatise *Of the Conduct of the Understanding* (see Locke, 1706). Rather than indifference, Locke unpacks the notion of 'indifferency', but as Lee (2013) argues, there is no stable distinction between the two. Indifferency in Locke's interpretation is a position of impartiality where one is indifferent to all viewpoints so that they can be weighed objectively. Taking this interpretation, to be indifferent means that the law has no stance towards non-normative and minoritized marriage practices and is a study in neutrality and impartiality, rendering its position harmless and even possibly positive.

However, there is more to indifference than we might think. It is not possible for the law to remain neutral, and a supposed lack of feeling is always more revealing than its presence. Inspired by Locke, Lee (2013) argues that when thinking through the meaning of indifference, the boundary between neutrality and disaffection is permeable. It implies an awareness of others' thoughts and positions while remaining calculatingly aloof from those thoughts and positions (see also Hollander, 2019). The impartial, neutral approach envisaged by Locke for indifferency includes devaluation and apathy. Where indifference is posited as taking the position of 'I don't know', it has additionally taken on shades of 'I don't care' (Lee, 2013). Therefore, indifference is not passive and neutral, but involves knowing while simultaneously not caring. The detachment and distance that indifference requires are constructed, and when thinking through the effects on marginalised and minoritised communities, Granzow (2020) argues that such indifference leads to dehumanisation and racialisation. By racialisation, I mean processes that result in people being categorised according to race or markers of their identity which are socially connected with race including religion (El-Enany, 2020). A lack of feeling is a lack of interest which is not neutral or harmless at all. By taking away feeling or sympathy, we become disconnected, and once that happens, we stop seeing each other's humanness; this can only be harmful.

Indifference is also an under-theorised aspect of colonial attitudes and mentality, which is why it is of concern for the present law around polygamous marriages celebrated in England. During and after colonial encounters, we can see the lack of interest in the colonies through the many violences that were visited on them and their inhabitants with no regard for their humanity. However, the insidious forces causing this lack of regard remain less exposed. Drawing on Rukmini Bhaya Nair's (1999, 2002) ideas, it is through the everyday humdrum bureaucratic and administrative functions of the imperial regime – of which law was a significant part – that we see indifference at its best. In the context of the colonisation of India, Nair (1999) argues that indifference was a way for the British imperial authorities to organise the complex domain of the subcontinent to challenge every element of civil society. Indifference formed part of a linguistic strategy of conquest to enable the colonial power to establish itself. This presented as emotional and cultural distance and provided the matrix through which it operated then, and still operates today, as coloniality. Corruption, graft and violence are the main subject of critical engagement in postcolonial studies, but these are symptoms of the underlying attitudinal structure of indifference. Ranging from ignorance through disinterest and all the way to inhumanity, indifference is the bedrock of these more prominent expressions of colonial power. Advancing this is Granzow's (2020) claim that indifference is more accurately a form of investment. It occurs through practices. Being indifferent requires an active commitment to being distant, detached and unconcerned. It is not passive or neutral.

Even as we negotiate the 'post' colonial today, institutions and powers, including law, display indifference towards those they govern and regulate. For example, Kolsky (2010) notes that a lack of secondary literature around forms of gender violence in colonial India indicates that they were of little interest to colonial authorities and parliamentary reformers at the time compared to the more sensationalised sati.[2] The 'common' abuse and murder of women was viewed by the colonial courts as a social rather than legal problem which should be handled by Indians themselves and so there was no inquiry into these offences by colonial reformers. The legal authorities were indifferent and therefore deemed Indian women unworthy of concern, leading to the women's racialisation and dehumanisation. This highlights once again that indifference is not harmless.

How does this indifference-led dehumanisation play out in the law today? When legal responses are indifferent to individuals affected by a legal issue, the law is neglecting their real-life experiences and the impacts of the law on their lives. The law therefore consciously develops in a way which results in it lacking awareness of the ones it governs. Inspired by Bhabha's (1983) work, which sees ambivalence deployed by the law as a colonial strategy of discriminatory power, I expand this to include indifference. As a strategy for discriminatory power, indifference creates the space for a 'subject people' who are subjected to stereotypes that are produced as knowledges to racialise, orientalise and cast them as inferior. In the case of polygamous marriages, this relationship form serves to racialise participants as the law is culturally and emotionally distanced from it. In displaying indifference by refusing for centuries to meaningfully engage with the legal framework around polygamy in England, the law has been manifesting a strategy of

[2] Sati is the practice whereby a widow sacrifices herself and burns on her husband's funeral pyre. The belief is that the wife will be rewarded greatly for her sacrifice. Instances of women being forced by their families and communities to engage in sati are well-documented.

discriminatory power that is used against minoritised individuals who marry in this way. Indifference to polygamous marriage is discriminatory, racialising and dehumanising.

Establishing Christian dominance over marriage law

There is no specific legal moment or detailed record of legal developments before the 16th century that we can scrutinise, and so we start with a broader scene-setting exercise to show the religious dominance over attitudes to polygamy. Polygamy is not alien to Britain. Milton observed that before Christianity arrived in ancient Britain, there were several early British polygamist kings, so the practice of polygamy by elite members of the community was present (see Patterson, 1931–38). In addition, there are records showing that when the missionary Augustine arrived to spread Christianity in Britain in AD 597, he asked Pope Gregory I what he should do regarding the polygamous Anglo-Saxons. He was advised that it was better to be tolerant of polygamy than condemn it (Chapman, 2001). For many, marriage is intertwined with religion. Religious guidelines and belief systems have shaped and continue to shape the ways that we define, enter and leave marriage. The legal debates around marriage and polygamy are in many cases also theological ones. This was the case even before Christianity became dominant in Britain with later Anglo-Saxon kings, such as Ethelred II categorising polygamy as a grave violation of divine law, in the same vein as incest and adultery in AD 994 (Witte, 2015). The reference to divine law is notable here as we see the religious basis for governing responses towards polygamy and by extension the formation and structure of marriage even during those times.

This interconnectedness of law and religion is worth exploring further in the context of polygamous marriage. Rivers (2017) argues that it is hard to evaluate whether English marriage law is Christian. He states that while there is nothing inherently Christian about the English legal understanding of marriage which reflects similar understandings of marriage from around the world, the Christian influence over English law is obvious in the state's regulation of formalities. Indeed, the Christian influences are undeniable. The establishment and persistence of Christian dominance in the British Isles means that law and legal conceptions of marriage are underpinned by Christianity (Kindregan, 2007). England remains a Christian country with the Queen as Head of State and Head of the Church of England. The Christian underpinnings of law are apparent and English law is not only Christian in origin but remains mostly compatible with Christianity. Rivers (2012) observes elsewhere that historically English law has been used as a tool to coerce Christian belief and practice in direct ways, and the direct effects of Christian teaching can be traced in the law around marriage and family. The point about coercion is vital because it feeds into later responses to polygamy, as we shall see.

More explicitly, before the Reformation, marriage was a religious institution under Roman Catholic rule. De Cruz even argues that for centuries the Church 'had exclusive jurisdiction over marriage and its consequences' (2010: 5). Any law being followed on marriage was inspired by Roman Catholic doctrine and canonical guidance. In these early Catholic times, monogamy was considered the norm which was unsurprising because the Roman Empire within which Christianity was born had criminalised polygamous marriage in AD 258 (Witte, 2015). However, the Catholic Church refrained from banning polygamy outright and dispensations permitting a man to take another wife remained possible. For example, in AD 726, Pope Gregory II answered a question of Bishop Boniface regarding marriage as follows:

> As to what a man shall do if his wife is unable through illness to allow him his marital rights, it would be better if he remained apart and practised continence. But since this is practicable only in the case of men of high ideals, the best course if he is unable to be continent would be for him to marry. Nevertheless, he should continue to support the woman who is sick, unless she has contracted the disease through her own fault [Gratian, *Decretum,* C.32 q 7. c.18].[3] (Talbot, 1954: 25)

This response clearly shows that the Catholic Church was willing to accept polygamous marriages in certain circumstances, but this was an exceptional permission for exceptional circumstances and did not translate into everyday practice. The ecclesiastical or religious courts in England presided over cases of polygamy which was treated as a spiritual crime attracting moral sanctions and community disapproval. Polygamy was frowned upon even though it was practised in early Britain and was never completely banned in Catholicism. We also need to keep in mind that Christian monogamy was the norm since in this pre-Reformation period, England was mostly populated by Christians. There would have been little interaction with non-Europeans – only perhaps through the crusades in Jerusalem, a distant land – and so English marriage regulation would not have taken into consideration anyone outside of the dominant majority-Christian populace. The Christian dominance over marriage law is therefore expected.

During this time when the law was an overt and intrinsic part of the religion, the real concern of authorities and leaders was upholding Christian ideals

---

3 The Pope cites a ruling in Gratian's *Decretum* (*Decreta,* pt ii, ch 32, q 7, can18), but I was unable to trace an English translation of this rule.

of monogamy while steering people away from a form of marriage which was displayed clearly by the revered polygamous leaders spoken about in the Hebrew Bible. The example set by these figures meant that polygamy posed a real challenge and provocation to the Church because it could be claimed that it was a form of Biblical marriage and therefore potentially acceptable (Vogel, 1991). A practice narrated in scripture is difficult to dismiss and this created difficulties for making monogamy the ideal and only acceptable type of marriage. Efforts were made to ensure that polygamy was not justified based on the ancient examples in the Bible. Instead, it was argued that these polygamous marriages were only background information for the people in the scripture (Onalaja, 2004). Moreover, the New Testament indicates that marriage should be monogamous, as demonstrated by the references to 'a man' and 'his wife' in the book of Genesis 2:24 (cited in Brooke, 1989); and in Deuteronomy 17:17, those who 'take many wives' are admonished, indicating another source which supports polygamy's prohibition' (Hillman, 1975). Polygamy was viewed as a part of pre-Christian religious history that should be confined to the cases mentioned in the Hebrew Bible, which were permissible through 'divine dispensation' (Hillman, 1975). The main concern at this point was to make sure that the reputation and character of these ancient leaders as role models were not questioned because of their marital practices. Thus, although there was no outright ban on polygamy, it was not encouraged either. The preservation and protection of Christian monogamy is therefore apparent from these early times and this approach governs marriage law today.

Distancing the behaviour of the ancient patriarchs in the Hebrew Bible from Christian marriage and the setting up of monogamy as the only marital form that can promote mutual rights and equality are early othering and orientalising processes. When leaders in the Hebrew Bible were held up as role models while their marriages were pushed to the background, there was a distancing process happening here. Their behaviour was exceptional because they inhabited a different time and space to later common Christians. This highlighting of differences is an orientalising process, but a more subtle one. It is a way for Church authorities located in Rome in the West, to authorise views on the Bible and its stories in the Middle East or part of the Orient. The differences, instead of being used to show how the Biblical figures were inferior, are marked out for relegation to the background of their stories. Their behaviour is excused because they were special but it is still frowned upon and certainly not tolerable in later Christian communities. In this way, they are orientalised to protect their narratives in the Hebrew Bible while achieving the Church's aim of protecting Christian monogamy.

In addition to the emphasis on Christian monogamy, the Biblical debates shaped discourses around the justifications for a ban on polygamy.

Monogamous marriage in the New Testament is described in the 'egalitarian language of mutuality and equality' (Witte, 2015: 69, referring to Ephesians 5: 31–2). Monogamy is positioned in Christian teachings as promoting equality between husband and wife. If monogamy promotes equality, then polygamy is set up as its inferior, unable to promote equality because the mutual rights of the husband and wife cannot be fulfilled if one person has multiple marriages. The passage in Ephesians 5 where this is shown goes on to model Christian marriage between a husband and wife on the union between Christ as bridegroom and the Church as his bride. Christian marriage should follow the example of the marriage between Christ and Church which is monogamous. The setting up of monogamy as the ideal for marriage as espoused by Christ himself ensures that any polygamous alternative will be inferior – another example of an othering process. Polygamy cannot compare to the monogamous ideal. While the emphasis on equality is used to justify the ban on polygamy, there is little interrogation of how polygamy may or may not uphold equality in a deeper sense. Polygamy is defined by what it is not, which leaves it orientalised and in a permanently inferior place even if it was practised by important figures in Christianity's history.

The Christian dominance openly expressed in legal responses to polygamous marriage from these earlier times also created the ideal conditions for the later development of imperial indifference towards polygamy in English law. When looking at the debates around the presence of polygamy and its permissibility in theological terms, there is a trend of thinking about it when the most significant concern about marriage in Christianity arises: divorce. Preventing and discouraging polygamy was important but still secondary to the fear of divorce. The introduction of 'simultaneous' and 'consecutive' polygamy into discussions shows this. Consecutive polygamy would nowadays be more commonly termed 'serial monogamy'. It involved a man divorcing and remarrying while his first wife was still living – a concept which is rejected in the New Testament. This 'great evil' regarding marriage was seen as consecutive polygamy since divorce is forbidden while there is no mention of simultaneous polygamy (Igenoza, 2003). As a result, polygamy was more of a concern for the Catholic Church when it facilitated a departure from the monogamous ideal or included divorce. This suggests that there was a comparatively indifferent approach towards polygamy that warranted attention only to reinforce the Christian doctrines around protecting monogamous marriage and preventing divorce. Such indifference explains the lack of formal developments around polygamy in the religious laws and courts for all these centuries because only one response was needed: an outright ban. It may have been included in theological discussions of the Bible, but it was used as a tool to uplift monogamy and then to reject divorce and remarriage. The designation of polygamy as secondary to other concerns about marriage and relationships continued and with time, took on increasing shades of indifference in its more insidious forms to dehumanise and discriminate.

Standardised marriage and standardised arguments: the 16th, 17th and 18th centuries

In the 16th, 17th and 18th centuries, we start to see sweeping changes to English law and governance along with the passing of two statutes indicating attitudes towards polygamy celebrated in England that remain prevalent today. I look at these three centuries together because developments in relation to polygamy were few and far between. The Holy Roman Empire officially designated polygamy as a criminal offence from 1532,[4] and the Council of Trent, also known as the 19th ecumenical council of the Roman Catholic Church, declared it an offence which could lead to excommunication (Vogel, 1991). There was little change from the previous approach of polygamy being an offence that had moral sanctions attached to it. In England, more dramatic changes in religious legal governance were happening brought about by the Protestant Reformation. The Reformation was triggered by one of the most high-profile divorce cases in English history: the divorce of Henry VIII from Catherine of Aragon. This case was steeped in religious debate and polygamy was considered as an alternative in the debates to dissolving this royal marriage. For some, the King having two wives was preferable to divorce and remarriage. In the end, the possibility of polygamous marriage was dismissed, and the divorce led to the English monarchy's break with the Roman Catholic Church (see further Bretschneider, 1963). Over this period, the main development in the English framework was the shift in authority over marriage away from the Church towards the monarchy and later, the state.

Until this time, disputes around marriage had been resolved in religious courts and with reference to Catholic doctrine. Earlier I mentioned that the monarch of England is both Head of State and Head of the Church of England. Bearing in mind the Protestant Reformation and the civil wars that occurred between 1642 and 1651 led to a shift in power from the Catholic Church, we need to think about the meaning of the shift towards the monarchy and then the state. Was authority over marriage truly taken from the religious authorities? The power struggle between Henry VIII and the Roman Catholic Church was instigated and driven by a marriage dispute. It was led by the monarch wanting the power to divorce and marry

[4] This criminalisation of polygamy is the precursor to the offence of bigamy that was first introduced in 1604. Bigamy was not yet a term used to describe the specific criminal offence which is why I refer to it as the criminalisation of polygamy here.

at will, but England's break with Rome was not a break with Christianity or religion. It was a break with the Catholic Church specifically. Due to the Reformation, the monarch became Head of the Church of England in addition to being Head of State, which meant that the power over marriage and its regulation was not removed from religious authorities and given to the monarch; rather, the two competing powers of Church and monarchy manifested in one person. The religious courts remained dominant in relation to marriage, but they were now applying Church of England doctrine which was ultimately overseen by the monarchy, and later the state. The Church's interests and motivations were aligned with the King's. In terms of the move towards state authority and a system of political democracy, the monarch retained their titles over state and church, even though they were more ceremonial in nature. With no official separation between church and state in England, this consolidation of power has created a model of governance that maintains the strong influence and dominance of Christianity over marriage and its legal regulation. Chatterjee (2010) considers the relationship between nation-states and religion in the postcolonial context to argue that the state does not withdraw from or deprioritise religious matters, but assumes the role of ultimate decision maker for them instead. The two cannot be separated even if there are attempts to formally do so. In taking on the role of ultimate decision maker for religious issues, the state becomes the ultimate enforcer of religious (in this case Christian) principles at the same time. Religion has therefore remained the deciding authority through this period and beyond.

From the Reformation to the English Civil Wars, these were turbulent times for England, and this continued through the 17th and 18th centuries (Lincoln, 2021). For this reason, scholars such as Rebecca Probert (2009) quite reasonably tell us that marriage law and regulation were not the only problems or concerns afflicting London and England during these three centuries. This could explain why there were so few developments around polygamous marriage and even why the criminalisation of polygamy by statute did not happen until 1604 – much later than in the rest of Europe. While this may be the case, I would argue that the dearth of legal attention or concern overall is also reflective of polygamy being considered a secondary concern to more pressing matters such as divorce and clandestine marriages. By emphasising that there were more important things to address, the law had formed the ideal conditions to express indifference towards polygamy. This indifference may have resulted from the need to be practical, but it developed into something more dismissive and troubling as time progressed.

In 1604 the statute 1 Jac 1, c 11, titled An Act to restrain all Persons from Marriage until their former Wives and former Husbands be dead, was passed to make getting married while your first spouse was still alive a common law felony offence which was punishable by death. The Act has been touted as the first time that 'bigamy' was criminalised (Bartholomew,

1958; Capp, 2009; Witte, 2015), and it is here that we start to see this term take precedence in the discourse around plural marriage. But what is bigamy? The word derives from the Latin *bigamia*, which was originally used in the Middle Ages to describe widows and widowers who remarried following the death of their first spouse. *Bigamia* was not a criminal status but an everyday social one (McDougall, 2010). As Bartholomew (1958) adds, bigamy did not involve marrying someone while already being in a valid marriage. However, it later assumed this meaning and became the label in English law for when a person is already in a valid marriage but goes through another ceremony of marriage which fulfils all the relevant legal formalities. Polygamy, the practice of being married to more than one person at the same time, encompasses marriages that are celebrated formally and informally in law, religion or custom around the world and therefore has a much broader meaning than bigamy in English law. Bigamy does not cover polygamous marriages that are celebrated lawfully in another jurisdiction or outside of the legal framework in the UK. The term 'bigamy' is not mentioned in the Act's title, and this is the same for the substantive provisions. There was therefore no official offence named 'bigamy' until the 1604 Act was transposed and updated into the Offences Against the Person Act 1828 more than two centuries later.

The 1604 Act has several characteristics which make it an interesting case study on the shaping and framing of the law. The preamble is straightforward, telling us that the Act is to stop 'evil disposed Persons' running to a different county or another place where they are unknown to marry while having another living husband or wife:

> Forasmuch as divers evil disposed Persons being married, run out of one County into another, or into Places where they are not known, and there become to be married, having another Husband or Wife living, to the great Dishonour of God, and utter Undoing of divers honest Mens Children, and others.

Before the Act, the religious courts dealt with cases of polygamy as a spiritual crime, and any second marriage would be held invalid. Based on the preamble to the 1604 Act, we can see that it was meant to achieve the same thing but entailed different judicial mechanisms and consequences. By referring to this behaviour as a 'great Dishonour of God', the influence of Christian canon is evident. This was not an offence against the community but against God, which means that its Christian foundation was still dominant. Thus the Act represents a continuation of existing legal attitudes and was not as monumental as we might think.

Looking at the provisions, there are some defences the accused could claim. One is that they had procured an ecclesiastical divorce or annulment:

> Provided also, and be it enacted by the Authority aforesaid, That this Act, nor any Thing herein contained, shall extend to any Person or Persons that are or shall be at the Time of such Marriage divorced by any Sentence had or hereafter to be had in the Ecclesiastical Court; or to any Person or Persons where the former Marriage hath been or hereafter shall be by Sentence in the Ecclesiastical Court declared to be void and of no Effect; nor to any Person or Persons for or by reason of any former Marriage had or made, or hereafter to be had or made, within Age of Consent.

Drawing on the case law from the period, Bartholomew (1958) argues that the Act was passed to respond to issues with the only available form of ecclesiastical divorce in this period: the *decree a mensa et thoro causa adulterii*. This was a form of legal separation granted by the ecclesiastical courts where the marriage was not dissolved but the couple no longer had to live together if a party had committed adultery. Prior to the Act, there was confusion about whether those with this decree who went on to marry another person should be prosecuted in the religious courts for polygamy. In *Rye v Fuliambe* (1602) Moo KB 683, it was held that the second marriage of someone with this decree would still be invalid, and therefore they would be an offender. It is likely that the Act was passed to prevent this result from occurring again and to protect people with this decree from being criminalised. Three cases – *Porter's* case (1637) Cro Car 461, *Middleton's* case (1638) Kelyng 27, and *William's* case (1641) March 101 – affirmed that the decree was part of the defence in the 1604 Act. The Act appears to create a distinction between the innocent and the 'wicked': to protect the ones who had tried to end their marriage with a *decree a mensa et thoro* before remarrying and did not intend to contract multiple subsisting marriages. This distinction between those who dishonour God and those who do not is also a mechanism to protect the ideal of Christian monogamy and the reputations of the innocent. Those who are married to another while their former spouse is alive are 'evil disposed', and so polygamy is for those who are disposed to evil, which by implication is unchristian. Protecting the reputations and status of those who have tried to remain monogamous is another way to uphold Christian ideals, telling people that if they engage with religious processes around marital disputes, they will not fall foul of the Act and be punished.

The circumstances around the passing of the Act also give us information about how the substance of the offence was constructed and how it was committed by people. In an examination of 350 bigamy cases from the late 16th century and 17th century, Capp (2009) notes that most bigamists were those who had simply moved on from old or failed relationships and entered new ones (what we would term 'serial monogamy' today). It was a very small category of bigamists who had deliberately deceived and abandoned their partners. This is challenged by Probert and D'Arcy-Brown's (2019) exploration of bigamy cases in the early 19th century, which found that a significant number of cases resulted in the defendant being punished with transportation. However, they ultimately conclude that while plenty of offenders were driven by greed, deceit and nastiness, many were more sinned against than sinner. This complicated picture provokes the question of why these 'sinned against' bigamists became offenders in the first place. There is one main explanation: lack of access to divorce. Up until the Divorce and Matrimonial Causes Act 1857, other than using the ecclesiastical court procedures mentioned earlier, the only way to end a marriage was by a private Act of Parliament. These procedures were all complex and restricted in scope, particularly for those in socioeconomically deprived circumstances (Shanley, 1989; Frost, 2019; Probert, 2019).

With such limited options, people wanting to leave an unsuccessful relationship had little means and opportunity to do so. They ended up walking away and moving on with someone else, which we can trace back to the original meaning of *bigamia* – the widow or widower who remarried. This is an example of serial monogamy and suggests that bigamy is a very specific type of polygamy: one that mostly arises through accident or fraud rather than as a conscious relationship choice by all parties to be actively engaged in multiple marriages. There is little to show that polygamy as a formal practice was even considered a viable possibility in English law. Bigamy was more a consequence of the struggles around getting divorced than a desire to be married to more than one person at the same time. This is borne out by the notion that with divorce becoming increasingly available as well as the increase in cohabitation without marriage, bigamy started to slip from legal attention, eventually becoming a 'rare and comical crime' (Soothill et al, 1999: 70). Again, we see how tangential and secondary the concerns around plural marriage have been to law and society in England. It may have been inevitable that bigamy was connected to a bigger issue like divorce based on the behaviour of people at the time, but this characterisation of being in multiple relationships as lesser and criminal has created the ideal conditions for the indifferent approach of today.

There was also an ongoing emphasis on harm to women as justification for bigamy being criminalised despite the scholarship telling us that many offenders were not malicious or disposed to evil. The harm to a second wife was central to this crime, with the powerful image of a deceived and exploited second wife spurring on lawmakers to justify its prohibition (Probert, 2019). However, this was just a smokescreen for the real agenda of protecting the 'stable' monogamous household under the Commonwealth model of marriage that began to take hold in the early 17th century. Under this model, the monogamous household was vital to stabilise the

English Commonwealth and its inhabitants. If citizens did not conform to this specific household structure, the state would be at risk. This brand of monogamy was wrapped up in patriarchal values with a male head of household ruling over the wife, children and servants (Witte, 2015). This echoes the way the word 'domestication' stems from 'dominate', as noted by McClintock (1995) when thinking about how the organisation of private households is weaponised to promote a way of life that is civilised and ideal. The cases with offenders who behaved maliciously are plainly visible, and there is no denying that in some cases there was exploitation and harm of victims. However, to justify the criminalisation of bigamy based on this minority when the majority were simply trying to negotiate their lack of access to divorce is more rhetorical than practical. The Act and the discourse around it were focussed more on the harms that bigamy causes than the harm of restricted divorce access for men and especially women which led to it in the first place. With divorce becoming more available, bigamy and the harms it caused have faded into the background along with any legal attention.

The 1604 Act remained on the statute books for more than two centuries until it was repealed and the offence was re-enacted and officially named bigamy in s 22 of the Offences Against the Person Act 1828. The later Act made several changes, such as removing references to God and stating that the offence was no longer punishable by death but by either seven years of transportation 'beyond the Seas' or two years of prison. The 1828 Act also started to account for international scenarios where a marriage was celebrated out of England so the offence was committed overseas. Following this, s 57 of the Offences Against the Person Act 1861 reproduced the bigamy provision in the 1828 Act and this remains in force today. People are rarely prosecuted for the crime now and it is treated more as a civil, rather than criminal offence with the marriage in question being annulled and victims perhaps receiving compensation (Cretney, 2005; Witte, 2015). Throughout its legal journey, we can see that the offence of bigamy has remained largely intact with very little change from 1604 to the present day. Indeed, in the 2015 Law Commission report on the 1861 Act, it was stated that they would not consider bigamy because it went well beyond the core offences of violence against the person and required much broader research and consultation to repeal or amend (Law Commission, 2015b).

Williams very optimistically proposed that the recasting of bigamy into a statutory common law offence would 'get rid of the present theological atmosphere of the law' which cast bigamy as akin to blasphemy and a 'profanation of a solemn ceremony' (1950: 427). However, bigamy became an offence in the first place due to the influence of Christian canon law (Shifman, 1978), and it would be very difficult to disassociate these origins from the offence and the reasons people became bigamous, because of restrictions on divorce that Christian practice dictated. The minimal change to the substance of the offence over centuries tells us that the concept of bigamy is still rooted in Christian faith and while people are unlikely to be criminalised today, the continued existence of the offence exemplifies the religious dominance over marriage law. The lack of change to this offence and the Law Commission's refusal in its 2015 report to engage with it meaningfully for the purpose of reform speaks volumes about legal attitudes towards it. It requires too much research and consultation to take legal action and because the offence has faded into the background in practice, the law has been left as it is. There is a calculated distancing between law and policy makers and the offence – it is not worth their time as there are more important issues to address and it is not used much anyway. They are indifferent and while people are no longer necessarily being prosecuted for it, this lack of engagement contributes to the larger picture of the English legal approach to plural marriage practices today.

The trouble with this indifference in the bigger picture is particularly evident when we think of the wider legacies of the offence and the 1604 Act. The first Act was a model for the offence being constituted in English Commonwealth and other common law states around the world. In particular, the North American colonies and states used the 1604 Act as a template until the 1900s (Witte, 2015). This religion-based offence was exported all around the world as a tool of colonisation, and although there is insufficient information, it is possible that its construction in the 1600s when colonial encounters had already happened, may also be attributable to the experiences of colonisers with societies where polygamy was being practised as a conscious family structure. To remain indifferent to the offence of bigamy is to remain indifferent to the colonial legacies of the 1604 Act which influenced legal responses to plural marriage practices on an international scale. The Act's translation into these different contexts shows its conformity and congruence with colonial processes. Remaining indifferent to this lasting legacy and the way that it has shaped law and policy around the British Empire and the Commonwealth is to racialise and dehumanise those that it was imposed on as part of the legal system that was a major tool for imperial rule.

Alongside the common law bigamy offence, the moral concerns with plural marriage forms caused a parallel narrative around clandestine marriages to develop from the early 17th century. There was an overwhelming fear and panic that clandestine marriages were happening in vast numbers and giving rise to harms including bigamy. These fears eventually led to the passing of the Clandestine Marriages Act 1753 which set out the formalities for a valid marriage and the standard form of marriage ceremony over which only an Anglican clergyman could officiate (Probert, 2009; Sokol, 2009). We need to explore the motivations behind the Act and the confusions around defining clandestine marriages to understand the links with bigamy. The 1753 Act is considered a landmark legal moment in the history of English marriage regulation. It is almost positioned as the answer to all the pre-existing issues with marriage and marks a dramatic shift from a more open, plural system that accepted multiple marriage forms to a narrow, restricted approach (Probert, 2009). Lemmings (1996) states that it addressed the confusion and frustration lawyers were experiencing with marriage law up to the 18th century. He further argues that there were two objectives behind the Act: first, to enforce patriarchy by facilitating greater control of parents over their children's marriages; and, second, to make marriage more public and legally certain in order to prevent bigamy which had terrible consequences for the transfer of property among the elite. These motivations show that the law was focussed on issues that people with money and property had around marriage, rather than on 'commoners', and that bigamy was a live concern despite having been criminalised over a century earlier. Moreover, bigamy was still bound up in the narratives of harm where vulnerable women remained at risk of being seduced into a bigamous clandestine marriage and ruined. There was a perception that the 1753 Act would fix this (Lemmings, 1996).

There are two questions we need to ask in relation to bigamy: How founded were the concerns that led to the Act? And how effective was the Act at tackling them? To answer these, we need to look at how these clandestine marriages were understood and I turn to Probert's (2009) leading work in this area which provides a forensic exploration of the Act. Probert informs us that clandestine marriages were a technical way to describe *only* Anglican Christian marriages that had failed to comply with the formalities set out in the 1753 Act: those which had taken place in front of Anglican clergymen but did not meet all the requirements of canon law. Marriages that were not carried out in front of an Anglican clergyman were not described as clandestine marriages because they were not seen as marriages in the first place. So, this Act was focussed on a very specific category of marriages in the Anglican Christian community. This narrow definition of clandestine marriages does not match the perception that the 1753 Act swooped in and changed the way legal marriage happened in England. The narrow focus of the Act also tells us that there was a specific community whose way of marrying was extremely important: those who practised Anglican Christianity. The passing of an Act that only speaks about Anglican ceremonies reinforced the dominance of this faith for English lawmakers and authorities. Linked to this is the question of how much of a practical problem these clandestine marriages were, and here Probert (2009) observes that the actual number of such marriages was perhaps less important than the perception that they were a problem. Probert (2009) undertook a detailed examination of case reports, marriage registers and other primary sources of law and information, finding that in truth, marriage in the Anglican Church was the clear norm, leaving little room for any alternative. In addition, there is significant evidence showing the devotion of English people to the established Anglican Church at the time demonstrating that people were very unlikely to dismiss Anglican marriage formalities (Probert, 2009). These clandestine marriages were simply not that common which shows again how little the 1753 Act did to change the system. It addressed a type of ceremony that was not happening often and it seems to have been propelled by fears about a small minority of difficult situations and misconceptions around what clandestine marriage was.

Marriage was viewed as less restricted before the 1753 Act because of the belief that people in England were able to self-marry which was then characterised as a type of clandestine marriage. In this context, self-marriage was thought to occur because of the contract *per verba de praesenti*, or precontract marriage, which involved an exchange of vows between a couple consenting to take each other as husband and wife from that time (Probert, 2009). The binding precontract created legal obligations between the couple that could be enforced in the ecclesiastical courts. However, there is a misconception that this was a valid form of marriage despite not fulfilling the formal requirements of a regular Anglican marriage. It is certainly not a clandestine marriage according to the statutory definition, because an Anglican clergyman did not have to officiate over the precontract. The precontract was a form of preliminary ceremony which, if enforced by the ecclesiastical courts, would compel the parties to undergo a fully compliant Anglican Church wedding – almost like a legally enforceable engagement ceremony. This did not have the same legal rights as a regular marriage and so could not be a self-marriage. Simply exchanging consent to get married without any of the formalities did not form a regular marriage. There is also no real evidence of precontracted couples living together before their church ceremony, which shows again that this was not a recognised way to marry (Probert, 2009). At this stage, we can see that the concerns around out-of-control clandestine marriages and self-marriage are not very convincing.

It is possible that the panic surrounding precontract as a form of clandestine marriage also stemmed from the perception that it facilitated bigamy. By being able to 'self-marry' through the exchange of consent, whether publicly or in private, opportunists could marry as many times as they wanted through precontract moving on to the next self-marriage whenever they wanted. The influential case of *Dalrymple v Dalrymple* (1811) 2 Hag Con 54 (hereafter *Dalrymple*) is responsible for causing confusion in this area because in the judgment the precontract in the case was described as a form of clandestine marriage. The case was heard long after the 1753 Act, yet the blurring of the line between clandestine marriage and precontract, along with the perceived large volumes of clandestine marriages, remained in the legal imaginary. One of the effects of this blurred line was that a number of people were prosecuted for bigamy when they had entered a precontract or non-Anglican marriage with one person but had then celebrated a full marriage ceremony with a different person.

In *R v Millis* (1843–44) 10 Cl & F 534; 8 ER 844 (hereafter *Millis*), the question of whether a precontract creates a valid marriage was examined at length. The accused was prosecuted for bigamy after he had undergone a Presbyterian ceremony in Ireland followed by an Anglican ceremony in England with a different woman. Millis was acquitted because, although legally binding, a precontract does not have the same consequences as a regular church marriage. It is not bigamy for someone who is precontract married to later marry a third party in a valid regular ceremony. This gives the impression that the confusion created by *Dalrymple* had been corrected but the judges were divided in *Millis*, and it was the presumption of innocence that led to his acquittal rather than the decision on precontract. Interestingly, no cases of bigamy involving a precontract as the first ceremony were reported before the 1753 Act and this was true for a long time after the Act was passed so the issues really did start with *Dalrymple* (Probert, 2008). The precontract was a publicly recognised marriage custom that was transformed into a cause for fear due to its conflation with clandestine marriage and bigamy. Bigamy and clandestine marriage were not rife or problematic in real, lived terms, but legal developments like the 1753 Act contributed to this perception. The overemphasis on clandestine marriages and bigamy around the 1753 Act shows the authorities' indifference in relation to the actual prevalence of these practices and their effects on society at the time. It is important to identify this as a dominant discourse that needs to be disrupted to ensure that clandestine marriages and bigamy do not remain the sources of panic and harm that they were portrayed as being. There is little to indicate that these concerns targeted polygamy in a wider sense, because communities in England were not practising it outside of accidental or incidental bigamy. Polygamy did not become a deliberate concern for legal authorities in England until colonial-linked immigration caused the entry of people from polygamy-permitting countries into the country as I discuss in Chapter 4. This helps us to view the effects of the mistaken assumptions around the 1753 Act with more nuance when we think about the forces that have shaped marriage regulation and how helpful this is for married people today.

The 1753 Act also sheds light on legal attitudes to non-Anglican and therefore non-normative marriage practices of the period. Under the Act, even Catholic ceremonies which had dominated before the Reformation, were not fully recognised because of the Anglican Church's dominance. It was not just Christianity that overwhelmingly shaped marriage law but Anglican Christianity which remains influential today. The Act did not make sweeping changes but it provides a legal snapshot of marriage before and after it was passed that tells us legal responses to marriage were mostly inflexible and designed to uphold the Anglican Christian ideal of marriage. From a practical standpoint, the population of England in the 18th century was not particularly diverse. In 1757 for example, it was speculated that two thirds of adults in London come from 'distant parts', although this was mainly referring to 'foreigners from all Protestant countries, and too many Papists' (Burrington, 1757: 37). Immigrants in this context were mostly European Christians and marriage ceremonies were affected by this demographic make-up with non-Christian ceremonies and communities highly under-represented in 18th-century England. The Act was written for and about Christians in England with Anglican marriage being the priority.

However, there is some accounting for non-Christian marriage through the exemption of Jewish and Quaker ceremonies from the requirements of the 1753 Act. Jewish marriages were a matter for Jewish law, and the 1753 Act exemption provided strong evidence of respect for Jewish marriage rites as the courts deferred to Jewish law and authority (see *Andreas v Andreas* (1737) 1 Hag Con (App) 10n; 161 ER 636; *Vigevena and Silveira v Alvarez* (1794) 1 Hag Con (App) 8n; 161 ER 636; *Lady D'Aguilar v Baron D'Aguilar* (1794) 1 Hag Ecc 773; 161 ER 748).[5] Additionally, as Judaism predates Christianity, it makes little sense to deny Jewish marriage recognition. However, we could also argue that polygamy predates Christianity, so this time-related argument is potentially limited. Perhaps more telling about this statutory exemption is the approach to the Quaker community and their marriages. The Quaker movement started in the middle of the 17th century and was therefore newer than the Church of England. Their marriages were also exempted from the 1753 Act but they were not viewed in the same way as Jewish marriages.

Quaker marriages were viewed with less deference than Jewish marriages and had even been described by Parliament in a 1694 statute[6] as 'pretended' though Quakers still had to pay the same taxes as those who engaged in Anglican marriage. This idea of pretend Quaker marriages was reinforced with situations such as that in *Dodgson v Haswell* (1730), PRO DEL/412, where a Quaker wanting to establish the binding character of their marriage

5 It is worth remembering that by seeing Jewish marriages as a matter for Jewish law, they were being treated as a matter for foreign law displaying their outsider status. In addition, despite their exemption from the 1753 Act, there was no certainty that Jewish (and Quaker) marriages were valid in *English* law. This confirmation came in the much later Marriage Act 1836 (Henriques, 1908; Probert, 2009).

6 An Act for granting to his Majesty certain rates and duties upon marriages, births and burials, and upon batchelors and widowers, for the term of five years for carrying on the war against France with vigour 1694 6 & 7 W 3 c 6, s 202.

ceremony had to present their case as enforcement of precontract rather than recognition of a valid marriage. This stands in contrast to the carefully documented evidence, investigations and procedures that made up the Quaker marriage process. These ceremonies were treated as though they were not serious, but the opposite was true (Probert, 2009). The caveat to all of this is that after the confusion in *Dalrymple* which allowed an exchange of consent to count for marriage through precontracting, Quaker marriages were assumed to be valid as long as there were witnesses (see *Deane v Thomas* (1829) Moo & Malk 361; 31 Rev Rep 738). The overall difference in treatment between Quaker and Jewish marriages informs us that the 1753 Act's exemption was not necessarily an accommodation or mechanism to respect these marriages. It is the case for Jewish marriages that the exemption was used to support the courts' deference to Jewish law and authority, but this should surely also have also been the case for Quaker marriage. It could be argued, as it was in *Vigevena and Silveira v Alvarez* (1794) 1 Hag Con (App) 8n; 161 ER 636, that Jewish marriages should not be expected to conform to Anglican rites since Jewish people were perceived to be 'anti-Christian', unlike Quakers, who did share Christian values, but I argue there is an additional reason. The supporters and drafters of the 1753 Act were largely indifferent to these nonconforming religious ceremonies. This does not mean that they felt nothing or were neutral towards them, but that the main aim of the Act was clearly about clandestine marriages in the narrow sense among the Anglican community in England. Other ceremonies were just that: other and maybe even anti-Christian – a dehumanising term which is orientalising and holds echoes of civilising discourses around what being Christian (or not) meant. The Act set the tone for present-day religious marriages that fail to fit within the existing framework favouring Anglican ceremonies.

The final observation from this period is drawn from the international context around the 1753 Act and the developments that preceded it. With the rise of the British Empire from the mid 15th century and its mission to reshape the world in its English image, the travel writings of New World explorers became increasingly popular in discussions in this area (Witte, 2015). The diaries of explorers contributed to negative perceptions of polygamous marriage in popular narratives. For example, in 1600 Leo attributed the barbaric nature of the African communities he observed to their polygamous households (see Leo, 2001). In this way, uncivilised polygamy was compared to the civilised, Western ideal of monogamy. This constituted an early use of orientalist and imperialist source material to other Muslim and indigenous people for their practice of polygamy. It is also possible that this marks the start of the constructed differences between polygamy and bigamy. 'Polygamy' is said to have disappeared from legal and political discourse in the 18th century with 'bigamy' taking centre stage as the preferred term for the designated statutory offence in England (Vogel, 1991). However, 'polygamy' was still being used in more cultural and social writings which suggests that it was taking on a more specific meaning – one in which its participants were racialised and viewed as a threat to the British imperial ideal of monogamy.

While discussing the high-profile Irish case of *Thelwell v Yelverton* (1864) 16 CB NS 813; 143 ER 1346 which dealt with a member of the Irish gentry accused of bigamy, Gill (2004) analyses the way in which concerns around an aristocrat engaging in polygamy were inspired by the hierarchy of marriage customs created as a tool for imperial order.[7] The hierarchy, which was organised from the primitive colonial customs including polygamy at the bottom through to civilised imperial monogamy at the top, was threatened by a well-connected Irish man having multiple wives. This threat to the security of monogamy also threatened the position of Britain as imperial authority and civiliser of the colonies. Polygamy was fast becoming a signifier of the colonies and colonial natives with those who practised it racialised through their association with this marital form. Bigamy was the offence being prosecuted, but in the House of Commons, while referring to this case, a Member of Parliament commented: 'It was said by lawyers, perhaps ironically, that a man might have a wife in each of the three kingdoms, although polygamy was not permitted' (Hansard, 1862: col 1201). This challenges Vogel's (1991) statement that 'polygamy' was disappearing from law and politics, showing that it was being used instead of 'bigamy'. Bigamy was always a narrow, specific offence, mostly committed because people could not divorce. It was no longer a concern in England, but polygamy was still worth the moralising panic because it was rife in the inferior, foreign colonies. So even though cases were about bigamy, the behaviour of the accused was described as polygamy. 'Polygamy' therefore did not disappear from discourse but became more prominent, and it signified the move away from domestic bigamy towards colonial polygamy. An additional point about this case is that it was not only about bigamy but also concerned the anti-Catholic legislation in force in Ireland which nullified certain marriages between Catholics and Protestants to protect the latter (Probert et al, 2018). Polygamy was again used as a smokescreen to obscure a deeper concern of the Protestant authorities, demonstrating the static nature of attitudes towards it. Against the backdrop of shifting terminology from 'polygamy' to 'bigamy', we do not see any real progress or developments around plural marriage for a long time after the 1753 Act as the law remained indifferent to the possibility of people in England engaging in polygamy. A complete

[7] See Erickson and McCarthy (1971) for a full account of the case.

ban and the prevention of clandestine marriages were considered sufficient then, and this still forms the foundation of the legal framework today.

Expanding options and indifference into the present day: civil marriage and non-marriage

Moving closer to the present day, the Marriage Act 1836 is presented as another significant legal moment which permanently introduced the option to marry outside of the Anglican Church. Before this Act, all marriages apart from Jewish and Quaker ones had to be conducted according to Anglican rites (Probert, 2022). With the 1836 Act, marriages could be celebrated in a place of worship that was registered for weddings or in a superintendent registrar's office as a civil ceremony. Civil marriage had already been introduced briefly into English law for a short time in the 17th century so it was not brand new to the system, but its permanent inclusion was a natural response to the times (Sokol, 2009). In the 1800s, attitudes were changing towards dissenting Protestants who had separated from the Church of England, and there were questions around whether forcing marriage conformity on non-Anglicans advanced the interests of the Anglican Church and community (Probert, 2009). The Act was also significant because it confirmed the validity of Jewish and Quaker marriages – another reflection of the change in attitudes towards diversity and dissent from the majority. These changes instituted by the Act point positively towards a marriage law framework that was more responsive and sensitive to the needs of non-Anglican communities, with the Anglican mode of marriage becoming less dominant – but how far was this really the case?

First, it is important to think about the drive for the 1836 Act. In a detailed exposition of the Act, Probert (2021) reveals that the Act was motivated by evidence that immigrant Irish Catholics were marrying before their own priests, which meant their ceremonies were not legally valid. There were lots of these religious-only ceremonies being celebrated and the cost of supporting the children of these marriages was falling on the parish they were born in. This led campaigners to argue for a ceremony that was an alternative to the Anglican standard which the Act duly provided. The Act prescribed the declarations and vows that had to be included in a valid marriage ceremony, but there was no mention of excluding religious content from weddings in those celebrated in either a registered place of worship or a register office. The evidence indicates that most weddings conducted under the Marriage Act 1836 involved religious rites (Probert, 2021; 2022). When the Act was originally passed, it was possible to have religious content in a civil ceremony. Therefore, while on the surface civil marriage represented a broadening out of people's marriage options, it was never intended to do away with the religious underpinnings of marriage. Further, it still mimicked the Anglican form of marriage, was reacting to diverse Christian religious practice, and was therefore constructed with Christian marriage in mind.

In the early 1850s, concerns arose where couples celebrated a civil ceremony and then had another church ceremony afterwards (Probert, 2021). The state became worried this would create doubt around the validity of marriages celebrated under the 1836 Act. To address this, the Marriage and Registration Act 1856 allowed parties to a civil ceremony to have another religious ceremony, but this would not supersede or invalidate the civil marriage and the second ceremony should not be entered into the marriage register. More confusingly, this express permission was taken to imply that a couple married by a registrar in a registered place of worship rather than the register office was not allowed to undergo a second religious ceremony. This led to the further provision in the 1856 Act that all religious content in civil ceremonies was prohibited. Through this, civil ceremonies were reframed as completely secular, moving away from the original flexible approach of the 1836 Act. The consequences of this in the 19th century were felt by Dissenters,[8] as their place of worship was unregistered for marriage but they did not want to marry in the Anglican Church. They had no choice but to marry in a register office with a ceremony that could not reflect their beliefs and the effects of this are still borne by minoritised communities today. Removing the religious content from civil ceremonies has not really created a neutral ceremony option, but rather an indifferent one which is still underpinned by Anglican dominance. This emphasises how little secularity represents the separation of religion from state to accommodate diverse religious rites and beliefs (Chatterjee, 2010).

The marriage rites of 'other' religions do not in themselves fulfil the requirements for a legally recognised civil marriage because they are too different from the Anglican template set out in the legislation. A religious ceremony like the Muslim Nikah ceremony for example, would not be enough to garner legal recognition, because it can be performed in any location, without prescribed words, without a written record or an authorised person present and still be valid in religion (Naqvi, 2020). As a result, Muslim couples can have religious ceremonies without mainstream legal recognition. This can lead to situations where members of such minoritised communities perform two distinct marriage ceremonies: a religious marriage and then a legally recognised civil ceremony. This represents the same gap that was noted in the 1700s with immigrant Catholics marrying in religious-only ceremonies emphasising just how little has changed. Anglican Christian dominance and the need to conduct a particular type of ceremony to

[8] Dissenters were members of non-established Churches and therefore were not Anglican Christians.

prevent marriages being denied recognition stretches back centuries. It is still possible under s 26(1)(a) Marriage Act 1949 for religious orders to register their places of worship for the purposes of conducting marriages, as part of the formalities for legal marriage in the presence of an authorised person or registrar. This would require, for example, a Muslim mosque or a Hindu temple to be registered and have an authorised person present so that couples could be legally recognised as married on the same day as the religious ceremony. However, the couple would still have to say the words derived from the Book of Common Prayer for the Anglican-inspired civil ceremony which can feel disruptive (Probert et al, 2022).

There is another legal consequence flowing from this two-ceremony convention which is linked to polygamy. The centuries-old approach of prohibiting polygamy is now set out in s 11(d) Matrimonial Causes Act 1973, which states that any polygamous marriage celebrated in England or celebrated internationally while one of the parties is domiciled in England is void. This seems straightforward, ensuring that if a domestic polygamous marriage falls within the Christian-centric view of marriage under the Marriage Act 1949 because it fulfilled enough of the requirements for a valid marriage or was celebrated abroad in a place that permits polygamy, it would be void. This is designed to prevent polygamy for those who treat England as their domicile or permanent home whether the ceremony is performed in England or abroad. However, the possibility of, and sometimes need for, two marriage ceremonies has created a gap that means polygamous marriages are still happening in England, just not in a normative legal sense. A religious ceremony, like the Islamic Nikah ceremony that has not taken place in a registered building in front of an authorised person complying with all the necessary formalities is also known as a religious-only marriage.[9] Over the years, the courts have developed a line of reasoning which classes this as a 'non-marriage' or, more recently, a 'non-qualifying ceremony' (Probert, 2013; Akhtar, 2020). Under the Marriage Act 1949, we are told that void marriages fail in some way to fulfil the required formalities for a legally binding ceremony, but when a marriage is void, a party to it can still apply for financial relief and therefore benefit from some legal remedies. The non-marriage is even more void than a void marriage which means that the parties to a religious-only marriage have no legally recognised relationship and are legal strangers, like cohabitants. If a couple undergoes their first religious ceremony but not the second legal one, the courts cannot annul their marriage, as shown in *A-M v A-M (Divorce: Jurisdiction: Validity*

[9] The descriptor 'non-legally binding ceremony' is favoured in the most recent research in this area to also account for ceremonies that fall outside the Marriage Act 1949 but are not religious (see Probert et al, 2022).

of Marriage) [2001] 2 FLR 6. Here, a couple's polygamous Nikah ceremony was performed in a private house, which may be acceptable in Islam but not in English law. This possibility of non-qualifying ceremonies means that a person can have one legal spouse and several religious spouses at the same time as a form of informal polygamy.

The attributes of non-marriage overall make it an undesirable status in law. By being more void than a void marriage, a religious-only marriage is situated as less capable of forming a valid marriage than even an invalid one. We should also remember that even the precontract marriage explored earlier had legal recognition and consequences despite not being a full alternative to marriage. While discussing void marriage in *Re Spence, deceased* [1990] 1 Ch 652, the judge described void marriage as 'only an idle ceremony [which] achieves no change in the status of the participants [and] achieves nothing of substance' (661). This may not have been completely accurate, but if a void marriage was remotely viewed as idle and achieving nothing of substance, a non-marriage is even less than this (Probert, 2013). If we think about what makes a void marriage, a marriage between a father and daughter would be void and therefore capable of attracting some legal attention, but a religious ceremony like the Nikah ceremony could not. This is insulting to the communities practising marriage in a way that fails to fit within the template provided by English law and may even feed into wider legal perceptions of their belief systems. The concept is not based in statute which only defines valid, void and voidable marriage, but has been constructed through judicial decisions as cases around religious marriages have gone to the courts. With this reactive approach, we can see a general indifference and lack of interest towards these marriages. Questions around these marriages have gone to court, and non-marriage – a way of describing a ceremony which is too far out of the realms of marriage – has been used as a convenient label without regard for the wider implications and message this sends to those affected by it.

Another attribute of non-marriage we need to be aware of concerns its origin. 'Non-marriage' was initially used to describe marriages conducted as part of a theatrical play – a fake marriage performed for entertainment. On this basis, non-marriage should be restricted to this original use, because placing religious marriages in the same category is discriminatory (Vora, 2016). Here, we see the emergence of racialising and dehumanising indifference. Religious ceremonies such as the Nikah ceremony, like the marriage rites of Hindu and Sikh communities, are being likened to fake ceremonies performed between actors who are entertaining an audience. Giving this label to these marriages while Christian ceremonies are viewed as real marriages shows an invested imperial indifference whereby minoritised marriages and those who celebrate them are othered. This is supported by the findings in cases such as *Gereis v Yagoub* [1997] 1 FLR 854 (hereafter *Gereis*), which involved a marriage in a Coptic Orthodox church. The church was not registered for marriage, and the parties knowingly ignored the advice that they would need a second civil ceremony. This was a non-marriage as the formalities for a legal ceremony had knowingly not been complied with, yet the judge declared the marriage void with the justification that the ceremony 'bore the hallmarks of an ordinary Christian marriage and … both parties treated it as such' (858).

In the later case of *Chief Adjudication Officer v Bath* [2000] 1 FLR 8 which concerned a Sikh ceremony, the judge stated that in *Gereis* 'some reliance seems to have been placed on the Christian character of the ceremony' (para 8). *Gereis* managed to escape the non-marriage designation because it was closer to an ordinary Christian marriage, and this reflects the obvious bias in favour of Christian rites from all denominations. The non-marriage status is racialising and dehumanising to affected parties, their marriages are not even deemed a marriage leaving them without the widely recognised legal status that others enjoy. It is orientalising and dismissive for these communities to need another marriage ceremony which fits with the legal Christian ideal. It is even more so because if the Nikah ceremony or another religious ceremony was performed in a country where it was recognised by the law of that country, it would be considered valid both overseas and in English law according to private international law provisions. That it is recognisable when performed elsewhere but not here is also racialising in the sense that other marriages can only be valid when permitted by other laws. There was some evidence of flexibility displayed in the first instance *Akhter v Khan* [2018] EWFC 54 decision to allow recognition for a Muslim Nikah, but the Court of Appeal later rejected this by reinforcing the relevance of non-marriage to the case while relabelling it a 'non-qualifying ceremony' (*Her Majesty's Attorney General (Appellant) v Nasreen Akhter and Mohammed Shabaz Khan (Respondents) and Fatima Mohammed Hussain and Southall Black Sisters (Interveners)* [2020] EWCA Civ 122). This new label is not an improvement; it still gives the impression that these marriages do not qualify as real marriages between real people. That there has been no effort to address the application of non-marriage to such ceremonies reflects the indifference of the law towards them and demonstrates how indifference can act as a strategy for discriminatory power. These marriages along with their participants are discriminated against leaving those involved in an inferior position: the fact that they facilitate polygamy shows how polygamy even in an informal form is viewed (or ignored) by the law.

Concluding thoughts

Legal responses in this area are complicated with polygamous marriages being either void or non-existent because of their structure. In this chapter,

I argued that this complexity stems from the dominance of Christian monogamy in English marriage law, which is further tangled up in colonialist indifference towards other forms of marriage. I started to narrate the legal story of polygamy in England by looking at specific moments that shed light on how the current framework has been shaped. There are not many legal moments for us to draw from, and even when they do occur, polygamy has always been a secondary issue that was used to obscure the real problems that people faced around access to divorce. In the name of preventing polygamy or bigamy, marriage formalities were set out in the Anglican image and divorce remained highly restricted. While divorce is now more accessible, not much has changed on the requirements for a legally valid marriage ceremony displaying the law's indifference and disinterest towards polygamy and other forms of marriage celebrated in England that may fall outside the scope of the Marriage Act 1949. Religious-only marriages that permit polygamy to happen informally today are at the bottom of the hierarchy in English marriage law and they are othered, dismissed and discriminated against. By describing them as non-qualifying ceremonies, they are even more defective than a void marriage, leaving parties to them with no financial relief or remedies. The use of 'non-marriage' to describe these ceremonies was noted as an issue, along with the hierarchy of marriage regulation according to religious group, which places Anglican marriages at the top in the Law Commission's (2015a) scoping paper on getting married. These issues feature in the review of wedding law by the Law Commission (2020; 2022), but as we have seen for centuries, there has been very little overall progression in legal responses and attitudes around polygamous marriages which continue to fail to take into consideration people's lives and experiences.

4

History and Conflict of Laws in Overseas Polygamy

Polygamy is recognised in law in many places around the world. In Chapter 3 I explored polygamous marriages celebrated in England. It was a tale of indifference, with English law showing little interest in domestic polygamy. In this chapter, I look at polygamy that is celebrated overseas which has attracted more attention than domestic polygamy, leading to two Law Commission reports in 1971 and 1985. However, these were published decades ago, so the level of attention is relative. When confronted with overseas polygamy, the English courts are usually deciding whether a polygamous marriage that is recognised by an overseas legal system should be recognised in English law. The courts look to private international law, also known as conflict of laws to help. This leads me to first explore the origins of this branch of law, to think about what influences the responses to overseas polygamy. Conflict of laws was developed because of colonial encounters and the desire to emphasise the difference and inferiority of non-European legal systems. This orientalist foundation governs responses to overseas marriages and when the courts look at these relationships, they are not just assessing the law of the place the marriage took place in, but the culture. I argue that current English law cannot be separated out from this context because these colonial influences determine the way overseas legal and cultural systems along with overseas polygamous marriage are assessed.

With more accessible case law around overseas polygamy in the English courts, I can examine legal attitudes and influences through patterns of discourse that appear in court judgments. This is inspired by Herman's argument that 'judges are active agents in the production of orientalist, racialized and Christian discourse' (2011: 20–1). Thus, the best way to discover what judges think about polygamy is to analyse what they say. This is why I carry out a discourse analysis of their decisions. Here, discourse analysis concentrates on instances where speech equates to action. A judicial decision is not just speech, but 'is intended to create an action, both in respect of the parties in the instant case and, where applicable, in future cases' (Harding, 2012: 434). By looking for patterns of discourse in these decisions, we can see what influences judicial perceptions of polygamy. I show how the imperialist mentality present in the statutory framing bears out in real-life interactions in the courts. I read and analysed over 50 cases heard in the English courts from 1866 to the present day which I sourced digitally on a mainstream English case law database using the keyword 'polygamy'.

From this analysis, I argue that there are three strategies in the English courts' responses to overseas polygamy: denigration, mutation and differentiation.[1] In earlier cases, the Christian imperialist influences are clear with polygamy being *denigrated* and not seen as a real marriage because it did not match the English definition of the relationship. Polygamous wives were not the same as Christian wives and were repeatedly characterised as concubines and 'slaves' which is denigrating to them as well. Polygamous marriages could not be dissolved by the English courts, parties could not seek financial relief, and polygamous wives could not be recognised as heirs to their husbands' estates. The early case law shows that polygamous marriages were more likely to be classed non-existent than void with no relief available for wives and children. The courts even struggled to acknowledge that monogamous marriages between non-Christian people could be classed as marriage. These marriages, though monogamous in practice, were celebrated in places that allowed polygamy. It was decided that they had the *potential* to become polygamous and they were therefore treated as if they were *actual* polygamy. With time, the courts and legislators started to see that treating these non-Christian monogamous marriages as if they were polygamous was unsustainable and they decided that the best way to address this was to mutate them. *Mutation* entailed the conversion of a potentially polygamous marriage into a monogamous one because the parties had later become domiciled in England. However, I argue that this forced non-Christian marriage into the imperialist-approved structure of Christian monogamy and is not the solution it is made out to be. Judicial language has now moved away from outright denigration of polygamy to the more subtle *differentiation* between polygamy and English marriage. Through this strategy, polygamous marriages are now recognised in English law but only for certain purposes when it suits the state or protects the public good and resources. Through these three strategies of denigration, mutation and differentiation, the courts have

[1] I have organised the discussion in this way rather than chronologically because these themes cropped up across multiple time periods. However, there is a vague chronological order according to when the themes present in the cases.

one goal: to preserve (Christian-inspired) monogamy and reinforce it as the ideal structure of marriage.

Private international law: conflict of laws or cultures?

Private international law, or conflict of laws, covers domestic cases between private parties that have 'foreign elements' (Bomhoff, 2008). A case may come before the English courts that requires them to consider the law of another jurisdiction and whether it should be applied to the situation in front of them. In family law this can occur when a couple marry abroad according to the law of that place, come to the UK and later seek a divorce in the English courts. Before the courts can grant the divorce in English law, questions may be asked about whether the marriage is legally valid according to the foreign legal system it was contracted in.

The origins of private international law are vague but predate the British Empire. Mills (2006) tells us that Roman law (an earlier imperial system) played a key role in its development, and the first attempt at private international law is widely credited to Aldricus in 12th-century Bologna. Aldricus argued that if a dispute is linked with more than one legal system, the court should apply the 'stronger and more useful law' (see Ehrenzweig, 1960: 647). This tells us that the conflict exercise is comparative and in some ways competitive as the conflicting systems compete to be applied as the ideal (Mills, 2006). The competitive slant to these conflict cases is the foundation for the wider relationship of international law to colonialism because it sets up a hierarchy of nations based on what serves European imperial interests. For example, as Koskenniemi (2011) explains, a group of men in Europe first recognised each other as colleagues in the international law profession in 1873 with the establishment of the Institut de Droit International. One of their earliest tasks was to decide what rules would govern the 'peaceful' division of Africa between European colonial powers, showing how bound up in colonial interests this discipline is. Later, this branch of law was geared towards tackling challenges around commercial disputes and securing the interests of the (European) international merchant when the world became more globalised from the 19th century (Okoli, 2019). Private international law as we see and experience it today was conceived by Europeans to benefit European interests against an imperial backdrop.

There is a debate around whether private international law can even be considered international law, which feeds into the competition and imperial superiority narratives. Mills (2006) states that earlier conceptions of international law underline the independence, equality and sovereignty of all states with a boundary between the internal and external affairs of the state. Dicey positioned private international law as an internal matter and part of domestic law. Without a sovereign, binding authority like a court or executive power to enforce private international law, he argued that we cannot claim it is strictly law (see Mills, 2006). In giving consideration to the 'sovereignty' of states, the recognition of private international law gives the impression that English law is respectful towards other states. However, when a conflict arises with UK (imperial) state sovereignty, these private international 'rules' are deemed discretionary and applied as a matter of goodwill. By characterising private international law as a national, internal matter that does not manage to meet the threshold for law, there is no competition with domestic English law. The conflict is resolved because English law takes precedence.

Muir Watt (2017) takes this further to look at the colonial. In colonial times, if private international cases came from 'foreign' places to the English courts, a legal fiction allowed them to proceed as if the issue had occurred in England. There was no need to apply or worry about foreign law. In the present day, where foreign law is pleaded by the parties, the plea is accompanied by a presumption of similarity between the foreign and English laws. The foreign elements must be convenient for the domestic courts, and if the foreign law's relevance is not pleaded in what the court deems a sufficient manner, the case proceeds as if it were purely domestic. This seems like a pragmatic approach which addresses the practical issues of applying foreign laws when the domestic court is not an expert, but it could also be viewed as indifference and as implying a sense of superiority. In Chapter 3, I showed how indifference is not neutral or harmless in law, but dismisses non-normative law and practice; and the law has a similar effect here. Private international law is portrayed as being concerned more with technical application of the law than with grander ideological concerns. This means critical accounts of its role in constructing empire or Eurocentric biases are not common (Muir Watt, 2017). More importantly, this portrayal obscures the fact that 'Western systems of private international law were constituted, to a large extent, to deal with the exotic by-products of colonialism in the field of family law' (Muir Watt, 2011: 380). They evolved to deal with questions around indigenous marriages and polygamy in an exclusionary way, solidifying colonial attitudes which persist today towards certain foreign marriages (Muir Watt, 2011).

The regulation of overseas polygamous marriages in the English courts cannot be separated out from this context around international law. Private international law was constructed to further the interests of European powers and their empire-building. Claiming that it is only focussed on the technical application of foreign elements obscures this. Guzman (2002) argues that the focus on sovereignty along with grand ideals has caused scholars to neglect the effects of conflict of laws on individuals and their behaviour. By emphasising this view of conflict as technical, almost machine-like in nature, those affected by it and their humanness have been ignored. Like the effects of indifference, the law as technical becomes a dehumanising force for those involved, particularly women in overseas polygamous marriages. The purpose of my exploration of the law is to disrupt this and focus on the effects on real people and their experiences. The law cannot be removed from the real people in family law who are affected, and we cannot forget that this area has developed as a framework to mitigate legal 'issues' relating to the foreign, colonial-linked family.

To achieve a contextualised disruptive approach, we need to reconfigure conflict of laws. Instead of a conflict of laws, I frame legal responses to overseas polygamous marriages as a conflict of cultures. According to Sinclair (1954), it is widely acknowledged that private international law operates at its best between legal systems that share a common tradition and culture and it must work much harder when the legal systems are too different. This may be positive. For example, Knop (2008) argues that private international law is a site of progress on multicultural issues where respect for group-based difference is the baseline and the limits of this are only questioned if there is a conflict. However, the background and history of conflict of laws tells us that this is an optimistic and unrealistic view.

There are two things that stand out about private international law: first, it is competitive; and second, it highlights the foreignness of non-domestic law. These elements are based on difference: how the foreign and domestic differ and how they compete because of these differences. But what is conflicting or competing? Is it just the law? Anghie (2006) suggests that the evolution of international law and the role of non-European societies in this field are better understood in terms of cultural difference – that is, it is cultures which are made to compete. Historically, the main factor which has defined a state in international law so that it is recognised and respected by others is sovereignty. Sovereignty, or the power of a state to ensure that the laws of its jurisdiction are binding is problematic. It was conceived according to European imperial understandings. Colonised nations were hardly ever recognized as being sovereign because their binding authority and systems of law were too unfamiliar and would prevent European international lawyers from achieving their colonialist agendas such as dividing Africa between European empires.

When legal systems are compared during a conflict of laws, they are marked out according to their differences but this is not a neutral comparison. The doctrine of sovereignty is part of a matrix of racial and cultural discrimination to establish imperial authority by creating a division between who is and is not sovereign. Sovereignty is explicitly bound up in cultural identifiers and processes that make European culture the normative standard against which sovereignty of all states is measured (Anghie, 2005). This imperialist division that cuts across sovereignty ensures that international law only recognises the sovereignty of certain cultures and laws: those which do not deviate from the normative European cultural standard. Private international law is not providing the site for cosmopolitan progress and tolerance for group-based difference, but is creating a hierarchy of cultures, legal systems and states. It responds to the conflict that it created in the first place by upholding a line between civilised Europe and the rest of the world.

Building on Riles' (2008) work, I posit that we would benefit from thinking through conflict of laws as though it were a conflict of cultures that is orientalist marking out the difference of non-European laws to treat them as inferior. We can then expose the racialised nature of conflict situations and the cultural normative standard formed by European perspectives that are shaped by the law and legal rules (Riles, 2008). Legal rules telling us what a valid marriage is reflect the dominant culture and shape the cultural understanding of marriage in a jurisdiction. When there is a conflict between two jurisdictions on what makes a marriage valid, the domestic court is not just commenting on the laws of both places, but also on their cultures and the people that are immersed in those cultures. The court does this through a lens of difference: comparing the laws by marking out their culturally shaped differences and then deciding whether to recognise and apply the foreign ones. The focus on difference and comparing laws to see which is 'stronger and more useful' is a type of orientalist, othering process that we are only able to see when we reframe conflict of laws as a conflict of cultures. The culturally minoritised community's foreign marriages are defined by how they are inferior according to national laws which others and diminishes their legitimacy in English law and culture. This then justifies the approach of not even seeing minoritised marriages as marriage or the women who engage in them as wives.

Denigrating polygamous marriages and wives: the empire speaks

Private international law was created because of issues presented before domestic courts with judges playing key actors in the legal, and therefore cultural conflict between legal systems. The prominence of common law means we should examine what has happened and is happening in the courts around overseas polygamous marriages to understand how the law and cultural responses to this relationship have been shaped. The importance of the courts is also demonstrated as we see how legislation trails behind case law and reacts to what judges have decided. In Chapter 3, we saw that the offence of bigamy governed polygamous marriages celebrated in the UK through the 1604 Act, the Offences Against the Person Act 1828 remaining on the books today in s 57 Offences Against the Person Act 1861. This offence included polygamous marriages celebrated overseas, so the first statutory responses to overseas polygamy and domestic polygamy overlap: 'Whosoever, being married, shall marry any other person during the life of the former husband or wife, whether the second marriage shall have taken place in England or Ireland or elsewhere, shall be guilty of felony' (s.57 Offences Against the Person Act 1861). Even if the polygamous marriage has been celebrated elsewhere, it will fall under the offence and individuals may be prosecuted. The wording of this was later repealed in part to limit it to Her Majesty's subjects in the Statute Law Revision Act 1892 (c 19), ensuring that it did not apply to those who were not under imperial authority. The continued existence of this offence shows the lack of development of criminal English laws around polygamous marriages even when celebrated overseas into the present day. In civil law, there was no statute until 1972 to regulate overseas polygamy, so we look to the courts for more information.

The first prominent conflict of laws case for polygamy in English law was *Hyde* in 1866, heard at the height of British imperial rule. Here, a former Mormon husband wanted to dissolve his marriage which had been celebrated in Utah according to Mormon rites. The husband left the Mormon faith and became domiciled in England while the wife married again in another Mormon ceremony. The question for the courts, so that jurisdiction could be established and the divorce granted, was whether the marriage was valid in English law. In private international law, a marriage is recognised if it is valid according to the law of the place where it was celebrated (Lord Collins of Mapesbury et al, 2012: 964). In the judgment in *Hyde*, Lord Penzance set out the first definition of marriage in English law:

> I conceive that marriage, as understood in Christendom, may for this purpose be defined as the voluntary union for life of one man and one woman to the exclusion of all others. (*Hyde* [1866]: 133)

In Christendom, which included England, marriage could only be between one man and one woman who voluntarily marry for life with no others involved. This has been criticised as unrealistic even for the 1800s, as it failed to account for divorce, adultery and forced marriage which existed then and today (Poulter, 1979; Probert, 2007). The only element which holds firm is that parties marry 'to the exclusion of others' (Calder, 2009). A polygamous marriage is void excluding it from past and present understandings of a valid marriage in English law. In *Hyde*, it was decided that an English legal divorce could not dissolve a marriage that had been celebrated in a polygamy-permitting country between spouses that follow a faith which allows polygamy:

> A marriage contracted in a country where polygamy is lawful between a man and woman who profess a faith which allows polygamy, is not a marriage as understood in Christendom … the English matrimonial court will not recognise it as a valid marriage. (*Hyde* [1866]: 130)

This marriage had never existed in English law or in 'Christendom'. Lord Penzance discussed the possibility of

> treating such first union as a Christian marriage, and all subsequent unions, if any, as void; the first woman taken to wife as a 'wife' ... and all the rest as concubines. (*Hyde* [1866]: 136)

but he ultimately decided against this. Finally, the judgment was confined to the case at hand:

> This court does not profess to decide upon the rights of succession or legitimacy which it might be proper to accord to the issue of polygamous unions. (*Hyde* [1866]: 138)

This leaves the door open for future cases to permit legal recognition for polygamy, but the judgment is not positive. *Hyde* introduces the key cultural conflict around overseas polygamy: the conflict between Christian and non-Christian marriage. The case comments on marriage as a cultural institution determining that polygamy is not a part of it because as with domestic polygamy, Christian dominance in English law determines that marriage is essentially monogamous (Smith, 1952; Poulter, 1976). Štýbnarová notes that 'Western doctrine ... was marked by its negative approach to recognising polygamous marriages, precisely for its "immorality" based on non-compliance with Christian values' (2020: 106). The lack of legal recognition for polygamous marriage prioritises moral Christian monogamy. The resolution to the 'conflict' is to choose the cultural ideal which conforms to the Christian values dominating English law and marriage.

In the language of the *Hyde* decision, we see various examples of imperialist, orientalist and sexist statements:

> There are, no doubt, countries peopled by a large section of the human race in which men and women do not live or cohabit together upon these terms. ... In such parts the men take to themselves several women, whom they jealously guard from the rest of the world, and whose number is limited only by considerations of material means. But the status of these women in no way resembles that of the Christian 'wife'. In some parts they are slaves, in others perhaps not; in none do they stand, as in Christendom, upon the same level with the man under whose protection they live. (*Hyde* [1866]: 133–4)

Said's (1978) definition of orientalism includes the notion of 'authorising' views of the Orient based on Western assumptions. The language of certainty employed in this excerpt through phrases such as 'no doubt' and '[i]n some parts they are slaves' fit with this. Lord Penzance's confident and assured opinion orientalises and dismisses polygamous marriage because it does not fit within his understanding of the ideal of marriage in Christendom. The remainder of the passage embodies an imperialist, Christian, patriarchal view of polygamous wives. For example, unlike a Christian wife, the woman here is not seen to be on the 'same level' as the man that takes her. This idea of being on the same level is encouraging at first, because it suggests that a Christian wife could enjoy a level of equality. However, with the words 'with the man under whose protection they live', the traditional gender roles of this era become visible. The idea that a woman cannot be on the same level as a man if she needs to live under his protection shows that the status of a Christian wife was also inferior.

With the imperialist and orientalist superiority displayed towards polygamy, the Christian wife held a higher value than the polygamous wife. In the judgment, polygamous wives are portrayed as lacking the protection of an English husband which can only be enjoyed by the Christian wife. This represents the perception that polygamously married women need to be saved from their marriages. When the judgment states that 'in some parts they are slaves', it is indicating a loss of agency and personhood. As 'slaves', these women are constructed as incapable of deciding the form of marriage that they engage in. This supports Johnson's (2014) critique of the orientalist presumption that polygamy automatically entails coercion (referred to in Chapter 2), illustrating how Christian imperialism justified denying recognition for polygamy. By imposing this assumption that polygamy entailed coercion, the idea that monogamy can also involve coercion is dismissed. Similarly dismissed is the idea that both polygamy and monogamy can be active, desirable choices for the women who live them.

For more than 20 years after *Hyde*, Lord Penzance's definition of marriage was ignored, until the case of *In Re Bethell Bethell v Hildyard* (1887) 38 Ch D 220 (hereafter *Bethell*), which was instrumental in developing the conflict of laws jurisprudence for overseas polygamy (Barratt, 2019). This case dealt with the monogamous marriage between an English domiciled man, Christopher Bethell, and a woman named Teepoo, of the Baralong tribe in Bechuanaland. Their marriage was celebrated according to Baralong custom but was held invalid in English law because it did not confer the same status on the parties as Christian marriage – Teepoo and the couple's child could not be recognised as heirs to his estate.

It was explicitly stated that Baralong marriage was being held up to standards of English civility and could not be recognised because it took place in an 'uncivilized country' and among people who were not 'so highly civilized as in England' (*Bethell* (1887): 225). This was not a question of conflict of laws but whether the colonised Baralong community's laws should be allowed to contribute to the growing body of private international law rules around marriage (Barratt, 2019). The decision was based on their 'inferiority' to English legal and therefore cultural values. The Baralong marriage was othered and orientalised as different and then classed as inferior on the basis that it did not take place in England among English people:

> The Baralongs had not any religion, nor any religious customs, and … polygamy was allowed in that tribe. (*Bethell* (1887): 221)

This connection between a lack of religion and polygamy is an example of Christian imperialism and orientalism. There is no indication of how it was decided that the Baralong have no religion. In his depositions, the chief of the tribe referred to Baralong custom, although whether this was rooted in religion or tradition was left unclear. By suggesting that polygamy only happens when participants are either non-Christian or have no religion, the discourse alienates the practice and its participants from England and English law.

Fryer notes that '[t]he golden age of British Empire was the golden age of British racism too' (1984: 165). Compared to the earlier *Hyde* case, the *Bethell* judgment had stronger racist undertones but *Hyde* involved a White couple based in the West (even if Utah is a former British colony) so racism had less of an overt part to play. In *Bethell*, the approach to the colonised Baralong was focussed on their inferiority as a

> barbarous or semi-barbarous tribe … beyond the limits of the British dominion. (*Bethell* (1887): 232)

To characterise a people in this way is dehumanising and insulting; to be barbarous is to be uncivilised, cruel, coarse and unrefined (Allen, 1990). Such racist discourse supports Mommsen's (1981) arguments regarding the use of racial and biological differences to bolster and underpin White supremacy and imperialism. During this golden age of empire, the inferiority of a colonised people was based on 'scientific evidence' linking physical characteristics to intellect and morality in what Fryer terms the 'pseudo-scientific mythology of race' (1984: 165). The view of the Baralong as 'barbarous', having no religion and permitting polygamy highlighted racial and religious differences. These differences were used against Teepoo and her child to deny them lawful recognition and a share of the deceased's estate. This approach shows that conflict of laws excludes certain legal systems and communities from recognition by measuring their values and identities against the European normative standard. It is imperial in nature and operation.

Dicey's rules, which have been compiled in a substantial volume known as *The Conflict of Laws*, are taken as an authoritative account of private international law in England and Wales. They cover various conflict of laws issues and set out how they have been 'resolved' (Lord Collins of Mapesbury et al, 2012). In line with Dicey's position (stated earlier) that conflict of laws jurisprudence is an internal matter and therefore cannot definitively be characterised as law, his work is widely known as 'Dicey's rules' rather than 'Dicey's laws'. The history of these rules around overseas polygamy is relevant here. The first edition of Dicey's *Conflict of Laws* was published several years after *Bethell*, and it used *Bethell* along with *Hyde* to assert that a foreign law would only be recognised when the foreign jurisdiction has 'reached a similar stage of civilisation' (to England) (Dicey, 1896). The Baralong were not regarded as being at this 'similar stage' so *Bethell* was not even seen as a genuine conflict case (Barratt, 2019). We need to bear in mind how these cases were explicitly used to manifest imperialist racialising attitudes towards systems and cultures simply for permitting polygamy, even when the marriage in front of the English court was monogamous.

This imperialist and orientalist approach focussed on cultural difference and non-Christian plural marriage is also evident in relation to the Chinese practice of secondary marriage. In Chinese law, a man could take a t'sip, or secondary wife, without undergoing a marriage ceremony and this granted her a position superior to a concubine or mistress (Morris, 1953; Greenfield, 1958). The cases of *Cheang Thye Phin and Others Appellants v Tan Ah Loy (Since Deceased)* [1920] AC 369 (hereafter *Cheang Thye Phin*) and *Khoo Hooi Leong Appellant v Khoo Hean Kwee Respondent* [1926] AC 529 (hereafter *Khoo Hooi Leong*) concerned the capacity of the t'sips and their children to inherit from their husbands' estates. In *Cheang Thye Phin*, the courts accepted the legitimacy of the deceased's t'sip and her children because her relationship was permanent in nature and the children were recognised by the father. As the secondary marriage adhered to Chinese law and there was no doubt surrounding the t'sip's identity, she and her children were allowed to inherit from the deceased husband's estate. Notably, the English court was not deciding whether the t'sip was a validly married secondary wife based on English law, but according to the Chinese law followed by Chinese residents in the Straits Settlements. However, the marriage was still being assessed in English law through the lens of cultural difference which is apparent when we look more closely at the language in the judgments.

In *Khoo Hooi Leong* and its subsequent appeal,[2] the appellant was unable to show that his grandmother was a t'sip rather than a concubine or mistress so that he along with his father, could inherit from his grandfather's estate. While expressing the view that the concept of t'sip is 'a little difficult for a Christian and western mind to grasp' (*Khoo Hooi Leong* [1926]: 533), the court was unable to recognise the grandmother for several reasons, including that she was a Catholic who had never abandoned her religion, that she was already married to another man, and that there was no element of permanence to her relationship with the appellant's grandfather. It was observed that as well as forbidding polygamy, Christianity 'prohibits illicit cohabitation' (*Khoo Hooi Leong* [1926]: 543) indicating the court's disapproval of the parties' conduct in Christianity.

2 *Khoo Hooi Leong Appellant v Khoo Chong Yeok Respondent* [1930] AC 346.

The courts treated the secondary marriage as polygamy, showing their unwillingness to differentiate between different forms of non-Christian plural marriage. The English courts' acceptance of Chinese law's overriding jurisdiction, not acceptance of the relationship, governed their stance. In *Cheang Thye Phin* it is stated:

> In the Six Widows' Case (*Choo Eng Choon v Neo Chan Neo* (1908) Straits Settlements LR 120) Hyndman Jones C.J. said in the Supreme Court: 'concubinage is recognized as a legal institution under Chinese law conferring upon the "t'sip" a legal status of a permanent nature, which subject to divorce entitles her to maintenance during her lifetime'. (*Cheang Thye Phin* [1920]: 375)

Concubinage was a legally recognised institution, and by recognising the t'sip, the English courts were not accepting the practice of secondary marriage but acknowledging it as a Chinese practice for Chinese people. This reasoning also contributes to the view taken in *Khoo Hooi Leong* where the appellant's grandmother was referred to in the grandfather's will as a 'Christian woman' (*Khoo Hooi Leong* [1926]: 534). The court found it difficult to accept the Christian woman was a secondary wife, implying that there is a fundamental incompatibility between Christianity and this practice. In following Christianity, this woman could not be in a relationship governed by Chinese law and custom. The conflict here was between her imperially approved faith and her disapproved marriage – the cultural difference between them was too vast, exposing the orientalising lens that the courts used to make sense of this relationship.

The courts' orientalist approach further confuses the practices of secondary marriage and concubinage and we start to see how the attitude towards the marriage impacted the status and view of the wife. In *Cheang Thye Phin*, the judgment suggests that the t'sip is also being identified as a concubine. However, in *Khoo Hooi Leong*, while it was claimed by the appellant that his grandmother was a t'sip, the court was unable to prove that she was anything other than a concubine or mistress. Through this failure to establish that the grandmother was a t'sip, the court suggested that there is a difference between a t'sip and a concubine and that they are not of equal status. However, this did not play out in the results. The judgment in *Khoo Hooi Leong* states that:

> The position of a concubine or mistress – this latter phrase is used by the settlor – or secondary wife under Chinese law and custom is peculiar. (*Khoo Hooi Leong* [1926]: 533)

The key term here is 'settlor'. The settlor's or coloniser's view was that the secondary wife is a concubine or mistress, and this influences the English judicial view of Chinese secondary marriage. This confusion between roles indicates that while the English courts do not view a t'sip as anything other than a concubine or mistress, they accept the existence of secondary marriage in Chinese law. Their engagement with Chinese law is a superficial performance rooted in racialised cultural stereotypes that ultimately conflate and combine the different relationship statuses of these women under the umbrella of 'non-Christian wife': a category defined by how it differs from the culturally superior Christian wife. That these women are not considered wives at all shows how they and their relationships are being denigrated by the courts.

As time passed and the British Empire started to formally break down, rather than just colonisers moving to the colonies, colonised people started to migrate and settle in greater numbers in Britain, bringing with them cultural and marital norms like polygamy. In *Hyde* and *Bethell*, the husbands in overseas polygamous marriages were White and English. The courts now started to face domestic cases with racialised, formerly colonised participants, and the cultural conflict between English Christian (White) and non-Christian (racialised) marriages persisted. The elevated status of Christian marriage continued into the 1950s and 1960s, with terms including 'union' and 'association' being used instead of 'marriage' to describe polygamy, reflecting the distinction between Christian marriage and non-Christian relationships. In *Matthew Olajide Bamgbose v John Bankole Daniel* 1952 14 WACA 111–15, the West African Court of Appeal used the word 'marriage' to describe both Christian monogamous and non-Christian polygamous marriages. However, the Privy Council stated on appeal that

> the courts of Nigeria attached to monogamous and Christian marriages a sanctity not accorded to polygamous unions by native law and custom. (*Matthew Olajide Bamgbose, Appellant v John Bankole Daniel and Others, Respondents* [1955] AC 107: 112)

The Privy Council corrected the first court's use of 'marriage' to describe polygamy, thereby displaying an imperialist, racialised response to the court system in colonial Nigeria as well as Nigerian conceptions of marriage. Native Nigerian law (and its native judges) needed to be corrected, and the distinction between marriage and polygamy needed to be reinforced. The Privy Council was not just racialising law but judges and marriage as well, showing the all-encompassing hierarchy of law and legal systems created by private international law.

Later, in *Shahnaz v Rizwan* [1964] 3 WLR 759 (hereafter *Shahnaz*), polygamous marriages became 'associations', distancing them from Christian marriages even further:

> The reason I think is one of policy, of morality as conceived first in the mid-19th century but surviving into modern times, that nothing should

> be done to blur the distinction between Christian marriage – marriage properly understood ... and, on the other hand, polygamous associations more resembling concubinage or slavery. (*Shahnaz* [1964]: 398)

While 'union' retains a sense of people coming together, 'association' is more removed from ideas of intimacy. A union could be a personal relationship, but an association is impersonal. According to the Christian, imperialist view that has been espoused by the courts since *Hyde*, a union or association can never equate to the social and religious institution of marriage. The relationships of those from other faiths are inferior and undeserving of the same level of recognition. In excluding polygamy from understandings of marriage, its inferiority is reinforced whether it is labelled a union or association. This then combines with the orientalist assumption that Christian marriage is the only form of marriage that is 'properly understood' as a matter of 'morality'. The labelling of the relationship as an association also leads to judgements about the status of the women that engage in it, because these problematic discourses are heavily intertwined. Polygamous marriages are 'concubinage or slavery' for women who need saving. This subordinates and denigrates polygamous wives, lowering their status to a concubine or 'slave' who is associated or united with a man rather than lawfully married to him. This manifestation of the cultural conflict between monogamy and polygamy emphasises the sexist elements that are wrapped up with the racialised nature of the cultural differences reinforced by the law.

Mutating non-Christian marriage: potential polygamy

In the judgments for both *Hyde* and *Bethell*, the marriages were not valid in English law. *Hyde* concerned a man whose wife had subsequently married again and was therefore married to two men at the same time: the marriage was *actually* polygamous. However, in *Bethell*, Teepoo's customary Baralong marriage to Christopher Bethell was invalid even though it was monogamous:

> [A] union formed between a man and a woman in a foreign country, although it may there bear the name of a marriage, and the parties to it may there be designated husband and wife, is not a valid marriage according to the law of England unless it be formed on the same basis as marriages throughout Christendom, and be in its essence 'the voluntary union for life of one man and one woman to the exclusion of all others'. (*Bethell* (1887): 233)

A marriage is usually considered valid if it followed the law of the place it was celebrated in, but the relationship in this case could not be recognised in England since Baralong marriage does not confer the same status on the parties as Christian marriage (Lord Collins of Mapesbury et al, 2012: 964). The marriage here was monogamous, but the Baralong community *permitted* polygamy. Christopher and Teepoo were married only to each other, but their marriage had the *potential* to become polygamous because it was celebrated according to a system that allowed polygamy. So, although monogamous in practice, it was still viewed as a type of polygamy. From this, it is evident that polygamy is being used as a smokescreen to denigrate any type of marriage which is not formed on the same basis as those in Christendom. Even marriages carried out in countries that permit polygamy but are in monogamous in practice are not spared from the courts' strategy. Polygamy is a convenient excuse – a minority practice used to characterise all non-Christian marriages as lesser and unworthy of being recognised.

The invalidity of potentially polygamous marriages was later confirmed in numerous cases including: *Risk (Otherwise Yerburgh) v Risk* [1951] P 50; *Muhammad v Suna* 1956 SC 366; *Ohochuku v Ohochuku* [1960] 1 WLR 183; *Sowa v Sowa* [1960] 3 WLR 733 (hereafter *Sowa*); and *Khan v Khan* [1962] 3 FLR 496. Because potential polygamy does not fall within the definition of marriage in English law, the courts were reluctant to accept jurisdiction for potentially polygamous marriages celebrated overseas and this meant that access to matrimonial relief or remedies could not be granted. In all these cases except *Sowa*, the courts refused to pronounce decrees of divorce or nullity. *Sowa* and its subsequent appeal dealt with a maintenance order, although it was again held that the wife from a potentially polygamous marriage was not entitled to seek such legal relief, so the message remained the same: even if a potentially polygamous marriage is monogamous in practice, it is no different from a marriage which is actually polygamous.

The lack of legal distinction between actual and potential polygamy during this period is both imperialist and orientalist. By characterising and treating potentially polygamous marriages in the same way as actually polygamous marriages, the law was being used to other and degrade those who had celebrated their marriage abroad in a polygamy-permitting jurisdiction. This meant that marriages celebrated in former colonies like India and Nigeria, were not considered marriages because of how they conflicted with 'English marriage'. The cultural difference between English and non-English monogamy turns around whether these marriages permit polygamy causing a conflict which is resolved by refusing recognition for all non-English marriages.

However, with time this approach became unsustainable and the courts started to recognise potentially polygamous marriages for different purposes, starting with *The Sinha Peerage Claim* HL Deb 12 December 1935 vol 99 cc 224–32 (hereafter *Sinha*). The House of Lords had to decide whether the son of the deceased Lord Sinha was legitimate and able to succeed to his father's peerage because his parents had been in a potentially polygamous Hindu marriage. Potentially polygamous marriages celebrated in India were discussed, and the ultimate finding was that they would be considered valid in England if they complied with Indian law. Therefore, Lord Sinha's son was capable of succeeding to the family peerage. The case had been helped by the clearly intentional monogamy of the marriage.

This change was possibly motivated by the desire to maintain the image of the empire as accepting and tolerant. In the judgment, Lord Strickland discusses 'religious toleration throughout the Empire' (*Sinha* [1935]: 225). However, the word 'toleration' represents reluctance. Brown argues that 'toleration' is limited and a 'token of Western supremacy' (2008: 182), centring the West as the standard for civilisation. We further see here how judges shape and construct polygamy as a construct which is given meaning through discourse. Not only does Lord Strickland's comment reflect broader societal norms at the time and the shift towards recognising the increased diversity in marital practices in the empire, but it also shapes the 'appropriate' response to polygamy – other non-Christian religions and their practices will be tolerated, but there is no room for full acceptance.

This token acceptance is reproduced in *Shahnaz*, the case I discussed earlier where polygamy was described as an 'association' rather than marriage. Here, a woman's contractual right to the dowry promised for her potentially polygamous marriage was enforced, showing that it was not unlawful. However, the court was careful to ensure that it was not the marriage or any right arising from it which could be enforced, but the right from the dowry contract. As in *Sinha*, it is likely that the marriage being monogamous in practice aided the court's cautious change in viewpoint. As explained by Judge Winn:

> Nor do I see any foundation in any of the decided cases that have been brought to my notice for any judicial ruling that that marriage involved any element offensive to the standards of decency accepted by the English law. (*Shahnaz* [1964]: 397)

The court was able to entertain the potentially polygamous marriages because its monogamous structure meant it was not 'offensive' or unlawful.

Moreover, the judge was conscious of the difficulties that women who are party to a Mohammedan marriage face after coming to the UK:

> It is better that the court should recognise in favour of women who have come here as a result of a Mohammedan marriage the right to obtain from their husband what was promised to them by enforcing the contract and payment of what was so promised. (*Shahnaz* [1964]: 401–2)

This sympathetic policy statement is possibly an attempt to adopt a proactive and humanising attitude towards the rights of women in potentially polygamous marriages celebrated overseas. It could also be explained by the courts getting used to seeing such cases as immigration to the UK from polygamy-permitting colonies became more prevalent (Shah, 2003). This led to a willingness to hear these women and their issues rather than outright dismissal.

However, the colonial saviour theme is also visible here, reflecting a persistent lack of development in cultural perceptions of gender and how they conflict with English legal understandings of the wife. The suffering of women who come here is attributed to their Mohammedan marriage rather than the courts' attitude to that marriage: it is the foreign culture and marriage that are the problem. The court enables a potentially polygamous wife to enforce her rights while it 'conceals the opposition between protector and protected' (Pathak and Rajan, 1992: 263). This protection comes at the price of othering the wife by blaming her relationship, the culture it is from, and the conflict it causes with English law. The court may be protecting her rights but it does so by taking on the role of magnanimous saviour; in other words, the law has saved her from her marriage and culture.

Potential polygamy may now be tolerable and valid in the courts at times, but not always. Dicey's rules tell us that polygamy is now recognised for most purposes, but there may be situations where the courts must decide whether a marriage is monogamous or polygamous. Without a legislative provision that tells us otherwise, a potentially polygamous marriage will be treated as if it were actually polygamous (Lord Collins of Mapesbury et al, 2012: 964). The official position to this day is that a marriage performed in a polygamy-permitting place according to the local legal system may still be treated as if it were polygamous even if the parties are married only to each other and are therefore monogamous in practice. So, little has changed towards non-Christian monogamous marriages celebrated in a place that permits polygamy: they are still being orientalised and denigrated in English law.

Looking more closely at the mechanics of this recognition for potential polygamy, the courts have deployed an interesting strategy through the principle of mutation or conversion. A marriage which was polygamous at its inception (because of where it was celebrated) but is monogamous in practice, can be mutated into a monogamous marriage when either party no longer has the capacity to take another spouse or they undergo another monogamous ceremony (Lord Collins of Mapesbury et al, 2012: 965). Mutation displays the courts' benevolence towards polygamy and its non-Christian participants, but what does it entail? It is a form of conversion which is almost religious: non-Christian monogamy (which is not really monogamous) into Christian monogamy. Kang'ara (2012) discusses how conversion strategies would require polygamous husbands who converted to Christianity in colonial Africa to choose one Christian wife and then abandon their other customary wives. The chosen wife would be legally recognised and monogamous while the other customary wives' marriages would be recast as adultery, leaving them traumatised. Cases like *Sinha* did not have such a dramatic effect on the parties, but conversion and the imperial adjudication over marriage validity was an 'important exercise of colonial authority' (Kang'ara, 2012: 353). Marasinghe (1978) comments that mutation was a strategy created by the courts to give matrimonial relief for non-Christian marriages in order to deal with the 'cultural problem' caused by polygamy which has wreaked havoc on the conflict of laws (see also Diwan, 1957). The blame is on the practice rather than the legal system, again making sure that non-Christian marriages are seen as the cause of the conflict and the problem without considering the part that the legal system plays in denying recognition for potential polygamy.

The supposed superiority of Christian monogamy is reinforced by the fact that mutation flows in one direction. You can convert a potential polygamous marriage into a monogamous one, but it is impossible in English private international law for a monogamous marriage to become polygamous (Lord Collins of Mapesbury et al, 2012: 965). The fact that this is a one-way process shows again the lack of balance in perceptions of polygamy. It cannot even be entertained that a monogamous spouse would want to become polygamous. This speaks to the ingrained orientalist perceptions of polygamy and potential polygamy as reserved for the non-Christian other and foreigner, and the belief that it should not happen in England among English people. I centre this colonial history to disrupt the discourses in the law which portray this as a sensible, practical way to accommodate minoritised and non-Christian marriage practices. The conversion of potential polygamy into monogamy is not a practical solution to a conflict of laws, but rather a way to portray non-Christian marriage as a cause of cultural conflict that needs to be forced into the Christian monogamous structure to be valid in English law.

For most of the 19th and 20th centuries, case law was the main authority for legal responses to overseas polygamy. However, with increased immigration to the British imperial centre and the courts needing to address more situations related to potential polygamy, it started to attract attention from law and policy makers for the first time. This led to several Law Commission working papers and reports as well as developments in legislation. Even though the courts had been recognising potentially polygamous marriages for certain situations since the 1930s as we saw with *Sinha*, the Law Commission did not publish a report on this until 1971. The report recommended the abolition of the rule set out in *Hyde* that polygamy and potential polygamy should be barred from matrimonial relief. This resulted in the Matrimonial Proceedings (Polygamous Marriages) Act 1972, which was then absorbed into the Matrimonial Causes Act 1973. s 47 of the 1973 Act determines that

> [a] court in England and Wales shall not be precluded from granting matrimonial relief or making a declaration concerning the validity of a marriage by reason only that either party to the marriage is, or has during the subsistence of the marriage been, married to more than one person.

By allowing access to the courts, individuals have the option to seek a legal divorce and other forms of matrimonial relief. Coupled with the courts' ability to make declarations of validity, a polygamous marriage can now be recognised for many purposes. However, the provision is couched in negative terms. For example, 'shall not be precluded' suggests that although the courts have the ability to provide relief or declare a polygamous marriage valid, they have no obligation to do so. Women in polygamous marriages are not automatically granted relief from the English courts, though no one, including women in traditional monogamous marriages, is guaranteed relief from the courts. Thus, the negative discursive construction of the provision is important to note, but this attitude is not specifically limited to polygamous wives.

In terms of validity, s 11(d) Matrimonial Causes Act 1973 provides that a marriage would be void if 'in the case of a polygamous marriage entered into outside England and Wales, … either party was at the time of the marriage domiciled in England and Wales.' In Chapter 3, I discussed void marriages and non-qualifying ceremonies, and showed that void marriages at least permitted the parties to obtain relief from the courts. This new development meant polygamy was now void and parties could therefore qualify for matrimonial relief. However, the report and resulting legislation continued to refer to potential polygamy reflecting the restrictive approach from *Hyde*.[3]

The category of potential polygamy remained authoritative during the Law Commission review in 1985. The report recommended that potential polygamous marriages be recognised as if they were monogamous, confirming the strategy of mutation that had been used by the courts since *Sinha*. The reason given was

> [t]he movement in favour of recognising polygamous marriages for very many purposes in our plural society is now so broad that we have reached the conclusion that … the civil law now draws no distinction between actually monogamous marriages on the basis of the nature of the ceremony. (Law Commission and Scottish Law Commission, 1985: para 3.6)

Referring to 'our plural society', the Law Commission accounts for the increased diversity in marriage practices due to increased immigration. Also,

---

3 There are many decisions which explain and apply this approach. See, for example, *Chetti v Chetti* [1909] P 67; *Srini Vasan v Srini Vasan* [1946] P 67; *Risk (Otherwise Yerburgh) v Risk* [1951] P 50; *Khan v Khan* [1963] VR 203; *Crowe v Kader* [1968] WAR 122; *Indyka v Indyka* [1969] 1 AC 33; *Radwan v Radwan (No 2)* [1972] 3 WLR 939; [1973] Fam 35; *Hussain v Hussain* [1982] 3 WLR 679; [1983] Fam 26; *Vervaeke v Smith (Messina and A-G Intervening)* [1983] 1 AC 145; *Lawrence v Lawrence* [1985] FLR 1097.

there was no practical reason to treat potential polygamy as polygamy rather than monogamy since the courts had been treating it as monogamy for years. But, as mentioned earlier, the strategy of mutation came at a price, and there are still situations where potential polygamy may be viewed as polygamous in English law. This raises the question of how much the recommendation and legislative responses changed orientalist views of non-Christian marriages.

The answer to this is not much. After the Law Commission report in 1985, it took a decade for the legislative framework to catch up with the 1973 Act being amended by s 5(1) Private International Law (Miscellaneous Provisions Act) 1995:

> A marriage entered into outside England and Wales between parties neither of whom is already married is not void under the law of England and Wales on the ground that it is entered into under a law which permits polygamy and that either party is domiciled in England and Wales.[4]

Potentially polygamous marriages are no longer automatically void unlike those which are actually polygamous. If an unmarried man domiciled in the UK contracts his first marriage in a polygamy-permitting place with an unmarried woman domiciled there, although the marriage would be potentially polygamous, it would no longer be considered void. The marriage would be treated as monogamous by the English courts. The rights of the married couple are upheld as if both parties were domiciled in the UK and celebrated a monogamous marriage in the UK because the marriage has mutated or been converted.

The 1995 Act was the last legislative development in English law around polygamy, showing again how little attention overall is given to these marriages. Arguably, this mirrors the indifference towards domestic polygamy, but these Law Commission reviews and the developments in the courts and legislation are more advanced. This is not necessarily hopeful: overseas polygamy has received more negative attention than positive because it is racialised and orientalised. Domestic polygamy is dismissed because it does not exist in the English legal imagination, whereas the overseas polygamy of racialised colonial natives who are coming to the UK and creating 'havoc' with their marriages is scrutinised much more. This is not just because of their marital structure, but also because of the perceived effects of their relationships on public resources and border

4 The case of *Suzia Abdin v Entry Clearance Officer, Dhaka* [2012] UKUT 00309 (IAC) states that the 1995 Act amendment is based on the recommendations of the 1985 Law Commission report.

control, which is where the focus of responses to polygamy has been found in more recent times.

Differentiating polygamy: protecting public resources

Moving closer to the present day, it became unfashionable to be overtly racist and imperialist towards polygamy. However, the courts still wanted to prevent it and their strategy progressed from explicit denigration to the more subtle differentiation hidden behind concerns for the public good and purse. For example, concerns about entitlement to public money started to arise where individuals – mainly women and children living in polygamous families – were deemed a burden on the state. The courts have protected state funds from 'abuse' by those in polygamous marriages as shown in *Imam Din v National Assistance Board* [1967] 2 WLR 257 (hereafter *Imam*). Here, a man abandoned his second wife and their children in the UK leaving them reliant on the National Assistance Board for financial provision. There was no denying that the wife and children were lawfully related to the husband under Pakistani law, so he could not

> avoid all responsibility and thereby throw the whole burden of maintaining his wife and children upon the public. (*Imam* [1967]: 218)[5]

Recognition of this polygamous marriage prevented the use of public money implying that the maintenance of the polygamous wife and children is a burden on the state. The husband in *Imam* had deserted his second wife after the death of his first wife and had only one living wife at the time of the desertion. The court recognised the marriage because although it may have been polygamous at its inception, it later became monogamous. This shows how the courts negotiate definitions of marriage to serve the public purse and prioritise state interests.

The court's attitude reflects the burgeoning privatisation of welfare favoured by conservative ideologies that are now at the heart of the neoliberal state in the UK. Societal institutions are increasingly expected to function for profit generation, so the line between the public and private sectors is blurred (Whitehead and Crawshaw, 2012: 233). In *Imam*, recognition of

[5] It is important to remember that this approach to public funds would also apply to monogamous spouses. It is further notable that in a recent case, a woman whose marriage was polygamous at its inception and celebrated lawfully in Pakistan was not barred from receiving a bereavement payment and widowed parent's allowance when the relevant social security regulations were read in line with the European Convention on Human Rights. It was a great help to the claimant's case that her marriage was monogamous for a significant length of time after her husband divorced his first wife. See *NA v Secretary of State for Work and Pensions* [2019] 1 WLR 6321.

the polygamous marriage removed state responsibility for the welfare of the wife and children, placing this family in a vulnerable position. Even with a legal order, there was no guarantee the husband would take financial responsibility leaving this woman and her children at the mercy of a man who had previously refused to fund their needs. The wife was undeserving of state aid because of her polygamous marriage, leaving her family in an untenable situation of financial insecurity.

The 1971 Law Commission report published soon after this case commented that the wife's lack of entitlement to social security benefits here was 'unfortunate and anomalous … [because she] … should be treated just like any English wife if she was in fact her husband's only wife throughout their period of residence in England' (1971: 42). This statement highlights the main source of suffering for women in polygamous marriages: judicial interpretations of their marriage which ensure they are treated differently and to their detriment. This different treatment others and orientalises them because their marriages are different from the monogamous ideal. Unfortunately, we see that the Law Commission's opinion made little difference to the case law.

The case of *Nabi (Ghulam) v Heaton (Inspector of Taxes)* [1981] 1 WLR 1052 (hereafter *Nabi*) dealt with the income tax relief of a man who had contracted two polygamous marriages in Pakistan. The husband could only claim relief for his first wife. During the *Nabi* decision, while interpreting the meaning of 'his wife' in the Income and Corporation Taxes Act 1970, the judge stated that

> to read the expression 'his wife' as meaning 'a wife' or 'any wife' would be to do too great violence to … the section. (*Nabi* [1981]: 1058)

In the judge's opinion, including polygamous marriage provokes a strong reaction that would cause significant damage to the section. This reminds us of the strong language used nearly a century earlier in *Bethell* where people who live in a society that permits polygamy were described as 'semi-barbarous'. In both cases, there is disturbance at the thought of polygamy, and even though the much earlier *Bethell* judgment was more explicit, the statement in *Nabi* demonstrates that these patterns of racialised cultural difference linger.

The courts recognised the two marriages as a mechanism to prevent the husband claiming two lots of tax relief – the benefit relating to the first wife remained intact. This harmed the second wife as recognition of her polygamous marriage deprived her husband of the second tax benefit. The decision impressed upon her that as a second wife, she was not worthy of the same status as the first wife and as her husband would not benefit from their marriage as much as from the marriage with his first wife, she suffered financial loss as well as a sense of inferiority. The message of inferiority running through *Iman* and *Nabi* is orientalist and patriarchal. Because their polygamous marriages were not suited to the welfare state's construction of marriage the wives were othered and seen as a burden. When compared to the much earlier *Bethell*, we see that while judicial attitudes towards recognition have evolved at this stage, the courts' aim remains the same: to deny relief and assistance to polygamous wives and their children. The problematic discourses surrounding polygamous marriages are still present in the case law at this time, impacting negatively on women.

Closer to the present day, the case law shows signs of the courts' willingness to consider the needs of polygamous spouses when money is involved. For example, in *R v Department of Health Ex p Misra* [1996] 1 FLR 128 (hereafter *Misra*), the two widows of a doctor, who were both lawfully married in India, were equally entitled via extra statutory concession to a pension under Reg 14(1) of the National Health Service (Superannuation) Regulations 1980.[6] The existing pension amount was divided equally between the two wives. No additional support was to be given to one over the other, and if one wife passed away, her share would not be given to the other wife.

This case shows that the courts can deal with polygamous marriage without being openly sexist, racist, imperialist or orientalist. *Misra* is interesting because the marriages of these polygamous widows were upheld ostensibly so that they may benefit. The courts were focussed on the money rather than the polygamous wife claimant, but were willing to uphold her rights provided there was no conflict with state interests. Snow and Jones (2011) state that a national shortage of doctors by the 1960s led to considerable overseas recruitment from former British colonies. Due to its recruitment of such a large proportion of staff from nations with formally recognised polygamy, the National Health Service could have expanded the pension scheme to accommodate immigrant personnel. However, unlike a monogamous wife, a polygamous wife is only eligible for half a pension which is damaging. The monogamous wife and her marital choice remain privileged and she is rewarded for her conformity to the dominant Western paradigm. Polygamous wives are denied access to a whole pension and treated differently based on the imperialist perception that a polygamous marriage has a fraction of the value of the ideal monogamous marriage.

Bibi v Chief Adjudication Officer [1998] 1 FLR 375 (hereafter *Bibi*) continues along this vein. Here, the widow of a Bangladeshi Muslim polygamous marriage was denied a widowed mother's allowance because the provisions only applied to the widows of potentially polygamous marriages. Interestingly, the judge was persuaded by the argument from the earlier *Imam* that

> [i]t would clearly be wrong for a man paying contributions on the basis indicated to reap benefits in respect of perhaps three or four current wives. (*Imam* [1967]: 221)

6 This provides for the entitlement of a widow to an annual widow's pension.

Bibi concerned a widowed mother's allowance, but unlike *Imam*, the husband in this instance was deceased so I question his reaping the benefits. By focussing on the man, the widow and her needs were sidelined based on her polygamous marriage. The polygamous widow was left to suffer consequences because the court deemed it 'wrong' to award her deceased husband's social security contributions to her. Women are again placed in a position of inferiority treated as an unfair burden on the state because of their non-monogamous marriage. Polygamous marriages are still being recognised to protect state interests and idealise monogamy. Underlying attitudes and approaches towards polygamous marriage have changed less than it would seem.

Another track of case law that is focussed on public interests concerns immigration and the entry of second spouses or children from second or third marriages into the UK. Polygamous marriages in this instance are recognised to prevent the entry of multiple spouses like in *Zeenat Bibi v Secretary of State for the Home Department* [1994] Imm AR 550 and *R v Immigration Appeal Tribunal Ex p Begum (Hasna)* [1995] Imm AR 249 (hereafter *Begum (Hasna)*). The immigration legal framework provides for the refused entry of such spouses and children. The framework refuses to grant a right of abode in the UK to a man's second wife if his first wife is already exercising that right in the UK. This limitation is another method of preserving monogamy in the UK, although the effectiveness is questionable since a man is not prevented from having multiple wives. The immigration rules state that only one wife can have the UK as her abode – the husband is still free to have more than one family abroad. The immigration context for these cases with selective legal recognition and differentiation is also telling. Immigration law is generally more interrogating towards marriage, as seen in the discourses around sham and forced marriages (Turner, 2020). This feeds into the narratives around immigrants and their marriages, whether monogamous or polygamous, needing closer scrutiny because they differ and are viewed as problematic by default. The validity of immigrant marriages and families is probed in racist and racialising ways which are not as visible in other areas of law. Polygamous wives and children are therefore subject to multiple orientalising processes, first as immigrants and then as members of polygamous families. Their relationships and entry into the UK are seen as doubly problematic for the state.

We can think about this further from two perspectives: that of the first wife who has a UK right of abode; and that of the subsequent wives who would be refused entry. The first wife can live, raise her family and stay with her husband in the UK. For any subsequent wife who must remain abroad, neither she nor her children can benefit as much from the presence of her husband. There is an inevitable distance in the relationship between a man and his second family, meaning the family life of the second family is not equal to that of the first family. I claim this on the basis that the second wives in these two cases would probably not seek entry and stay in the UK if the benefits did not outweigh all other difficulties associated with emigrating. It is understandable that a wife would desire to be with her husband in the UK and it must be a source of suffering and hardship for her to live without him.

This is illustrated in *Begum (Hasna)* where the appellant

> has always lived with her mother in a house which is shared with her brother and his family ... her brother considers it unacceptable that his sister should be condemned to her present life, being separated from her husband. He feels it is a matter of shame to his family that his sister has never gone to her husband's house to live with him. ([1995]: 1)

Hasna Begum was living in a difficult situation away from her husband while he lived with his first wife and their children in the UK. The reference to 'shame' uncovers another form of harm to women in polygamous marriages which is not as apparent in existing literature. In Chapter 2, I explored harm as a tool to promote negative perceptions of polygamy with scholars like Kaganas and Murray (1991) concluding that patriarchy is the real harm. The brother's shame because the applicant lives with her maternal family is a harm resulting from patriarchal legal attitudes towards polygamy. *Begum (Hasna)* shows the consequences suffered by a lawful polygamous wife. Despite having official recognition in Bangladesh, refusal of entry to the UK left her to live as a single woman supported by her brother. We also cannot underestimate the emotional impact of her living situation being associated with 'shame' by her own family member.

The same attitude is displayed towards the children of polygamous marriages who are denied entry and even legitimacy, as shown in *Azad v Entry Clearance Officer, Dhaka* 2000 WL 1918688 (hereafter *Azad*). The child here was the son of a man and his third wife. Although valid in Bangladesh, the parents' marriage was void under s 11(d) Matrimonial Causes Act 1973 because the father's UK domicile meant he could not contract further polygamous marriages. This meant that the child was not born of a legally recognised union and could not claim legitimacy for the purposes of entry into the UK. These labels of 'unrecognised marriage' and 'illegitimate child' are damaging. That the relationships between all involved are being differentiated from English legal understandings of marriage and parentage is denigrating to the couple and their child.

Another case in which the courts denied entry to the child of a polygamous marriage was *ECO New Delhi v SG* [2012] UKUT 00265 (IAC) (hereafter *ECO New Delhi*). This took *Azad* further by discussing women along with children in relation to polygamy. Here, the daughter of a man and his third wife could be excluded from entry because:

> There is a legitimate aim in excluding from admission to the United Kingdom a woman who is a party to an actually polygamous marriage

> and that aim justifies the indirect effect of that exclusion on the child of such a marriage, in that it will be more difficult for the child to satisfy the immigration rules relating to sole responsibility and circumstances making exclusion of the child undesirable.
>
> The legitimate aim here is not limited to considerations of numbers alone, but to deter the formation of polygamous households in the United Kingdom. Such a policy is well within the state's discretionary area of judgment. (*ECO New Delhi* [2012]: para ii)

It is legitimate to exclude a polygamous wife and by extension her children. Such exclusion is justified to discourage polygamous households. Again, the courts recognise the polygamous marriage to serve the public interests of limiting immigration, rather than serving the wives and children affected. Some consideration was given to the interests of the child. The child's current care and welfare were weighed against her prospective care and welfare in the UK, with the finding that her current lifestyle was satisfactory and in fact, her standard of living would be higher as she benefits from 'overseas remittances' with the UK resident father's support. The wishes of the mother and child were easily overridden to serve policy objectives.

Later in the same judgment it is mentioned that

> the modest contribution to the discouragement of such marriages in Nepal or elsewhere is a legitimate aim in pursuit of morals and the rights of others particularly the pursuit of gender equality. (*ECO New Delhi* [2012]: para 47)

The question of morality and polygamous marriages arises again in this recent case, displaying the continuing presence of orientalist discourses in the case law. At several points, it is stressed that the child was not denied entry because of her parents' marriage but because she failed to meet the relevant criteria in the immigration rules. Why was it then necessary to explain and commend the discouragement of polygamous marriages 'in Nepal or elsewhere'?[7] The authoritative commentary on polygamy and its danger to gender equality is also problematic. Monogamy does not guarantee gender equality and to assume so is damaging for all married women.

Immigration cases have also involved attempts to invoke the European Convention on Human Rights in the UK regarding respect for private and family life, the right to marry and the prohibiting of discrimination. One of the earliest indications of the judicial approach to human rights in polygamy is found in ECmHR Appl 19628/92, *Bibi v UK* (Dec) 29 June 1992. The applicant

---

7 I interpret this as 'everywhere'.

complained that under Article 8 of the European Convention on Human Rights, her right to respect for family life was infringed by the UK's refusal to allow her polygamously married mother into the UK. She also argued that her mother was discriminated against on the grounds of sex as her father was allowed to choose which of his wives would live with him in the UK. Reid observes:

> The Commission found that excluding surplus wives was a legitimate aim under the second paragraph of Article 8 for the preservation of a Christian-based monogamous culture dominant in that society (as pursuing the protection of morals and of rights and freedoms of others). It also recalled its findings in an unpublished Dutch case that a Contracting State cannot be required to give full recognition to polygamous marriages in conflict with their own legal order, referring to bigamy laws. (1998: 277)

There was no evidence of an Article 8 infringement as the mother's exclusion pursued the legitimate aim of preserving monogamy. There was also no finding of discrimination as the exclusion stemmed from polygamy, for which the UK was not answerable under the European Convention on Human Rights.

A few years later, the court employed tortuous logic based on gender equality to differentiate polygamy from monogamy under the guise of protecting the public good. It was argued in *Khan v UK* (1996) 21 EHRR CD67 that the UK government had infringed the applicant's rights under Article 8 of the European Convention on Human Rights by refusing his second wife entry when his first wife was already resident in the UK. Although the application was deemed inadmissible, the government argued that the second marriage had not been prevented by UK law in this case. The refusal of entry for the second wife was partially justified by the assertion that the multiple husbands of a polyandrous woman would not be permitted entry and stay as it would 'not be conducive to the public good'.

This is the first mention of polyandry in the case law and no explanation or justification for the statement is made, giving the impression that the state is trying to demonstrate an equal approach to both polygyny and polyandry. Interestingly, this case represents a shift in attitudes reflecting the consciousness of sex discrimination. Throughout the case law, polygamous marriages, most of which have been polygynous, have been orientalised and held up to Western idealised standards of monogamy (Beaman, 2014). By contrast, in *Khan v UK*, a polygyny versus polyandry stance was taken to refuse entry for *any* polygamous spouse. By addressing polyandry, the UK avoids claims of sex discrimination under Article 14 of the European Convention on Human Rights, because it would refuse entry to all individuals in polygamous marriages regardless of their gender. The authorities have changed the comparator from monogamous marriage to gender. Malik explores the use of comparators in discrimination law, arguing that 'comparison is too individualistic and does not take sufficient account of the social context' (2007: 79). Polygyny is much more common than polyandry and women are more affected by judicial attitudes towards polygamous marriage than men, indicating a deliberate strategy to construct a comparator which is harder to challenge.

The phrase 'not be conducive to the public good' signifies the priority given to public interests as the UK government argues that the public would be negatively affected by a polyandrous husband being granted entry into the UK. Employing the 'public good' justification shows that polygamy is still being othered based on orientalist 'knowledge' that it is contrary to the public good and different from the ideal of monogamy. This links with the welfare cases explored earlier where women in polygamous marriages were portrayed as a strain on the state because their residence in the UK impacted on public resources and finances. Women in polygamous marriages are viewed in terms of their difference to the mainstream version of marriage in the UK and suffer as Hasna Begum did.

Concluding thoughts

In this chapter, I explored the legal and judicial treatment of polygamous marriages celebrated overseas. Starting with a discussion of the private international law that governs this area, I showed how the law is still bound up in colonial understandings of marriage which racialise and orientalise polygamous marriage and polygamous wives. The imperialist attitudes towards polygamy affect how this relationship is treated in practice by judges in the courts. From outright racist statements in the 1800s through to the subtly orientalist finding that polygamy is not compatible with the 'public good', we can see that overseas polygamy, like domestic polygamy, has been shown very little consideration or exploration that is sensitive, nuanced and aware of its imperialist baggage. Drawing on the conflict of laws scholarship, I also showed that the courts and legislation are reproducing a conflict of a different kind: a conflict of cultures which others and dismisses cultural communities where polygamy has been legally recognised for centuries. Over time, the courts have denigrated polygamy as not being good enough to count as a marriage; mutated potentially polygamous marriages into monogamous ones even though they were actually monogamous in the first place; and differentiated between polygamous marriages based on whether it suited the state for them to be recognised or not. The law is severely underdeveloped in this area because it is convenient and easy to maintain the status quo. This legal exploration has been important to establish the need for legal change, but it is incomplete without thinking about the real needs of women. I now turn to their stories to see how their experiences and lives have been affected by perceptions and reactions towards polygamy.

5

Tensions in Religion and Culture

Noreen

I've been married and divorced twice so far; I've got two young children. My first marriage was arranged with someone in Pakistan. I wouldn't say I was forced into it; I was sort of pressured into it. I was 16, he was 33. I went on what I thought was a holiday to Pakistan and came back to the UK married, and then didn't go to college, ended up working. I went back to Pakistan one more time and then realised that I couldn't actually do it so I told my parents that I wanted to get a divorce.

I left home at 18 and that's when I met my children's father. I got with him ... obviously the family weren't happy, so I can imagine why as well – he's White, he wasn't in the same race or culture or anything. I had children with him and we were together for four years before I got married to him.

The second you sign that piece of paper for some reason, everything seems to change, and I don't know if it's the pressure of 'Oh we're married now – it's not like I leave you at any time.' For some reason that just tends to have an effect on some people. And the way that he became Muslim, I don't think that that helped either. I think he did it for me and the children, not realising that he'd have to stick by it. He was obviously practising in front of my face but not sticking to it behind my back and when I found out I felt deceived and felt that my religion had been made a joke out of. Two months later we ended up breaking up and then a year later we got a divorce, and I've now been divorced for over a year since my second marriage. After the divorce, I was looking for a husband because I wanted to settle down. I've got two daughters – they're 3 and 2 – and I thought their dad isn't around much at all and he's returned back to his old ways. I hope to bring them up in the right way, and I realised that not only do I need a husband, but they need a father.

Pakistanis can be very close-minded and backward-looking, and they have a completely different mentality. A lot of Pakistani boys wouldn't marry a divorcée, or their parents wouldn't accept it. But Islamically it's a good thing to do that, to marry a divorcée or a widow or somebody who's got children. As soon as I say that I'm twice divorced and have two children, men don't wanna know, and on top of that, my children are mixed race and it's blatant, and even if the guy could accept that, their family wouldn't and it would cause so many issues. I just need somebody that can father my children in an Islamic way, who can help bring them up knowing what's right from wrong Islamically.

I went on some of these marriage websites, and that's where I met this guy and we started talking and he told me he was looking for a second wife. Before we started talking in terms of, you know, on a sort of romantic level, he was opening up saying that, you know, a similar thing happened. He started to change … practising Islam and sorted himself out. And everyone was telling him that the next thing you should do is get married, and there was somebody that was in his family that didn't have any parents, so he kind of thought, as a Muslim man, he had a duty to take care of her.

I said from day one that I've never been the girl that would be able to handle a situation like that, but the more that he started opening up, the more I realised that (a) I had feelings for this person and (b) I realised that maybe there's not actually much between him and his wife, which made it … it sounds awful, but it made it easier for me to handle being a possible second wife. So we kept talking and then, you know, those feelings turned into love, which without marriage, we realised was wrong so we need to get married.

I've not just walked into this – me and my mum and even my dad, we've done so much research into this to make sure that what he's doing at the moment is Islamically correct, which means that we've looked at surahs and ayahs of Qur'an, Hadiths and everything. It feels like it would be a good thing for both him and me to do, and my mum spoke to the local imam here, just to get it right. There's a lot of reward for being one of many wives, being able to control your anger and your jealousy and things like that. There are times – and I'm still a woman at the end of the day – where I wish I could have him all to myself. We're not even married yet, so I can imagine … but I am willing to overcome that.

With his first wife, it caused a lot of drama. She wasn't happy. I spoke to her and my mum spoke to her, and she just couldn't handle it at all, so we decided to put a stop to it. But with the way things were, we decided to go ahead with it. To begin with, it's going to be difficult, because obviously then he's planning to tell his first wife again, but not until after it's done. And Islamically, he is able to do that. It doesn't matter when he tells her, as long as he does.

In the law, when you get a registry marriage, it's great because if your marriage is registered in the UK, you have all these benefits, these rights if you were to get divorced or your husband or wife were to die. Islamically,

> if your spouse is practising, you still get those same rights whether the marriage is registered or not. Now that's another reason why I would want to marry someone who was practising, because it doesn't matter whether the marriage is registered in the UK or not. If they are full-on practising Muslim and they have a love for their religion, me and my children as stepchildren, will have the same rights that we would have if it was registered in the UK.
>
> I would like it ... if I had the chance, I would be registered, just because it's nice for your marriage to be recognised everywhere. A Nikah is not really recognised in the UK unless you register it, so technically in the eyes of the law, if they haven't registered it they're not married, which is a sad thing to do. Well, it's not sad, it's just kind of like 'oh, OK' kind of thing. For me, it doesn't make a difference but it doesn't really make me happy either.
>
> I wanted other women to know there's more to it than people thinking 'oh the man is just being greedy – he's got his bit on the side and his main wife.' It's more than that. There's love between him and his first wife, they've got children together and a family together, and I completely can understand that. It's not that I find it easy – it's just that I've learned to accept it.

Noreen, a 23-year-old British Pakistani woman who had been married twice before spoke with me the day before her polygamous Nikah ceremony. She got in touch with me after a national charity kindly shared my advert for the project on their website. Her path to finding me was different from that of most of the women who spoke with me. Each of her three experiences of marriage has been unique and they are rich with religious and cultural insights into her relationships and life choices. Her story, along with those of the other women who talked with me, shed much-needed light on the real experiences that the law has neglected so far when addressing religious and cultural considerations for minoritised communities and their marriage practices. In this chapter, I centre these experiences and perspectives to develop the discussion around cultural conflict and differences initiated in Chapter 4. I draw from the 26 semi-structured interviews I carried out with women from various religious and ethnic backgrounds to analyse their understandings and attitudes around religious and cultural identity in relation to marriage and polygamy. Broadly, I asked them about whether they saw marriage as a religious or cultural institution; what they considered to be the religious and cultural consequences of marriage; and what their cultural upbringing and religion or personal belief system caused them to think about marriage and polygamy.

Noreen referred to religion and culture throughout her story, and I start by unpacking the significance of these two concepts for marriage and polygamy. Their importance should not come as a surprise if we think about how much religion – more specifically, Christianity – has shaped understandings and responses towards marriage in English law. I first argue that because of this legacy we need to be aware of the Eurocentric ideals that have shaped the use and understandings of religion and culture. This is most apparent when we see how culture has become a way to exclusively describe the lives and practices of minoritised people. For members of the social and cultural majority community, culture and religion are difficult to identify and express (Roald, 2004). This is because they are so embedded in the social order they become invisible. For minoritised people this is not the case, yet their religious and cultural values are simplistically defined as the opposite of the majority's: they are all 'other'. Mainstream institutions assume that all minoritised religions and cultures are the same pushing them into a single box labelled 'other cultures' (Jivraj and Herman, 2009). In the literature, this manifests in how minoritised people are said to have a 'religio-cultural identity' rather than seeing religion and culture as possibly distinct for the individual (Abbas, 2003, 2010; Olds, 2010; Lim et al, 2014; McGrath and McGarry, 2014). All the beliefs and values which differ from the dominant majority are seen as the same and should therefore be treated the same – there is no nuance to account for their uniqueness. By collapsing minoritised religions and cultures in this way, they are orientalised and othered by institutions and systems including the law. In Chapter 4, I showed how the law considers minoritised identities, practices and values as a matter of 'cultural difference' with no understanding of people's lived realities. The orientalist collapsing processes that led to this need to be disrupted.

The relevance of a combined religio-cultural identity was rejected not just by Noreen, but also by the other women who spoke with me. Religion and culture were often mentioned in the same breath, showing that they are linked but their relationship is troubled and at times they work against each other. For Noreen, her cultural community could not accept her status as a divorced single mother, but her faith gave her multiple options because her past relationships should not be an obstacle to her marrying again. The conflict between religion and culture was framed in a particular way: religion is supportive and empowering for women, while culture oppresses them. This is particularly visible in experiences and stories around marriage and polygamy. Inspired by Jacobson's (1997, 1998) work in this area, I therefore argue that in line with women's interpretations of religion and culture, they should be treated as dual and alternative sources of identity. They are related but there needs to be room for them to differ and conflict.

Seeing these markers as dual and alternative also helps to negotiate the simplistic positioning of religion as empowering and culture as oppressive in women's stories. This 'good versus bad' paradigm provides an alternative account to the orientalist story of religion as the oppressor, but it facilitates minoritised cultures being denigrated by the mainstream as part of the cultural difference framework that we see in law. Minoritised cultural practices and relationship forms are placed at the bottom of the ladder because in imperialist interpretations they are backwards, primitive and cause women to be treated badly – so they need saving by the White coloniser. My intention is not to dismiss women's experiences of culture as oppressive, but to complicate it. I argue that instead of culture or religion, the real culprit behind women's oppression is the gendered double standards imposed on women which result from the influence of the patriarchy on their cultural and religious norms. It was the patriarchal influences on Noreen's cultural community that led to her being marginalised because of her divorced status showing that the decision to engage in polygamy goes beyond religion and culture. It is therefore too limiting to say that experiences of polygamy and the decision to practise it are part of women's religio-cultural identities. While Noreen's religious beliefs were unable to overcome that patriarchal marginalisation, they did give her the opportunity to practise polygamy. That said, the choice to be polygamous did not erase her marginalisation so there was a limit to how far her religious practice could empower her. Polygamous wives are still subjected to orientalist othering discourses and seen as inferior because of their difference from the monogamous norm but polygamous husbands are not. Without exposing this underbelly of patriarchal oppression, we end up serving the dominant orientalist agenda that depicts minoritised religions and cultures as inferior because they are different. The dismissal of polygamy in law should not be justified on the basis that it is too different from the imperialist-approved standard of monogamy and because of its association with minoritised religions and cultures.

The importance of religion and culture

I start by making the general argument that religion and culture play a significant role in shaping experiences and attitudes towards marriage and polygamy for women, so they are relevant to developing our understandings of how they live out their relationships. In previous chapters, I showed how much Christianity and the emphasis on cultural differences affects mainstream responses to polygamy. It comes as no surprise that the influences of religion and culture reach beyond the law and affect everyday perceptions of marriage. These two concepts came up repeatedly in the stories around relationships and marriage, as shown by Noreen's situation:

> 'I ... felt that my religion had been made a joke out of [by my second husband] ... I just need somebody that can father my children in an Islamic way, who can help bring them up knowing what's right from wrong Islamically.' (Noreen)

Noreen's second marriage breakdown was based on her husband not sharing her view on the importance of religion and the consequences of this for her children. The centrality of religion to her life as a Muslim is clear as she made an open commitment to the faith which is then interwoven into her everyday experiences. In further examples:

> 'In terms of my parents, they don't have that because, well, in my dad … my dad's side, they're Jamaican, but the culture is not really about marriage – it doesn't have that aspect, and also my mum … my mum's side, she never got married – yeah I don't know much. All I know is from the religious side coming to Islam – I didn't really see myself getting married til, yeah …' (Gul)

> 'Yeah, I think that my idea of marriage in this really traditional way and that it should come before children is definitely related to religion. So I'm a Catholic and all my mum's family are Catholic. … Although I wouldn't identify myself as being religious, it's quite interesting that I still draw that comparison.' (Lauren)

> 'I think, culturally, marriage is highly valued, especially within Asian culture.' (Maariyah)

These were responses to questions concerning the links between marriage and religion, culture, law and society. I asked whether marriage was a social, religious, cultural or legal institution and then whether people were viewed differently in society, religion, culture and law after marriage. By drawing through the importance of personal context, some interesting observations arise. Gul was a Muslim revert and marriage had not previously impacted on her understanding of relationships, because the culture and environment that she had been raised in did not emphasise marriage. In Islam, extramarital relationships are forbidden which is why reverting to Islam and the increased role of religion in her life completely changed her perceptions of marriage. At first, this seems like religion is the main influence, but we can also see that culture still played a role by telling her that marriage is not that important. Lauren on the other hand, had been raised with a traditional conception of marriage which was heavily influenced by her White Catholic background. She herself found it interesting that despite not being religious, it was religion that governed her ideals on marriage and family. Lauren and Gul came from different ethnic and religious backgrounds, but for each of them, the emphasis and role of religion was quite similar in relation to marriage. From yet another perspective, Maariyah tells us that marriage is highly valued in her Asian culture. These statements show us that any exploration of marriage, including polygamy, must pay attention to the concepts of religion and culture. This is especially vital when we think about how law and mainstream society are dominated by a narrative underpinned by specific religious and cultural ideals about what marriage should look like.

These reflections provide a starting point for understanding perceptions of polygamy and marriage in the UK, but we should also look at women's experiences and perspectives of religion and culture. We often take religion and culture for granted in life without really thinking through what these concepts mean. When I asked people how they would define culture for example, they repeatedly expressed that it was a tough question. These concepts are highly complex and there isn't a universal way to define them, but the statements of the women who spoke with me provided some patterns in their understandings.[1] For religion, it was generally in reference to a specific faith or belief system, like Catholicism or Islam, that women discussed their experiences. This means that when I refer to religion, it is led by their comments and experiences that were mostly rooted in the institutionalised and formal observance interpretation. As our discussions centred mainly on marriage and polygamy, the frame of reference was narrower, so the women's comments mostly spoke to religious principles or prescriptions around family life. My explorations of culture are similarly led by multiple minoritised women's references to culture as a way of life. The phrase 'way of life' appeared repeatedly in the narratives when women were asked to explain culture. According to Jenks (2005), when culture is seen in this way, it acts as a social category interpretation. By comprising our 'whole way of life', culture becomes so all-encompassing that as a social category interpretation it could also cover religion. This provides the foundation for a close relationship between the two but also blurs the boundaries between them which is where we later see the confusion that leads to the idea of a religio-cultural identity.

While the discussions of religion and culture are led by the women's interpretations and stories which include some overlap, there is another big issue attached to the way that we take them and any definition of them for granted. This is not as visible in mainstream writings, and so it arises out of what we are not being told by the literature. Religion and culture do not exist in a vacuum, which means they have a particular context. They have been developed, theorised and applied in a formal disciplinary sense as part

1 There is a vast array of scholarship that looks at the concepts of religion and culture, with the main message that defining them is complex and subjective. See, for example, Durkheim (1915), Weber (1965), Sahgal and Yuval-Davis (1992), Featherstone (1995), Archer (1996), Selfe and Starbuck (1998), Fenn (2003), Roald (2004), Jenks (2005) and Hopkins and McAuliffe (2010).

of a bigger picture which is easily forgotten. For example, Asad (1993) argues that anthropologists studying Muslim beliefs and practices must understand how religion was conceptually and practically formed in the modern West, because it is integral to modern Western history. As a result, there is no need for a universal definition of religion, because it is constructed in historically specific ways. Similarly, Dubuisson (2003) asserts that religion is a Western construct and central to the formation of Western values and representations. He further argues that the concept of religion is too Eurocentric and heavily based on Christian experience. Even after we accept that religion represents different things, it is still based in this context and has been constructed with reference to European Christian practice. Therefore, to define a religion, we do so against the baseline standard of European Christianity. This means that when we talk about or refer to religion, there is an unspoken assumption that Christianity is the subject of the discussion and the paradigm for what is meant by religion. By adopting this default viewpoint, the literature is limited in its ability to tell us about religions other than Christianity. In the mainstream, religion means Christianity practised by Europeans. From this, we see that other faith and belief systems are less visible and therefore less accounted for. Most belief systems predate European Christian practice, so there is also a question of whether the term 'religion' is even helpful for minoritised communities that are not Christian. If the term and concept of religion are rooted in the Western Christian view, is it even applicable or helpful to those with different beliefs?

This question is even more affecting if we think about the historical context for Christianity in Europe and its use in the civilising mission as a tool for colonising the mind. If religion is associated with a system that was weaponised against people to justify stripping them of their rights and humanity under imperial rule, it cannot reflect the lived realities of minoritised peoples. Yet this has been neglected even in critical scholarship. Donaldson and Kwok (2002) discuss at length how feminist scholars have paid attention to intersecting identities, including race, gender and sexuality, in colonial contexts but ignore the crucial role that religion has and continues to play. In existing scholarship, understanding religion goes hand in hand with recognising that it is synonymous with Western understandings of Christianity that orientalise and ignore the lives and experiences of racialised women (see also Rajan, 1993). Religion as a concept is too well established for me to dismiss it and propose an alternative, especially since the women in this project also spoke of it as a matter of fact. When I discuss religion here, I view it critically as a tool that has been used against women but one which has also been disrupted and reclaimed by them.

Culture has its own troubling history and context. In later work, Kwok (2012) shares that while culture has become a buzzword in the academy across many disciplines, this attraction to culture and its analysis gloss over its past. The women who spoke with me described culture as a way of life: something that tells us how and why we do things a certain way. It is an important part of our identities and lived realities. However, this very broad understanding of culture is not as broad as we think. From cultural diversity policy finding purchase in Europe and North America, to the emphasis on celebrating world cultures and ways of life, there is an underlying pattern to these discourses and initiatives (Isar, 2006). When we talk of culture, we are talking not about the mainstream, but the minoritised. Culture is another way to talk about difference from the majority. Culture in this 'way of life' sense is not something for White people to live by or concern themselves with. It works to address those who are 'culturally diverse', and so culture as a concept becomes articulated and spoken into existence when there is a need to make sense of something that differs from the dominant narrative.

Culture has been constructed and deployed in this way to respond to a postcolonial world. As European empires started to break down and colonies regained independence, imperial powers needed to find new ways to identify and imagine the difference between the West and the rest of the world. Balibar (1991) argues that relying on race, nature and biology to show how the colonised natives were inferior was no longer acceptable. But these imperialists did not want to let go of their superiority, so they needed to find another way to enforce the inferiority of the former colonies and their people. They settled on culture to achieve this (see also Phillips, 2007). Race was no longer the differentiating factor but culture, using the origins and development of cultural difference as a mechanism for comparison. We see that same cultural difference mechanism governing the conflict of laws today (as discussed in Chapter 4).

Narayan (1998) frames this way of creating images of cultural differences as 'cultural essentialism' whereby privileged Western subjects engage in a form of cultural imperialism by constructing 'cultural others' based on how they differ from those situated in Western cultures. By focussing on difference, they obscure the ways that those differences create the 'other' in the first place. These cultural differences are not pregiven and an uncontested truth, but are formed as part of imperialist othering processes to impose Western superiority on former colonies. Culture and religion are both part of ongoing historical and political processes that centre Western, Eurocentric understandings of these concepts in mainstream society and the existing literature.

These processes which essentialise non-Western ways of doing and living culture and religion have another interesting consequence. Narayan (1998) draws on the practice of sati, or widow immolation in India to show how certain practices have been determined as central to 'Indian culture' despite not being that prevalent among the majority in India. Because of imperialist understandings that were advanced as part of the authoritative definition of Indian culture, sati has come to be seen as a central practice that characterises Indian culture and Hinduism as backward and cruel. The colonisers defined 'Indian culture' in a way which was favourable to their own 'civilised' culture and religion. The same has happened for polygamy. Polygamy is a minority practice which has been subjected to historical and political manipulations to cause people to fixate on its difference and its supposed deviance. Cultural difference is therefore about establishing cultural deviance from the imperial standard. Through this, imperial powers tell their stories about other cultures because while imperialism's main battle was over land, this was decided in narrative (Said, 1994). The power to tell the story or block other stories about a land and who is deserving of it based on their way of life provides a key connection between culture, religion and imperialism (see also Schutte, 1998). Where religion and culture are concerned, there is always one religion and culture that has the upper hand: that of the West. Through its power to tell authoritative stories about other cultures and religions, it diminishes them and those who follow them.

These dominant framings of culture are reflected in perceptions of minoritised people in the here and now. For example, in her work on British Muslim girls and education, Basit shows that over the years, the main concern of the state around minoritised individuals has shifted from race to 'religion and ethnic distinctiveness' (1997: 435). Race is not relied on as much any more to establish differences; religion and ethnicity, including culture, are used instead. Whether it be clothing associated with religion or the level of education girls receive, differences are perceived in terms of religion and ethnicity markers rather than race. This shift may be due to racism being viewed as unacceptable, or it may be because it is easier to associate minoritised issues with religion and culture – it is difficult to say. Regardless, religion and culture play a role in forming individual identities and social relationships. Religion and culture are both individual and collective; they permeate every level and structure of society, so they are impactful and important, but they have a price (Castelli, 2001). These markers form part of power structures and processes that highlight the differences of minoritised people, dictating the experiences and perceptions of their identities and relationships. Minoritised women like Noreen and their relationships are painted as images of cultural difference, with their religion and ethnic distinctiveness emphasised as the reason for their marginalisation rather than the power structures that have marked them out as different. In this way, these dominant framings reinforce the idea that culture and religion drive minoritised people's behaviours and practices. This creates a radical othering process in which minoritised people are driven by their culture and/or religion, while those in the modern West are motivated by morality. These concepts of religion and culture have become rigid and definitive of individual actions and behaviour where minoritised people are concerned, which leads to cultural (and racial) stereotyping (Phillips, 2007). Throughout this chapter, when I discuss religion and culture, I do so based on the premise that the women shared their stories while operating in a system which sets out to caricature and orientalise minoritised religions and cultures. It is very difficult to avoid internalising these systemic framings, and while I am optimistic that the women's disruptions to the dominant narrative are effective, they are not going to fully escape the legacy of the problematic tropes surrounding minoritised religions and cultures.

The emphasis on religion and culture to define difference is evident when we compare the understandings of minoritised and (majority) White women in the UK.

> 'I think culture's quite a difficult thing to pinpoint anyway, but I don't think … I don't know whether being British … or what being British is – maybe someone who acts traditionally British, I don't know.' (Lauren)

> 'I actually struggle with culture for me, because culture tends to be attached to religion in a way, so when you talk about, well we don't talk about British culture, because I'm in it … so I don't really know if I'm being honest in that I guess I'm probably like, you know, Christian.' (Grace)

> 'Erm, I suppose it's like a way of life, I guess, erm, I dunno, it's not something that I've really thought about as a White British person. It's not something that I'm aware of. I'm only made aware of it when I go to America; it's like … oh, or talk to Americans, I should say … like you realise how much different your way of living is.' (Brenda)

Roald explains that there is no need for a person to search for or think deeply about their identity if they are 'part of the mainstream culture or belong to the majority in society' (2004: 185), and we see this demonstrated in Brenda's views. Culture is more difficult for an individual to identify and express when they are a member of the social and cultural majority. Culture and to a degree religion, are taken for granted by the majority because they are part of the furniture. The majority culture and religion are so ingrained in the social fabric and infrastructure they become almost invisible. This makes it difficult to distinguish between the two, which as we see later, is not the case for minoritised people. Both Lauren and Grace have mixed feelings about culture – they are unsure about what it means and whether it matches their lives and identities. Lauren does not refer to society, but her mention of Britishness shows that she links her cultural identity to being part of the White ethnic majority. For Grace, there was no clear separation between religion and culture. As a White British woman with a Christian background, Grace was less sure of the role of culture in her life. The invisibility or inapplicability of culture caused her to retreat to religion to help make sense of it and define it. These ambivalent statements by members of the ethnic majority reflect the way that culture has been moulded into something that only concerns racialised and minoritised people. Because it is not generally relevant to the ethnic-majority women, they are less invested in culture and its influence on their identities.

Jacobson argues that scholars often 'treat religion as a component of ethnic identity' (1997: 238) and this is also displayed in Grace's narrative. By combining religion and culture, these two concepts governed her White British identity, but it was not possible for her to separate them out. The difficulties shared by Grace and Lauren suggest that they have not previously interrogated the idea of culture in as much depth as the minoritised women. Minoritised women were a lot less hesitant with their definitions. For example, Daliyah shared that:

> 'Culture's just a way of life. It's traditional, the way you perceive things, the food's different, the language is different. Two different worlds – the West and Pakistani … two different things.' (Daliyah)

As a British Pakistani woman, Daliyah's minoritised ethnicity provided the context for her definition. Culture was a marker of difference between her two worlds. The boundaries between the West and Pakistan, between food and language, show the importance and role of cultural identity for minoritised women. As Basit (1997) notes, ethnic distinctiveness is the new focus for the minoritised, and culture may help to make sense of their distinctiveness as they search for their identity. They engage in this search because they have more moving parts to contend with: they not only have to negotiate their personal religious and cultural identities but also must do this within the 'dominant discourses of secular-liberal Western-European society' (McGrath and McGarry, 2014: 949). For the majority-White woman, culture does not serve the same purpose, so she spends less time thinking about it and has a less developed response to questions about it.

A further way of interpreting these responses is that being interviewed by a woman of colour like myself could have affected the way that questions were answered. The White women who spoke with me might have been careful with their comments for fear of saying something that could be construed negatively. However, the contrast between the mixed feelings of the White women and the more confident way that the minoritised women spoke of culture is suggestive of the ways that certain identity markers become heightened and visible when, and because, they differ from the mainstream (see Roald, 2004).

Collapsing religion and culture

The confusion that we see with Grace's use of religion to define culture and her combination of the two markers indicates a wider issue about how they are understood. This issue has cropped up in existing research as well. In some of the literature in this area, religion and culture are mentioned together without being defined or differentiated. As I said earlier, scholars give in to the temptation to treat them as a matter of common sense or general knowledge and because the meanings are so obvious, there is no need for clarification. For example, Cohen (2009) discusses religious and cultural diversity in France but uses religion and culture interchangeably with no explanation. Hall et al argue that religion and culture should not be separated because the 'division cannot be easily sustained and can be shown to be premature or even false' (2003: 43). Beyers goes further to argue that studying religion requires us to also study ethnicity and culture because 'religion is determined by culture, but religion also influences culture' and their fates are interwoven (2017: 2). This is further demonstrated by feminist theologians Kwok (1991) and Chung (1996), who point out that Christianity has never been a pure religion, but has consistently adapted elements from different cultures since the start.

Due to the various difficulties in discussion of religion and culture, there has been a trend in the literature of collapsing these identity markers into a singular religio-cultural identity. This single identity appears to represent the intersection of religion and culture along with their individual but connected existence (see, for example, Abbas, 2003, 2010; Olds, 2010; Lim et al, 2014; McGrath and McGarry, 2014). That religion and culture are connected is borne out by the real experiences and views of the women who spoke with me, but I argue that they should not be combined or considered interchangeable as they have been elsewhere. By combining them, we essentialise them and make their particularities invisible (see also Han, 2017). This pushes them into the background so that we take them as a given and fail to recognise how they are historically and politically constructed to other and orientalise minoritised people and communities. Moreover, the notion of a religio-cultural identity is difficult to reconcile with the multiple, intersecting and competing religious and cultural identities that minoritised women hold:

> 'So I'm a Muslim, erm, we all follow the same religion but parents and that, they have kind of brought us up in the belief that this kind of caste … so, for example, if you're a Misri, Pathan whatever, you're a caste, so you have different expectations. So the more higher rank of a caste you are, you have to be extra religious, you have to be extra observant.' (Aiza)

Aiza talks about how Muslims all follow the same religion but the added dimension of caste influences the level of religious observance. This shows the multiplicity of her identities and their impact on one another. While caste has an influence over religious practice, it did not originate in Islam – it is a unique marker that is linked to religion. To collapse two identity markers like religion and caste – a social class system that stems from cultural background – oversimplifies them and their individual roles in forming our identities and perceptions.

Jivraj and Herman (2009) observe that in the courts, non-Christian beliefs are frequently equated with cultural values. This subordinates religions other than Christianity and downgrades their status to culture, telling us that there is a hierarchy between religion and culture with religion, defined by Christianity, considered superior. Christianity is therefore being compared to the wide category of 'other cultures', which encompasses non-Christian religions. By oversimplifying and forcing them all into a single category, minoritised religions and cultures are less visible to mainstream institutions, systems and processes. This lesser visibility means they are given a more negative consideration and are subordinated along with those who follow them. Taras (2013) notes that in Islamophobia or fear of Islam, religious, ethnic and cultural prejudices are bundled together, though it is religion that is supposed to be the cause of the fear and mistrust. Islam is defined by the mainstream as this jumble of religion, culture and ethnicity, showing us how this collapsing of the prejudice based on these three markers into Islamophobia leads to misconceptions about Islam in the first place. What are perceived to be the negative characteristics of all three are combined to create the image that they are all negative attributes of the religion. Mainstream political discourse ignores the problems with this approach, which racialises 'non-Western' cultural and religious values (Taras, 2013).

Basit states that the 'misinterpretation of religio-cultural values is not uncommon' (1997: 436), but I go further to problematise the category of 'religio-cultural' itself as a misinterpretation of minoritised identities. This leads me to look for another approach which accepts that religion and culture are closely connected and affect each other while treating them as distinct, to avoid them becoming essentialised and collapsed for the convenience of the majority. I adopt Jacobson's (1997, 1998) theory of religion and culture being 'dual and alternative sources of identity', which she developed in her work with British Pakistani youth. Jacobson argues that religion and culture are 'two sources of identity which in practice are extremely tightly bound up with one another but which at the same time, are increasingly commonly regarded as the bases of separate or even alternative self-definitions' (1998: 10). She builds a framework based on a 'religion-ethnic culture distinction' which distinguishes universally applicable religious teachings from the more limited application of culture (Jacobson, 1998: 129). As Cora noted:

> 'If I say I'm from a particular ethnic group in Nigeria, OK, erm, unfortunately I couldn't say we have a culture as Nigerians. There are many ethnic groups or nationalities. So if you ask me my culture, I will be talking about the Igbos cos I am Igbo, so I would be talking about the Igbos and how they live, because we live differently to other ethnic groups.' (Cora)

By saying there is no Nigerian culture, Cora emphasises that culture operates on a smaller scale which is closer to her and not as universal as her Christian faith which she practised in Nigeria and in the UK. Jacobson's framework is helpful for noting these nuances between religion and culture. She argues that it is important to make an analytic distinction between an individual's commitment to a 'universalistic religion with a global reach and membership of a [cultural] social group which is linked to place of origin' (Jacobson, 1998: 9). Further, this analytic distinction matched what the young British Pakistanis she spoke to felt about religion and culture. For these children of Pakistani immigrants in the UK, ethnicity was a natural or given as they were born into their British Asian culture but religion was a matter of personal choice that entailed reflection and active commitment. The retreat of these young people towards religion as a separate base of identity stemmed from their diasporic social environment being full of contradictions. Their Pakistani values required them to operate within boundaries set by their parents that were different from the majority-White population. However, Jacobson's informants noted that the appearance of staying within these boundaries was more important than actually observing them. It was fine for a young woman to talk with a fellow male college student in public as long as no one else saw and misconstrued it as inappropriate. This was confusing for the young people as they dealt with adaptation or translation of the norms of their parents' place of origin into their current UK context and lifestyle. Religion on the other hand, was much more clear cut for them. They found themselves turning to religion for guidance as a way to cope with the confusion that their British Pakistani values provoked. Therefore, it was not religion that was likely to form part of ethnic identity, but culture.

There is another reason that religion and culture as dual and alternative is a good fit for women's experiences of polygamy and disrupts the dominant discourses around this minoritised relationship. I argue that the singular religio-cultural identity prevents women's use of religion and culture as tools to disrupt discourses that are negative and undesirable to them in their lives and relationships. In Summayah's words:

> 'I guess again I'm not sure if this would be culture or religion but I think with regards to the South Asian community erm if you're a woman of an older age and unmarried, I think that that can lead to a stigma being associated.' (Summayah)

Summayah was not sure whether the stigma of being unmarried and older came from culture or religion which displayed her difficulty with understanding where one ends and the other begins. They could intersect and both be responsible for the stigma, or one of them could, or even neither. We cannot unravel religion and culture fully, but like Jacobson, I am also led by the opinions of the women I spoke with on their relationship and how they interact:

> 'Er, culture, I define it as, as where we from, society … everyone sees culture and religion as pretty much the same thing but they're not.' (Noreen)

> 'So, for me, culture is everything … all the traditions that your family might do that are not from the religion – that's, for me, what culture is. Culture in a more general sense … in a secular society if we go out, erm … I think that would be a good definition to say … the traditions that one is used to. And usually culture comes from countries rather than from religion. Because I know that in my Indian culture, we share a lot of traditions with Hindus … so that doesn't mean that those traditions come from the Hindu religion or the Muslim religion – they come from India and so are practised across different regions and different religions. So when I think of culture, it means traditions and practices that come from different countries, practised by different faiths. Because they don't come from religion – they come from places that the people are from, if that makes sense.' (Maha)

When we collapse the two markers into one, there is no conceptual room left for them to conflict; there is an assumption that by occupying the same space in our identity, they operate in harmony. This does not reflect the everyday lives of women. Religion and culture can and do collide, they even may be at odds with one another, so at times we need to see them as distinct to allow them to disrupt one another. For Noreen and Maha, religion and culture are not the same. Noreen disagrees with the common perception that they are 'pretty much the same', and Maha explains in detail how culture is linked to place rather than religion, since there are similar cultural practices for both Muslims and Hindus in India. By distancing culture from religion, we see how the analytic distinction between them is necessary to reflect real views and experiences. It is more appropriate to see religion and culture as dual concepts to account for this technique that some women employed.

Looking more closely at this duality, there is a strong tension and hierarchy between religion and culture when they interact. This tension was experienced and expressed in relation to the (mis)treatment of women.

> 'A lot of Pakistani boys wouldn't marry a divorcée, or their parents wouldn't accept it. But Islamically it's a good thing to do that, to marry a divorcée or a widow or somebody who's got children.' (Noreen)

> 'I think Islamically women are given equal. It says you should treat your wife like a princess and not drive her like a slave. I think it's more cultural. It's nothing to do with religion.' (Daliyah)

> 'Christianity its having to live according to the tenets as spelled out in the Bible, a woman is expected to submit to the husband, OK, erm, even then again, I could say that it's more of cultural than religion, because here in the UK, I'm still a Christian, I still attend churches the way I did in Nigeria. But the way, it's not that same way it's preached in my culture, about submission, that's not the same thing that's being expected of women here. You're expected to respect your husband, yes, the way your husband should respect you.' (Cora)

In these excerpts, it is women, their treatment and concerns that suffer when religion and culture collide and conflict. For Noreen, Pakistani cultural opinions of divorce went against Islamic teachings, while for Daliyah and Cora, perceptions of the wife and her role differed in religion and culture. Their experiences suggest that the interaction between religion and culture is negative and results in the mistreatment and oppression of women. Noreen, Daliyah and Cora set these markers up as opposing forces, and these were structured the same way for all of them. Cora's observations centre on her experiences as a migrant who has experienced church preaching as a member of the cultural majority in Nigeria and as a minoritised woman in the UK. It is therefore interesting that she associates the submission of women with her culture rather than Christianity. Religion was constructed as positive, but culture played a negative and oppressive role in their lives. In religion, women are princesses who are worthy of respect, and divorce is not a stigma. Culture on the other hand, limits the marital prospects of divorcées, permits women to be treated as 'slaves' and encourages their subordination.

This good religion/bad culture dichotomy has been observed in other research around minoritised women. Bolognani and Mellor look at the marriage choices of British Pakistani women and discuss a religion versus culture model which 'uses "culture" with an automatic negative connotation and, as an ethos, is based more on reputation and family ties than on "genuine" religious principles' (2012: 213; see also Bolognani, 2009). Culture is not just harmful but also to blame for the abuse of religious principles. Religion is further seen as empowering and a source of agency that increases women's confidence and access to rights (Bolognani and Mellor, 2012). Through the experience of marriage and being a wife, culture is increasingly viewed as an impediment to religion rather than an integral part of it, which leads to women dissociating themselves from culture and attaching themselves more closely to their faith (Van Herck and Drigo, 2019).

The way that the religion–culture clash was portrayed by the women also meant that there was a clear winner to the battle. Culture was always the one that overpowered and dominated religion and then caused harm to women. As Karimah notes:

> 'culture is basically man-made and they make it so strong … they have some issues, why issues are there is because they don't have knowledge of the deen. If they will come to their religion, they will find out the solution for all these problems. They don't have to worry about this stuff.' (Karimah)

From this, we see that Karimah is dissatisfied with the outcome of the battle between religion and culture. She talks about culture being so strong it can dominate religion by either overriding it or closing off certain interpretations of it and therefore shaping how it is practised. While culture is man-made, she implies that religion is divine and should have the higher and more powerful status. The term 'man-made' is also interesting – it could be referring generally to humankind or given the prefix 'man-', it could be androcentric. Men are the ones who make it, and they make it so strong because they do not understand religion or how it can solve their issues. Karimah is therefore challenging the way culture favours the men who made it and she does not see the situation improving unless they come to their religion. Religious principles around family life are being overpowered because they are misunderstood or not understood at all. The problem is with people rather than the faith, although there is an idealism here that neglects how certain manifestations and practical applications of religious doctrine and principles are also man-made. In the end, Karimah's argument is more focussed on degrees of human influence and her view is that culture is much more man-made than religion with its divine origin.

This portrayal of religion as the key to respect for women and their empowerment and equal treatment has an important implication for these women and their relationships. It allows women to disrupt the dominant discourse that their religions are responsible for their oppression. This discourse is one that we see time and again in the West as 'non-European religion' is collapsed into culture and designated as inferior. The women I spoke with reject this characterisation of their beliefs and values. For example, Noreen expressed:

> 'I don't think they understand that. [They] assume that [when] we Asians get married, "Oh the wife's meant to be a slave and the man is able to hit her". That's not religion – that's culture. Religiously, a man is not allowed to lay a finger on his wife. Religiously, a woman is not obligated to do any cooking, any cleaning, nothing at all.' (Noreen)

Along with the others, Noreen is openly defensive against criticism of her faith, stating that Muslim women are exposed from a young age to ideas around their role and rights. From my personal experience, I have sat through numerous Islamic talks by women scholars about the rights of women; and we know the famous line from the Prophet Muhammad's (peace be upon him) final sermon where he states that women should be treated with kindness. It was important for Noreen and the other women to clarify that religion does not incite the mistreatment of women – unsurprisingly, they want to defend the belief system that they follow. Women in Islam enjoy an elevated role and status, and are not obliged to perform labour or accept abuse; but for this defence to be effective, there must be a reason for the harm that does take place – and that is culture. Naber's work on young Arab Muslim women demonstrates that Islam is used in this context to 'transform gender hierarchies' (2005: 486). The young women Naber spoke with used religion to challenge and disrupt patriarchal norms enforced by their Arab culture. Having studied their faith and learnt about women's rights in Islam, they would question the restrictions their families would place on them, pursue their higher education, challenge workplace harassment and become more devout with their religious practice. Noreen does the same: by sharing her knowledge of the wife's rights in Islam, she is disrupting the dominant story that religion is responsible for women's abuse. This rejects the popular misconceptions of Islam as oppressive and backwards for women. Such a disruption would not be possible without recognising religion and culture as alternative sources of identity.

Noreen also used religion to disrupt dominant narratives around the limited marital choices available to divorced women by choosing to engage in polygamy. Although religion encouraged her to marry for a third time, culture limited her marital prospects because of her relationship history and single motherhood. Religion directly opposes the cultural stigma against marrying a divorcée. Unfortunately culture still appears to win this round as we see from Noreen's experience of facing prejudice for being twice divorced. She was aware that marrying a divorcée in Islam is a "good thing", but she remained helpless in the face of cultural norms dictating otherwise.

Helplessness is a key quality that surrounds women living and narrating the religion–culture clash. Bolognani and Mellor (2012) argue that religion as a tool for women's empowerment and its ability to disrupt against culture is limited. Even though women like Noreen and Cora use their knowledge of the religion to counter undesirable cultural practices – such as the stigma against divorce and how wives should submit to their husbands, there is little evidence to show that they are successful in convincing their families and communities that they should reject culture and exclusively follow religious teachings. There are questions about how helpful it is for us to record instances of women using religion-based arguments to assert their rights when they speak with us, without later returning to see whether they were successful in their efforts. It is not just about who can speak, but who is being listened to and whether that results in positive change for women. Bolognani and Mellor (2012) argue that this good religion/bad culture divide is therefore better understood as a social construction that helps women to make sense of their lives but is not necessarily effective when faced with other power structures.

We should not dismiss the power of religion to disrupt quite yet, because there was evidence of women using religion to defy culture and then acting on this. There are positive results that I can report. Noreen's decision to become a polygamous wife was connected with what she identified as cultural prejudices towards her divorces and motherhood. The result of her religion–culture clash, where marrying a divorcée is positive in religion but negative in culture, can be seen from two perspectives. First, she decided to enter into a polygamous marriage because she felt restricted in her choices. This can be taken from her original intention to look for a monogamous husband before meeting her fiancé and her statement that polygamy is viewed negatively in her culture:

> 'The people in my family that are more culturally orientated, they wouldn't like it, they wouldn't be happy.' (Noreen)

Second, her decision to become a polygamous wife can be interpreted as privileging the religious permissibility of polygamy over the cultural dislike of it. She pursued her Islamic right to be in such a relationship and was able to marry a man that she had feelings for. She therefore disrupted Pakistani cultural norms to marry the person she wanted to be with. Noreen also defied the argument that women are unsuccessful in convincing their families of religion's superiority, because we clearly see her parents were supportive and took an active role in the marriage arrangement process. It is possible for women in some instances, when they feel religion is on their side, to disrupt cultural perceptions that make them feel helpless. This demonstrates the processes of negotiation and reflexivity around these concepts and how women engage with them (Pande, 2015). Noreen was not able to prevent cultural stigma towards her relationship history but with the help of her religious beliefs, she could decide how to react.

If we continue to see religion and culture as interchangeable, we will be unable to see the fascinating ways that women overcome restrictive and orientalist perceptions of their identities in the West. We need to make sure that there is this conceptual space for religion and culture to disrupt as well as operate in harmony. By creating this room to manoeuvre, we can also uncover other forces that structure and organise their tense relationship. We need to examine this dichotomy more deeply, and that requires me to carry out some disruptive work. Is there another explanation for what is causing women's oppression besides holding religion and/or culture responsible?

Complicating the dichotomy and orientalising perceptions

Throughout this chapter, I have looked at the importance of religion and culture along with how they manifest and are used by women in their lives and relationships. The trend of seeing religion and culture as distinct and at odds with each other cropped up repeatedly for the minoritised women I spoke with. They drew a battle line between religion and culture to explain how religion supports and empowers them, while culture undoes this. I want to scrutinise this further because, as we saw earlier with the difficulties of defining these markers, if they are so nebulous and uncertain in themselves, can we really characterise them as good or bad? My position and location as the one recording these experiences means that I risk conveying the wrong message about what women told me. For this reason, I follow Khan's (2005) path of stating from the outset that my argument is not to dismiss this dichotomy around religion and culture – it is these women's lived reality and one that they have developed through their observations and experiences. I want to offer an additional or alternative account of female oppression in religious and cultural contexts. Instead of holding culture, religion or both responsible for women's mistreatment, I argue that it is patriarchal gendered double standards that are to blame.[2] This is evident in a general sense for

[2] I draw on Cooper's definition of patriarchy as a 'gendered organizing framework composed through a series of historically emergent articulations between gender and other social practices' which 'benefits men ... enabling [them] to exercise power in ways not similarly open to women' (1995: 10).

marriage, but also specifically for polygamy. These double standards are further wrapped up with imperialist and orientalist forces that operate to create a relationship and spouse hierarchy placing polygamy and polygamous wives in an inferior position to monogamy and monogamous wives.

The frustration towards culture's dominance and its oppressive effects for women were expressed repeatedly.

> 'I just think it's a backward culture, I think it's very patriarchal, I think it's very centred on the men, and it's very hypocritical. And that doesn't just apply to my culture but … you know, if a Pakistani man wants to stay out late at night, he can, and no one will say anything to him. A Pakistani woman, she would be labelled and all sorts of things would be said about her. For me, being in a relationship, there's been plenty of things said about me but nothing about my boyfriend – nothing's said to him, because it's fine, he can be in a relationship.' (Farha)

> '[N]ow people only explain to the girls that, "Don't do this and this". But you're supposed to explain to the boy – like when my son was growing up, I would say to him "don't mess around", cos I go, "they're somebody's sisters and daughters" … I think that's where people go wrong, you know, cos it's alright for boys to go out and do things like that, but when it comes to the daughter, they think … you know, hell breaks loose. So you have to think of these things both ways.' (Jamilah)

At first glance, culture is the culprit here: in Farha's view, girls and women are treated worse because of the backward culture; and according to Jamilah, boys have more freedom. Looking more closely at these comments, they acknowledge that women are subjected to different standards. These gendered standards stem from the concern that women are 'cultural carriers' who pass their cultural values down to future generations (Sahgal and Yuval-Davis, 1992: 7). Women are therefore characterised as guardians of their families' moral integrity and honour, so more attention is paid to their behaviour, especially in intimate relationships (Liversage, 2014; McGrath and McGarry, 2014). Farha and Jamilah each describe the higher level of control and scrutiny that women and girls experience compared to boys and men. As a young woman, Farha fell prey to her hypocritical and patriarchal community and culture when she was perceived negatively for having a boyfriend but nothing was said to him. Jamilah spoke from her position as a mother trying to educate her son and combat patriarchal influences by asking him to reflect on his behaviour towards women.

There were some further nuanced perspectives on what leads to women's mistreatment and oppression that support my alternative account:

> 'I think the disadvantage is that people pick the religion and use it as a justification, especially when it comes to men, for their own patriarchy. Because I think a lot of Muslim marriages … are inevitably intertwined with culture as well, you can have a lot … a lot of patriarchy in the marriage. I've seen it myself – especially in Muslim marriages, erm, from our community. And it all comes down to the fact that they don't follow the religion correctly and then they use religion as justification for not letting a woman go out, or forcing the woman to wear a *niqaab* even when they don't want to, or not letting a woman go out to work even if it's a permissible environment. So that's the only time marriage has a disadvantage … but I think that the religion doesn't have a … doesn't play a part in the negative consequences of the marriage. I think it's the way that people follow the religion and the actions of people who claim to be religious but are actually not following religion in the correct manner.' (Maha)

This was Maha's answer when asked what she thought were the advantages and disadvantages to marriage in religion. In her case, culture and religion were not the problem in themselves. Instead, it was how religion was used to justify patriarchal behaviour in marriage. The defence of religion by holding patriarchy and incorrect religious practice responsible advances Karimah's earlier statements about people being ignorant of religion. It is interesting that Maha noted the intertwining of religion, culture and patriarchy in marriage. Patriarchy is the combination of male privilege and power with female subordination that defines women primarily through their relation to men. In Maha's comments, we see the ways within marriage that women's lifestyles and choices can be dictated by men so that they cannot exercise power in ways that men can (see further Majeed, 2015). Introducing gender and patriarchy into the discussion complicates the simpler religion–culture dichotomy described by the women. According to King (2004), gendered issues and treatment are ubiquitous in religion because gender and religion are mutually embedded. The same is true of culture, and by remembering this, we can analyse the relationship between religion and culture in a more sensitive way that uncovers how the tension between them arises rather than just blaming culture. Indeed, Dube argues that no culture is 'absolutely negative' or 'wholly pure' (2002: 116). These markers are multilayered and affect individuals and communities in many ways because they are important to us. They perform a fundamental function for the formation of individual and collective identities. Culture is seen as a way of life and religion is similar even for those like Lauren, who was not religious but identified Catholicism as influential on her views of marriage. Where gender and the treatment of women in marriage are concerned, religion and culture are viewed as the source of harmful stereotypes and oppression with little attention given to the traditional patriarchy that they are moulded and practised within. Religion and culture are better seen as social variables that mirror mainstream gender codes like any other social field (Winkel, 2019). This reflects their dynamism and the fact that they influence and are equally influenced by one another and other social categories like gender. Declaring that culture or religion is the source of any problem for women is limited, since they are deeply rooted in people's lives:

> 'A Pathan is a subdivision of a group in Pakistan. I think it originates in Afghanistan and they are very traditional, I think their traditions and culture haven't changed for hundreds … thousands even of years. And you're expected to carry that on, erm, in order to associate yourself with the culture.' (Summayah)

Summayah's cultural background flows from thousands of years of historical traditions, and in her view these have not changed. If women in this cultural community have been treated the same for thousands of years, it cannot just be the culture that is doing this. The culture is not fully negative or pure, so there must be something else impacting on the values being passed down. I argue that it is the patriarchal double standards imposed on women because we cannot separate gender out from religion and culture. Experiences of polygamy are nuanced and need to be seen as broader than a manifestation of women's so-called religio-cultural identity. By reducing them to a religio-cultural or even just a cultural issue therefore, we risk missing the intricacies of the various dynamics around women's lived experiences.

We also see this when considering the impact of gendered double standards and patriarchy on culture in relation to polygamous marriages. This presented in the overarching cultural disapproval of polygamous marriages shared in participants' narratives. More generally, participants used the label 'taboo' to describe cultural perceptions of polygamous marriage:

> 'No I think in my culture, polygamy is one of those things, it's taboo and it's more for people who are really religious.' (Imaan)

For Imaan, religion and culture represent polarised views of polygamous marriage, while other participants observed that there is a certain type of cultural reaction to polygamy:

> '[I]n my culture it's quite taboo, so people do look down upon men who have several wives. So even though those men explain it or justify it by religion … especially in the cases where a man has had an older wife and he's gone to Pakistan or Kashmir and he's in his

sixties and married a female who's in her twenties, that's especially frowned upon, because it's seen as disgusting that the male is after young meat.' (Kiara)

The underlying sentiment here is revulsion towards an older man marrying a younger woman. Interestingly, Kiara cited religion as the justification for polygamy which in her context refers to Islam. However, in doing so, she implied that in these situations, religion remains insufficient to pacify people and mitigate their reactions of disgust. This shows again that when religion and culture intersect and clash, religion is overwhelmed by the cultural response to polygamous marriage. In these women's lives, culture proved to be the domineering force governing perceptions of marriage and the boundaries of acceptable or approved behaviour in relationships.

The association of polygamous marriage with marriage between older men and younger women is also noteworthy because there is no mention of similar relationships arising outside the polygamous context. While it is apparent that an older man can marry a younger woman monogamously, Kiara specified that a factor in people's disgust relates to the man already having an 'older' wife. This theme surrounding the tension between cultural disgust and religious permissibility was further intersected with gender, revealing the prevailing gendered double standard I have been talking about.

> 'I think that for a man, polygamous marriage is good in the way that it's seen as acceptable, it's fine, it's good, you know. But if a woman did this, it's so wrong, it's like she's committing a really big crime.' (Aiza)

> '[I]t's not a good thing and … there's a degree of shame around it because, erm, I definitely hear that shame in relation to women. So if a woman is one of many wives, then she's deficient in something, because she's not enough for her husband.' (Juweriyah)

> '[M]aybe it's a cultural thing, but it just seems, it's just acceptable for men to have more than one wife.' (Maariyah)

> 'I wanted other women to know there's more to it than people thinking "oh the man is just being greedy – he's got his bit on the side and his main wife".' (Noreen)

From these comments, we can see that cultural views on women who engage in polygamy are openly negative. These women are culturally shamed, criminalised and made to feel deficient. By contrast, as Aiza asserts, polygamy is "good" and "acceptable" for men, demonstrating the difference in treatment.

This thread of inferiority running through cultural attitudes towards polygamy situates it below monogamy in the marriage hierarchy, which (as I discussed in Chapter 2) is steeped in the orientalist assumptions of monogamy's superiority (see Phillips, 2010). Polygamous wives are subjected by their cultural communities and mainstream society to othering processes in cultural and gendered terms. The disparity in cultural treatment of polygamous wives and husbands ensures that women in these marriages are deemed inferior to monogamous wives, but there is nothing to suggest that polygamous husbands are considered inferior to monogamous husbands. This shows how cultural responses towards polygamy are profoundly gendered and based on orientalist assumptions of polygamous wives as less worthy than monogamous wives. This is especially troubling because it plays into the orientalist's hands and leads to the minoritised culture being rejected while 'closely befriend[ing] imperial strategies of colonizing' (Dube, 2002: 116). Noreen picked up on this orientalist cultural perception as a reason why women engaged with this practice:

> 'I read one story, there was a woman that was past the point of, you know, having children, and I think she was in her forties, late forties, and she just wanted to get married just so that she could say to everybody, "look I'm married now" ... there are women out there who have no choice but to enter into a polygamous marriage and it's sad that those are the reasons, but it is understandable, you know, because again that's what culture does – that's not religion, where a woman gets to a point where she feels like she's second best. If it's what a woman wants to do, then there's nothing wrong with it, but it's sad that culture does that to a woman, where it's not good enough because she's past a certain age or she has children or because she's been with somebody else, you know, and it makes a woman feel, "oh I'm not worthy enough ... to be number one".' (Noreen)

She discussed women who feel pressured by their history and age to see polygamy as a way out of the stigma of being unmarried but in doing so, are made to feel unworthy and 'second best'. She emphatically attributed this to culture, demonstrating that for some women, where marriage is concerned, there is no escape. They still suffer from negative cultural labelling: for being unmarried and unworthy or for being polygamously married and unworthy. Furthermore, this suffering is a form of spirit murder defined as 'the generic disregard for others whose lives qualitatively depend on our regard' (Williams, 1991: 73). When women in these relationships are othered because they do not conform to the dominant monogamous paradigm, a specific narrative of being unworthy of being wife number one is imposed on them which is injurious to them and insulting. These women are placed at the heart of the religion–culture intersection, but neither religion nor culture alone inflicts their injuries. Patriarchal interpretations and meanings ascribed to the term 'wife' have intertwined with the orientalist hierarchisation of marriages to harm them.

There is another worrying consequence to the orientalist cultural othering of polygamy and polygamous wives: the silencing of these women:

> 'I've come across it a very small number of times, but I think it's one of those taboo, almost a taboo subject – that if someone is in a polygamous marriage, we shouldn't really discuss it. It is what it is and we should just get on with it. I think it's just one of those things we don't talk about – one of the many million things that we don't talk about.' (Farha)

When Farha states that "we should just get on with it", this indicates that the orientalising processes affecting women in polygamous marriages also silence them. Culturally, people may disapprove of polygamous marriage, but they remain silent on the matter with little open discussion or awareness of the harm that this approach can cause. Ali situates this silencing of Muslim women 'in a matrix of patriarchy ... as well as the impact of Orientalism on contemporary European culture ... [because] ... there is a culturally embedded assumption that women should know their place ... and oriental women are too ethereal to have a place at all' (1992: 101). This is the most dangerous consequence of any othering process because it takes polygamous wives' voices and inhibits their agency. It excludes their experiences from discussions around polygamy so that there is no possibility of them speaking out against the dominant perceptions of polygamy and their lives to show how they exercise their agency in the patriarchy-driven system around marriage.

There are further questions about these perspectives and the position of the women who hold them. Most of these women were not polygamous wives themselves (Noreen was about to take on the status but was not yet a polygamous wife). However, they all shared the experience of knowing someone or knowing of someone in their family or community who was. They therefore straddled the line of having more insider knowledge than most but still being outsiders who did not have direct, personal experience. Insider and outsider statuses around practices like polygamy are political and situational (Kusow, 2003; Carling et al, 2014). These women were sharing normative judgements about polygamous wives compared to polygamous husbands and how they are part of a larger system of power and privilege (Vanner, 2015). Through the positioning of those speaking about polygamy and deciding whether it is right or wrong, we see how culture is part of a bigger picture that includes gender and power relations. Polygamy and its participants are spoken about more and judged more by those in the community who observe rather than experience polygamy themselves. Farha was quite vague and general when she said that no one talks about polygamous marriage and that although this affects men as well, due to the gendered double standards in culture women suffer more.

Women not only have to face charges of inferiority as individuals, but are also left without a platform to discuss the issues and cultural concerns around polygamy. Men are privileged: their reputations remain intact regardless of their relationship history or marital choices. Their behaviour may be 'frowned upon', but they are not held accountable in the same way women are. In fact, the lack of openness benefits men who wish to abuse polygamous marriage. Without encouraging people to think about, question and then challenge patriarchal perceptions of women in culture, we cannot address the different harmful and subordinating forces that they experience. These forces operate in all situations and contexts. Women are othered and treated as inferior regardless of their marital status but the orientalist cultural hierarchy of relationships places monogamous wives in a privileged position over polygamous wives and unmarried women. Culture is held solely responsible for the mistreatment and oppression of women when it is patriarchal values which are really to blame.

Concluding thoughts

Noreen's story showcased the role of religion and culture for minoritised women in the UK and the influence of these two markers on marriage and polygamy. She wanted to speak with me to raise awareness that there was more to being a polygamous wife than being a 'bit on the side' for a man who was greedy enough to want more than one marriage. Her intent was to disrupt the mainstream narratives around this relationship. After showing that religion and culture are important for women, I looked at these concepts more closely to show how complicated and overwhelmed with colonial baggage they are. Minoritised religions and cultures are often lumped together and collectively defined as 'other cultures', and this underpins the cultural conflict we have seen play out in the law. There is also a temptation to collapse religion and culture into a single religio-cultural identity. Not only is this orientalising, it was soundly rejected by the women I spoke with.

There is no denying that religion and culture are connected and overlap but this connection is troubled. For the minoritised women, these markers had to be separated out to help them negotiate the oppression and mistreatment they face in their families, communities and society. This need for separation led me to position the markers as dual and alternative sources of identity. The women thought their faith was too important to cause their oppression and when looking for an explanation, culture was a ready target. They saw culture as overriding religious values and leading to women's subordination in life and marriage. But there was potential for women to disrupt their conditions of oppression. They disrupted the imperialist messaging that their othered religion is oppressive by expressing the ways religion empowers them and upholds their rights. Religion also gave them the opportunity to challenge and speak out against problematic cultural values.

My concern with this dichotomy of good religion/bad culture was that it seems unrealistic to hold either of these solely responsible for the unacceptable treatment of women. In addition, there is a risk of feeding into orientalist narratives about women and polygamous wives from minoritised backgrounds being mistreated because of their 'other culture'. I argued that patriarchal double standards imposed on women are the real problem in these situations. This is the case in a general sense and for polygamous wives who are held inferior to monogamous wives and treated with more disdain than polygamous husbands. Experiences of polygamy are therefore shaped by more than religion and culture, so it is overly simplistic to see decisions to live in this relationship as part of a single religio-cultural identity. Polygamous wives are being othered and silenced and this needs to be addressed by thinking in a more sensitive and nuanced manner about what is behind their subordination.

6

Complicating Harm and Gender Equality

Jamilah

I got married just before my 14th birthday, so I feel a bit embarrassed because, you know, when you look at your kids, you can't imagine them being married to someone at that age. I knew I was young, but my parents talked me down, saying: 'You're getting married, just do the Nikah, I'll bring you back.' But I ended up staying there. Eight months after the marriage, I came back and had my son, and then I went back after two years but it was hell. My husband was really violent and abusive. When two people argue, it's just going to get worse, and of course I didn't want to bring my kids up in that atmosphere so I just used to stay quiet and take the punishments. Whatever money I got, I used in the household, and whatever my ex earned was in his pocket. I thought he was putting it away for us and the kids, but I didn't know he was going to do the opposite and run off with it.

Now I blame myself because I should have spoken up, but at that time, we were having problems and my brother passed away, and he was only like 19; my other brother wasn't getting on well, and my other sisters were married and they were having problems. So one day I sat down and thought, 'does my dad need my problems on top of him?' I couldn't really tell my dad, because my dad's been through a lot in his life to then think 'all these kids aren't happy' as well.

While my dad was alive, I think he was a bit in control. But after he passed away, my ex started being bold in front of the kids. Then he got married again and he didn't tell me about it. I found out through other people, and he finally admitted it. He went to the second wife's house and he saw her family. They said they were fine – she could stay in Pakistan. But as soon as they got married, they wanted her to come over to England. The rules changed, so: 'Now you've got our daughter, we want you to divorce your first wife.' My ex used to say to me: 'You coped with the physical and mental abuse all these years, so why not this?' I think when he got married, he

> stepped over the line, because before that there was always the hope that he'll get better one day.
>
> Near the end of the marriage, it was really violent and the kids noticed as well. One day we had a big fight and I was crying, and my daughter came and asked, 'what's wrong?' and I said, 'your dad.' She went downstairs and told him off and he said, 'oh, your mum hit me back!' That was the first time I'd done that, and she turned around and said 'good!' I was upstairs crying and my son came and said, 'Mum, it's not worth it.' I was saying 'what's gonna happen?' and he turned around and said, 'whoever comes in your life is gonna be better than him – no one's gonna be worse than him. So that's when I decided enough is enough. I made my mind up – I wanted to separate.
>
> After the divorce, I found out that my son was sometimes sending him money. I said to my ex: 'You're a healthy man, you're supposed to earn for your second wife and then for the kids, but if you can't do it, then why keep her? It's your duty, not my son's duty. There's me trying to not make my son do so much, but you're getting the money off him.'
>
> I feel like I'm happier now. My kids are bugging me to get married again – I'm scared you know. I'm just waiting for Mr Right to come along.

Jamilah's story could quite easily justify the saviour narrative that we have seen repeatedly in the legal responses to polygamy (discussed in Chapters 3 and 4). She was subjected to so much abuse and harm before being forced into polygamy. So what does her story tell us? That polygamy causes harm and inequalities? These charges have been levelled against polygamy for centuries, and in this chapter, I complicate this dominant narrative. From the outset it is important for me to establish that the aim of this chapter is not to demonstrate whether polygamy is harmful or unequal. To take this approach would legitimise the problematic question of whether polygamy should exist which underpins much of the debate in this area as I observed in Chapter 1. It is not my intention to defend polygamy, but rather to disrupt the foundations of the arguments around harm and inequality and the consequences of relying on them to reject polygamy. While women may experience harm and inequalities in monogamous marriages as well as polygamous ones, the existence of monogamy is not questioned in the same way as the existence of polygamy.

The stories and experiences shared in this chapter are from women's responses to questions in the semi-structured interviews around polygamy and Islam. I asked the women who spoke with me whether they had any experience of polygamy; what they knew about polygamy in Islam; and what their thoughts were on the multiple-wife structure and gender equality in Islamic polygyny. Most of the narratives in this chapter are from Muslim women, but there are contributions from several women who are not. It is not surprising that the most detailed insights, views and experiences on Islam and polygamy came from the Muslim women since it is part of the belief system that they are living in. This book covers not just Islamic polygyny,[1] but it provides an interesting case study because polygamy is overwhelmingly associated with Islam (Zeitzen, 2018). Further, of the major world religions, Islam is the only faith where polygamy is still acknowledged as permissible subject to the guidelines that I broadly explain later.

I continue where I left off in the previous chapter with the argument that women spend their lives tangled in a web of patriarchal power relations – a web in which all the harms and inequalities they suffer are produced and effected on them through culture, religion and marriage. I view the two forces of harm and inequality as overlapping, but it is useful to think about gender inequality separately (I look at constructions and responses around it later). Patriarchy is about power – the way it is distributed and concentrated among us in ways which lead to women being treated as inferior – so I begin with the concept of power. Based on the experiences shared here and my consideration of the wider context that women live in, I first argue that women experience harm and consequently gender-based inequalities because the patriarchy and the way it structures power underpins society and reinforces their subordination. A lot of attention has been paid to the argument that polygamy should not be recognised in law because it is harmful, and through the stories shared with me, it is apparent that polygamy has been used to harm women. Jamilah's encounter with polygamy was brief and part of the broader set of terrible abusive experiences she was subjected to her in marriage with its patriarchal underpinnings. However, only one story dominates the mainstream: polygamy is harmful, it hurts women and children, and must therefore be stopped and excluded from legal definitions of marriage. Many women spoke to me of gendered harms and abuses in a variety of situations, but there is a disparity in the way those situations are treated for women in polygamous marriages. When considering violence against women in monogamous relationships, scholars focus on the patriarchy and unequal power relations to explain the victimisation (see, for example, Mojab, 2012; Doĝan, 2013; Grewal, 2013; Brown, 2014). When a woman is not in an intimate relationship but still experiences gendered harm, again her experience is situated in relation to the wider forces at work in society. The experiences of women in polygamous marriages do not attract the same level of nuance or contextualisation. Polygamy is othered and this contributes to the wider othering of minoritised people and practices without looking more closely at the root causes. There is no meaningful

[1] Polyandry is the form of polygamy in which one wife is married to multiple husbands; polygyny is the term used for polygamous marriages involving a man married to multiple wives.

interrogation of polygamy being used as a harm, because it is convenient to leave things as they are.

The argument that polygamy upholds inequalities is similarly deployed without nuance. Equality has traditionally been described as people being deserving of the same treatment, but this 'equality as sameness' approach does nothing to help us make sense of inequality and polygamy. It instead reinforces the misconception that monogamy promotes equality better because there is only one husband and one wife who based on numbers alone are equals. I use Cooper's (2004) 'equality of power' framework instead to shed light on misguided notions of equality in polygamy. This framework posits that no individual should have more power to impact on their surroundings than anyone else, but due to organising principles of inequality, such as race, gender and class, some individuals may be prevented from exercising as much power as others. The framework aims to identify, challenge and undo these organising principles, including those sustained by normative principles like formal gender equality. Gender equality was challenged by some of the women in this project because they found it unhelpful when applied to religious-based polygamy and the treatment of Muslim women. This leads to the question of whether equality is the lens that we should use to look at practices like polygamy, whose legal recognition is denied because it does not uphold traditional ideals of equality in the West. While I discuss this in the context of Islamic polygyny, there is a broader discussion to be had here about formal gender equality as the standard we apply for women who, because of their personal beliefs, choose to live in relationships or behave in ways that oppose this standard. There is a developing branch of literature that argues we should think about women's decisions to seemingly conform to patriarchal standards in the context of their agency. This helps us to move away from the default position of seeing polygamous wives as victims to seeing them as agentic, thereby avoiding the colonial saviour narrative. By dismissing polygamy because of harms and inequalities and ending our engagement there, we end up silencing women's voices and the potential for learning about the range of experiences and stories they have of polygamy. The stories shared here show us how the current approach limits our awareness and understanding of this relationship and women's voices on it. We need to move towards a more developed and nuanced engagement with the harm and equality arguments around polygamy that are not stuck in patriarchal, colonial understandings and render women invisible.

Polygyny in Islam

Many (although not all) of the experiences included in this chapter come from the perspective of Muslim women, so it is helpful to explain the background to Islamic polygyny where a Muslim man can have up to four wives at once. Arguably, Islam is the only remaining major world religion which permits polygyny to be practised, but there are a lot of different opinions on how this translates into the ideological position Muslims adopt in real life. Moreover, polygamy has never been a common or dominant form of marriage in Muslim communities, although many people see Islam and polygamy as deeply linked (Zeitzen, 2018). Polygyny was practised in the Bedouin-Arab community that the Prophet Muhammad (peace be upon him) was born into before the advent of Islam. It was not a Muslim innovation, and many of the first Muslims were already engaged in it due to pre-existing tribal customs. In AD 625 the Battle of Uhud took place between Muslims and pagans who rejected the message of Islam. Many Muslim men lost their lives leaving behind widows and orphans without any support (Jawad, 1998; Alsunaid and Almofadda, 2014). The dwindling numbers of men in the Muslim community were faced with the dilemma of providing for these women and children while ensuring that they remained in the faith. There was a risk that the women would feel compelled to marry non-Muslim men for support and protection (Ahmed, 2021). To remedy this situation, the following Qur'anic verse was revealed:

> If you fear that you cannot treat orphans with fairness, then you may marry such women as seem good to you: two or three or four of them. But if you fear that you cannot do justice, marry one only or those you possess. This will make it easier for you to avoid injustice. (Zayid, 1980: Surah an-Nisa, Verse 2)

Monogamy is preferred and is practised by the majority, but polygyny is permitted in Islam if it is not 'for someone's fancy or indulgence'; so rather than being born of religious ideology it was permitted for practical reasons (Sanasarian, 1986: 215). Interestingly, there are two broad camps of interpretation for the Qur'anic ruling. One position is the strict approach that polygyny can only happen where no injustice is visited upon the wives, but achieving justice is impossible (Husni and Newman, 2007). This view is supported by another verse in the same chapter of the Qur'an:

> In no way can you treat your wives in a just manner, even though you may wish to do that. Do not set yourself altogether against any of them, leaving her, as it were, in suspense. If you do what is right and guard yourselves against evil, (you will find) [the Lord] Forgiving, Merciful. (Zayid, 1980: Surah an-Nisa, Verse 129)

If it is impossible to treat your wives in a just manner, there is no way to fulfil the essential criterion of avoiding injustice, so polygyny should not be practised. Scholars in this camp limit polygyny to its historical context because the social, political and economic conditions facing the Muslim community now are no longer present to justify polygyny (Abduh, 1979; Khan, 1988).

This is contrasted against the more 'classical interpretation', which speaks to the commitment of trusting the divine wisdom behind polygyny. In this camp, there are special circumstances where polygyny is justified for men who can treat their wives equitably and justly. Responding to the argument that justice between wives is impossible, scholars rely on the last sentence of the second verse:

> If you do what is right and guard yourselves against evil, (you will find) [the Lord] Forgiving, Merciful. (Zayid, 1980: Surah an-Nisa, Verse 129)

This qualifies the requirement for justice and, as Jawad notes: 'The kind of equality demanded by the Qur'an is one that is humanly attainable. Absolute equality is obviously not attainable on the plane of human emotions and love. But a sincere attempt at treating one's wives equally is possible' (1998: 44).

Human weakness is acknowledged in Islam, so intentions are a major aspect of behaviour. If someone intends to do justice and uphold equality and acts according to that intention, the Lord will be forgiving and merciful. This is where the contemporary practice of polygyny is situated emphasising the spiritual consequences of sincerely intending to treat wives with justice and equality. When this is not the case and Islamic polygyny is used to subject women to injustice, the religious rulings are being disregarded. There is no grey area to justify the behaviour of a man who does not care about treating his wives justly. In such cases, polygyny is not sanctioned at all. It gets complicated when someone is sincere and feels as though they can practise polygyny with a 'clear conscience' but, as I discuss later, in a patriarchal world, there is always a risk of injustice.

This brief explanation of Islamic polygyny provides the context for my deeper discussion of equality and harm. As polygamy is practised beyond Islam and beyond the 'other', this section is intended to disrupt the narratives that marginalise polygamy and lead to the experiences of polygamous wives, whether Muslim or not, being delegitimised and dismissed.

Polygamy as harmful and unequal?

In Chapter 5, I shared women's descriptions of how men are given more freedom, opportunities and rights. Women identified cultural strictures as the reason for this differential treatment and I complicated this by arguing that gendered double standards are to blame. It is a similar story for the harm and inequalities suffered by women. In the previous chapter, culture was the culprit; in this chapter, the culprit is polygamy. To start, women expressed the disadvantages they experience compared to men in a variety of situations regardless of their relationship status:

> 'In some cultures, they always say bad about the woman, a man can get married ten times and they won't say a word … I think that people shouldn't say to a woman that once she gets to a certain age she can't get married.' (Jamilah)

For Jamilah, male privilege in the form of freedom to remarry without criticism stemmed from gender interacting with culture. This double standard was similarly experienced by others:

> '[Marriage is p]rison, I would say because, erm, once a woman gets married … in my culture, a woman stays at home … cooks for the husband. It's a duty. … Basically, before marriage, it's like your parents are controlling you; after marriage, it's your husband who's controlling you.' (Aiza)

While Jamilah's comment was in relation to divorce arguing that women should be free to move on and remarry, Aiza's statement as a single woman related more generally to women before and after marriage. In Aiza's experience, the balance of power in a woman's relationships always leans away from her. This imbalance in power relations is not attached to a particular type of marriage; rather, women's subordination happens because of gender interacting with other social relations that uphold male privilege.

This is also noted in the literature. For example, Kaganas and Murray (1991) demonstrate female disadvantage in South African customary polygyny where women bear and take responsibility for children, yet parental rights are vested in men. They conclude that 'most examples of inequality simply point to a variety of oppressive, patriarchal features of the … marriage' (Kaganas and Murray, 1991: 127; see also Sweet, 2013). The source of inequality here is the oppression and patriarchal features of the relationship rather than its structure. They proceed to argue that '[t]he treatment of women as property, sexual stereotyping and domination are not limited to polygyny, nor are they practices that can be shown to be inevitable in polygyny' (Kaganas and Murray, 1991: 128). These types of issues with domination and sexual stereotyping were experienced by interviewees in this study even when they were not in a relationship, as with Imaan:

> 'I was organising an event or something and at work, so at work we have a volunteers database and we also have a WhatsApp group for

the volunteers … there was this one guy in the group … he started messaging me off WhatsApp and … he started asking me if I was married and I said no, and then, er, he continued to message me … and it kept going on and on and on, and it was very inappropriate to me because, I mean, I take my work very seriously and to have someone from work message me at midnight … I felt a bit violated, especially as I had told him twice to not contact me. … And then I had to get a manager involved who was a man, and it wasn't until then that he stopped messaging me … it is a bit disgusting as well that I have to be under the authority of another man to feel like I am protected.' (Imaan)

Imaan, a single woman in her early twenties, suffered this treatment in a professional situation and the harm was related to her not being married. She felt "violated" by her harasser's behaviour and even though she told him to refrain from contacting her, he ignored her. His disregard for professional boundaries and invasion of Imaan's personal life demonstrates that the gendered power structures they live in made him think it was acceptable to transgress those limits and behave oppressively towards her. The most revealing facet of this story is Imaan's reaction to the action she was compelled to take. She tried to address this man's harassment alone but was unsuccessful and had to ask a senior male colleague to deal with it. The disgust that she felt was not only towards her harasser but towards the system which made her helpless against this man's behaviour. It was only when she sought the protection of another man that her abuser stopped, and this is the problem. The system not only means a woman can suffer harm but also leaves her without an independent way out. A cycle of harm occurs where a man is needed to stop another man. Until the system and structures which give rise to this female vulnerability and helplessness are exposed, challenged and changed, women in all situations and relationships remain at risk of harm and gender-based inequality.

When I refer to gendered double standards, I am talking about one of the effects of patriarchy. The chief influence on how women are treated is not the form of their relationship, or lack of relationship, but patriarchy. Patriarchy is an organising power structure that institutionalises the suffering experienced by women. Cooper interprets patriarchy as 'a specifically gendered organizing framework composed through a series of historically emergent articulations between gender and other social practices. … Constituted by, and in turn constituting, social interactions, processes, and relations, patriarchy benefits men … enabling [them] to exercise power in ways not similarly open to women' (1995: 10). Patriarchy is determined by the exercise of power, so I need to establish what is meant by power before showing how its distribution leads to women suffering.

Power has been subject to various interpretations and definitions which traditionally fall into two broad camps. First, power is a 'commodity which some people, or class of people, may "own"', meaning certain people possess it and then wield it over others to dominate and restrict' (Smart, 1989: 7). On the surface, this seems quite useful in that it represents a dichotomy of power/powerlessness. Power is distributed among the haves while it never reaches the have-nots. The claim that polygamous marriages give rise to harm and inequalities fits well within this model – in these relationships, men own the power to dominate women. This is then used to justify the lack of legal recognition of polygamous marriage on the basis that polygamous wives can never possess or exercise power and cannot be anything but a 'slave'. This model has been criticised by feminists because it does not leave room for women to be anything other than helpless victims and it fails to recognise their capacity for resistance or agency (Oksala, 2017). These shortcomings have pushed feminist theorists to conceive of power in a way which accounts for women's strengths, actions and resistance – a model that sees power not as something which is owned or possessed, but as a positive ability to act. In this interpretation, power is 'the human ability not just to act but to act in concert' (Arendt, 1970: 44), and the focus is on bringing about change or transformation. Liberal feminists have modelled power as a positive resource that should be distributed among all members of society to create equal opportunities for women to gain economic and political power (see for example, Friedan, 1963). In this model, the ways that women like polygamous wives exercise their ability to produce change within their families could be recognised. It also provides the possibility of seeing polygamy as a tool for change and resistance in the hands of the women that engage in it.

However, both conceptions of power miss a crucial detail that reflects their mainstream foundations: they focus on the individual's abilities and relationship to men (Oksala, 2017). They struggle to account for the systemic or structural elements of power, which are experienced disproportionately by those who are minoritised and subordinated. This focus neglects the power structures that dominant and subordinated individuals operate within, as all their beliefs and practices are shaped in the same environment (Foucault, 1980). In addition, it is increasingly difficult to identify where power is located. Individual and group identities are multilayered 'amalgams of advantage, marginalization and repression' (Cooper, 1995: 13). Taking Jamilah's experience as an example: she stated that her father was "in control" and after his death, her husband started "being bold in front of the kids". This shows that although her husband was the oppressive and dominating force in her life, his behaviour was constrained by her father. Her father provided a counterbalance to her husband and while she was abused during her father's lifetime, his death made her even more vulnerable. Here, even the abuser was under the control of another party, demonstrating the complexity of power. Jamilah further discussed how her choices and capacity to act were affected by her parents and children, but this was part of the wider systemic context that facilitated her being a child bride in the first place. Forcing a child to marry and later forcing a woman into polygamy is not simply down to individual behaviour, but the social structures in place that permit and in some ways sanction this.

With these criticisms in mind, scholars started to find Foucault's understandings of power more useful, particularly because he starts with the argument that we should not be looking for the centre of power or those that are in power. We should instead construct a 'microphysics of power' that looks at the margins and how power manifests in families, the workplace and everyday practices. The idea is to look at power relations from the bottom up, because power is relational, diffuse and capillary (Foucault, 1978; see also Oksala, 2017). When we see power as flowing around systems, processes and institutions from the details of our everyday lives upwards, we can also see power as capable of operating in productive, fluid and creative ways. Here, power is a force that in theory can flow in any direction and manifest anywhere. However, there are limits to this. In his later work, Foucault notes that even though power relations are fluid, they tend to become stabilised through institutions, so the flow of power is restricted and it is concentrated in certain places. Institutions use laws and codes to gather power in certain places and for certain people so that power relations become rigid and mobile (Foucault, 1997). These institutions then engage in processes of normalisation using power to discipline and condition individuals and societies so that they conform to normative standards. As a result, there is a limit to the resistance and agency that individual women can express as they negotiate the structures and systems that shape power relations where 'non-conformities are marked and punished with a view to correcting the deviation' (Bell, 1993: 66). For a practice like polygamy, its nonconforming structure is marked out through a lack of legal and social acceptance which can in turn discipline its participants and push it underground. In this way, legal and social processes shape and influence how relationships are perceived and practised. Cooper's (1995) interpretation of patriarchy (mentioned earlier) uses this concept of power as a creative force which interacts with the social before becoming solidified into a gendered structure that perpetuates female subordination. How does this translate into women experiencing harm because of polygyny?

It has been repeatedly noted that polygamous marriages are objectionable because they are harmful and unequal. As Beaman observes, '[s]tories of underage brides, women married off without their consent and lost boys permeate these discussions' (2014: 6). Brooks (2009) adopts the position that greater harms are attached to polygamous marriage for women because it is structurally inegalitarian in practice and theory. Polygamy is inegalitarian in a practical sense because it is rarely polyandrous, so women do not have the opportunity to engage in polygamy in the same way as men. In addition, polygamy is inegalitarian in a theoretical sense, because it is discriminatory against same-sex relationships and because a polygynous husband can divorce any of his wives at will, but the wives may only divorce him, not one another. This leads to the conclusion that polygamous marriages are incapable of existing outside a patriarchal framework. In other work, Parekh (2010) argues that polygamous marriages are harmful because spouses feel 'dispensable', while monogamous marriages provide ideal family conditions and a better prospect of spousal equality.[2]

Brooks uses empirical studies conducted in other countries to support his arguments, asserting that there is a 'case to believe that polygamy is linked to an increased likelihood of several harmful effects' (2009: 112). One such study, involved interviews with individuals living within the Bedouin-Arab structure of polygyny to gain insight into family functioning and relationships. It concludes that '[e]conomic, educational, health and emotional arguments are given in favour of monogamous unions' (Slonim-Nevo et al, 2008: 206). However, it is also stated in the same study that 'polygyny itself may not be detrimental to family members' adjustment, and in cases where the family functions well … adjustment … will not be impaired' (Slonim-Nevo et al, 2008: 197). The contradictory statements here reveal the difficulty of providing definitive evidence for polygyny being the harm because correlation is not the same as causation (March, 2011; see also McDermott and Monroe, 2018). In addition, there is little to show how or why the findings of this research should be generalised and applied to other contexts.

This approach of classifying polygamy as harmful and unequal is founded on the discourses of imperialism and orientalism. Polygamy is othered and set up against the ideal of monogamy so that any assumptions about it are accepted without question because it deviates from the ideal.[3] If the basis of assumptions about polygamy being harmful and unequal are not critically examined, the danger is that women who are not polygamous wives are portrayed as being at less risk of harm, which can diminish their experiences.

Existing literature provides us with responses to these claims of harm and inequality, which we can initially draw from. The gendered nature of polygamy which is operationalised through the higher rates of polygyny is

2 These are just some examples of the scholarship making these claims, which I have included for illustrative purposes. For further insight, see Calder and Beaman (2014).

3 Beaman (2014) discusses how polygamy has acquired a differentiating function to distinguish the monogamous and therefore civilised *us* from the polygamous and uncivilised *them*.

a challenge for feminists. However, scholars like Brake question whether 'marriages within religious traditions that subscribe to gendered spousal roles [should] be deprived of recognition' (2012: 199). In doing so, she criticises the use of gender roles in monogamous marriages to frame polygamy as a harm:

> polygyny is structurally inegalitarian as monogamy is not. … But … in some communities – and in U.S. law within living memory – monogamy is structurally inegalitarian in its spousal roles, just as polygyny is: It gives the husband the dominant role. It might be said that not all monogamous marriage is patriarchal – but not all polygyny need be. (Brake, 2012: 198)

Polygyny is being compared to a specific form of monogamy: the idealised version which is supposedly neither patriarchal nor unequal. The simplistic comparison being carried out here between polygyny and monogamy is problematic because the 'comparison is too individualistic and does not take sufficient account of the social context' (Malik, 2007: 79). To expose this, Brake undertakes a contextualised comparison between monogamy and polygyny in the 'small patriarchal religious communities within which polygyny tends to be located in the United States' (2012: 198). From this exercise, she finds that polygamy's 'problematic features are not sufficiently different in kind from existing male-female monogamy to justify differential treatment' (Brake, 2012: 200). This demonstrates the importance of context to determine the dominating influence on harm and gendered roles (see also Shrage, 2016).

The women who spoke with me observed that they knew or were related to other women suffering though polygamous marriages which had been imposed on them. But is polygamy a symptom or a cause of this harm? In Jamilah's case, the public insult of becoming a polygamous wife was the final straw after a lifetime of marital abuse.

Maariyah also described the use of polygamous marriage as a harm:

> 'my cousin sister's got [Crohn's disease]. … It's quite personal but she wasn't always able to look after his needs, so he's got another woman … I think he's married to her Islamically. … It was really difficult for her to deal with … that her husband was going to do this and … well I felt because he's from Bangladesh and he came over here having married my cousin sister and, it's like, she's given him a son and a daughter and, erm, yeah, she would devote everything to him and she has. But, erm, in the end he didn't feel like she was fulfilling her duties as a wife.' (Maariyah)

In this situation, the husband contracted a further marriage because he was dissatisfied with his marriage to Maariyah's cousin after she developed a long-term illness. Polygamous marriage was 'done to' Maariyah's cousin, leaving her with no choice but to unhappily resign herself to the situation. Moreover, a sense of betrayal is evident in the statement that this man was able to emigrate from Bangladesh because of his marriage to her cousin, implying that his quality of life improved thanks to this marriage. Maariyah felt that her cousin had been a devoted wife and mother, but instead of being supported by the husband, he publicly expressed his dissatisfaction by marrying again. That harm can result from imposing polygamous marriage on women cannot be denied, but there needs to be a deeper examination of the context around this.

Cora's interpretation of her grandmother's situation provides a different take on the cause of harm:

> 'Oh, don't get me into my grandmother's situation. It was not positive, but I don't want to say it was because she was in a polygamous marriage. If she was not in a polygamous marriage, perhaps her situation would have brought polygamy in, because she only had female daughters, she had only female children, she didn't have male, which was quite disadvantageous. Even if there were rights in the marriage, she wasn't on the same level with every other person.' (Cora)

Cora takes a balanced view towards polygamous marriage and her refusal to blame her grandmother's suffering on polygamy is interesting. Instead, she blames the attitudes attached to her grandmother having daughters. This highlights the influence of patriarchal attitudes over her grandmother's experiences. Her grandmother's experience and abuse resulted from something that was out of both her and her husband's control.

A similar experience was recounted by Sharan:

> 'One of my aunts … her husband had two wives and that was quite acceptable because, erm, although she had a son, her children kept dying and it was quite acceptable for her husband to take another wife. … My aunt was treated very badly.' (Sharan)

Despite having a son, Sharan's aunt was treated badly because her other children did not survive and this again displays how polygamous marriage can perpetuate suffering. From these narrations and Maariyah's, we see that polygamous marriage is locked into a cycle with punishing attitudes towards women and their 'failure' to meet the needs or obligations of their relationships. For Maariyah's cousin, although not stated explicitly, it was suggested her husband felt dissatisfied with their physical relationship, which suffered because of her illness; for relatives of Cora and Sharan, perceived concerns about their fertility played a part in them being treated badly. In certain societies, perceived fertility issues can be equated with a 'failure of femininity', and there are misconceptions of fertility as a 'women's issue' (Batool and de Vissec, 2016: 181:). This is sexist as the women are forced to live in a system that blames and punishes them through perceived concerns around fertility.

This system stems from patriarchal attitudes towards women and their roles in society. As Sharan stated, it was "quite acceptable" for her aunt's husband to marry again when her children kept dying – the key word here is 'acceptable'. It was acceptable for Cora's grandmother to be harmed and treated as not on 'the same level' as everyone else because she had no male offspring; it was acceptable for Maariyah's cousin to be subjected to a polygamous marriage after she became seriously ill. The notion of 'acceptable punishment' for women in these situations comes from the patriarchal privileging of male desires and needs rooted in the priority given to husbands and sons.

Taking Noreen's story (in Chapter 5) as another example, she shared that her fiancé's first wife was extremely unhappy with his pending second marriage. As an orphan with few family members, the first wife's main source of support was her in-laws. However, when asked about their position on the matter, Noreen clarified that the fiancé's family had chosen not to be involved, leaving the first wife without any support. Despite Noreen being positive about her polygamous marriage, the negative experience of the first wife cannot be ignored. It cannot be denied that because Noreen's husband was dissatisfied with his relationship with the first wife, that wife was made to suffer. In this relationship, the imbalance in power relations was evident from the start. The husband had viewed the first marriage a favour to the first wife based on his pity for her orphaned state. It was implied that she should be grateful he married her at all and that she had no right to complain about his pending second marriage.

These negative experiences all demonstrate that abuse, harm and suffering were present in these women's relationships. Polygamy was being used to harm them although they were already suffering from pre-existing harms including the stigmas associated with fertility, only having female children and being unable to meet their husband's needs.The deployment of polygamous marriage as a tool to harm women is underpinned by the pre-existing imbalance of power in the relationship. This is upheld by the patriarchal structures within which these marriages are formed and operate making it acceptable for men to disregard their wives' feelings.

By advancing a more contextualised engagement with the harm argument, it is possible to make space for a wider range of women's experiences of polygamy which may challenge the dominant narrative. It is important to 'utilize narrative or storytelling as counter-stories to the master narrative, the dominant discourse' (Berry, 2010: 23–4). The dominant narrative is that polygamous marriage is an inherently harmful practice and always victimises women. This is a manifestation of the imperialist telling an authoritative story about this relationship to establish its nonconformity and deviance. As a counter-narrative to the 'polygamy as a harm' critique, we can explore the extent to which the dominant narrative is reflected in women's everyday lives and realities.

Noreen exemplifies a woman who engaged with polygamy on her own terms. She had actively chosen to marry a man for whom she had developed feelings with full consideration of his personal and marital circumstances:

> 'I wanted other women to know there's more to it than people thinking "oh, the man is just being greedy – he's got his bit on the side and his main wife". It's more than that.' (Noreen)

While discussing her motivation for sharing her story with me, it is clear she wanted to address the negative perceptions of polygamy that she had encountered. It is especially interesting that she addresses her counter-story to "other women". She wanted other women to know that polygamy does not have to stem from a man's greed or desire to have multiple partners.

In another example, Farha described a polygamous marriage that had positive aspects:

> 'From my personal experience that someone I know got married in North … Western Frontier Province and then … and then he also got married to someone else here … his wedding in Pakistan was arranged … but he also ended up falling in love with a woman here, so he married both of them and he was treating both women equally … and the situation was kinda, the man was told that if he ever broke the first marriage that the wife's family would go and kill all of his family members.' (Farha)

Farha's story represents a different contribution to the 'polygamy as harm' debate. The polygamous situation that she recounts does have harm with the first wife's family posing a threat to the husband's family. The harm in this case was external and displays that the powerful husband can also experience powerlessness. Although the husband was being forced to remain in his first marriage, he was still willing to fulfil his responsibilities towards his first wife. There is a developing body of literature on offences which are committed to protect a 'value system predicated on … honour' (Gill and Brah, 2014: 73). 'Honour'-based violence is often associated with 'respect, esteem, dignity, reputation and virtue', and the threat that Farha describes falls under this category (Gill and Brah, 2014: 74). Here, the first wife's family threatened to kill the husband's family if he divorced her because the insult of the wife's divorce to their reputation would be unacceptable to them. Pierre Bourdieu (1977) argues that 'honour' is played out publicly and the public arena gives rise to 'honour'-based[4] criminal behaviour. The opinion of others matters because people feel that it impacts on many aspects of family life and livelihood. In this way, the husband in Farha's narration would injure his first wife's family 'honour' by making her a divorcée. The husband entering a polygamous marriage was not deemed dishonourable here; rather, this was an acceptable compromise given the complex patriarchal forces at work.

That 'honour'-based crimes are concerned with protecting women from loss of reputation or virtue demonstrates how entangled they are with patriarchy. Women are policed and 'defended' in the name of 'family honour', but men are never controlled in the same way. The threat to the husband in this case was related to the stigma of divorce for the first wife's family. The 'polygamy compromise' in Farha's story is further rooted in patriarchy since the husband was able to find a solution to this problem which generally worked for him and kept his family safe. If the situation had been different and the first wife had been unhappy with the idea of both divorce and polygamous marriage, there would have been no tolerable alternative for her.

Another theme from the conversations presents polygamous marriage as a positive structure in which co-wives can develop and maintain a bond of sisterhood.

> 'My dad's aunty … we never saw them like, er, two wife for one man – we saw them like sisters.' (Humayrah)

> 'I have seen it when I went to Ghana. I saw two women – they were really close and then my grandmother told me they were married to the same man … yeah … I thought it was quite interesting, the way they were, you know, so together. They were like sisters, almost like twins – it was interesting.' (Gul)

Here, relationships between wives are centred. The idea of sisterhood provides another insight into perceptions of polygamous marriage. Under one interpretation, by representing polygamous wives as sisters, the marriage is being sanitised for the public by taking the husband out of the equation. In this way, the marital relationships are being dissociated from sexuality while validating the female homosociality between co-wives (Bailey, 2015). However, this approach is problematic because it still attaches a sense of shame to polygamy by removing its key characteristic as a marriage so that it becomes more palatable to the masses. Another interpretation drawing

[4] Scholars place 'honour' in quotation marks to express their disapproval of associating such violence with 'honour', because there is no honour in this patriarchal crime. See, for example, Reddy (2008).

on bell hooks' (1986) work, sees Humayrah's and Gul's examples as stories of sisterhood and solidarity. Traditionally, male supremacist ideologies encourage women to believe that their value is obtained through their bonds with men like their husbands, and other women are 'natural enemies'. When women unlearn this and bond with each other, they learn the true meaning of sisterhood, living and working in solidarity. The sisterhood exhibited by polygamous wives is a disruption of these male supremacist ideologies but also of the White liberal feminist approach that calls for solidarity in the face of common oppression. This conventional form of solidarity sees women as only victims which is demoralising. hooks (1986) argues that women's bonds should be based on their shared strengths and resources and that this is the essence of sisterhood. By building and living these bonds, polygamous wives construct their own meaningful family relationships which can provide a place of comfort, solidarity and disruption. Polygamy is a complicated and dynamic practice that in many cases has been imposed on women as a harm. However, that does not take away from the possibility of women finding opportunities for empowerment, agency and disruption through polygamy. By dismissing polygamy on the basis that it causes harm, we neglect these experiences of disruption and solidarity.

Polygamy and gender equality

So far, we have seen how gendered inequalities and harm are rooted in patriarchal power structures that women must negotiate throughout their daily lives. In Chapters 3 and 4, I explored the English case law around polygamy which in recent times has started to re-emphasise that this relationship fails to uphold or enable equality for women and should therefore not be encouraged in the UK. How helpful is this argument? Equality has been scrutinised in many contexts and disciplines, from legal philosophy to economics highlighting its importance (examples include Dworkin, 2000; Nussbaum, 2000; Baker et al, 2009; Sen, 2009). Historically, it has been framed and deployed in a formal sense to achieve sameness – that is, things that are alike should be treated alike (Aristotle, 1925). Attaining this same treatment is the mission of mainstream liberal feminism as they prove that women are like men and deserve the same opportunities.[5]

The 'equality as sameness' approach is also favoured by the law, and we see this in anti-discrimination doctrine. All forms of discrimination are the same – for example, racist discrimination and sexist discrimination

---

[5] For discussions and critiques of the liberal feminist formal equality mission, see, among others, Williams (1982), Williams (1991), Cain (1990), Cornell (1998), Bartlett (2012) and Boyd (2015).

are the same – which means they can be dealt with in the same way. However, the law is oversimplifying discrimination and equality here. Formal equality fails to understand that equality is not always attained when people are treated the same (Verma, 1995). Critical feminist scholars have exposed the limits of formal equality in law showing that it does not provide for the needs of those who are discriminated against or mistreated on more than one ground. Minoritised people suffer the most because their differences are not understood or even accepted by the legal system. For these reasons, the current legal approach to equality is limited. The rejection of polygamy is based on a standard of equality that is not realised for people in the first place. Again, questions are being asked of polygamy that are not asked of monogamy. At the same time, there is no easy answer to whether any of these relationships can uphold equality in the patriarchy and what the consequences are of dismissing polygamy on this basis.

The formal approach to equality was visible in women's views that the overwhelming prevalence of polygyny (multiple-wife marriages) means polygamy is unequal. As Maariyah expressed:

> 'I think [Islamic polygyny's] unfair … because of … the way women can be treated that they're dispensable, and they're not. They don't have as much value as men. So, it's almost like if a man can have up to four wives, then four women are the equivalent to one man.' (Maariyah)

Maariyah's strongly worded perspective on Islamic polygyny shows the implications of a formal equality framework. The perception of Islamic polygyny is that the one dominant husband is equal to their four wives, so a wife is worth a quarter of the husband. Arguably, this is the popular view of all polygynous situations. This simple formula proves that polygyny is unequal because it is not possible for a woman to have the same weighting as her husband. This statement around equality points to the patriarchal attitudes underpinning the practice of polygyny. For women to be valued as a fraction of the man shows how deeply ingrained patriarchal attitudes are. Under formal equality, marriage is constructed around monogamy where the two spouses are viewed as perfectly equal. Polygamy is forced into this construction with the husband on one side of the equation and all the wives grouped together on the other side. This diminishes polygamous wives and relying on the equality argument to reject polygamy reinforces this troubling perception of them.

Another example of how the equality argument is embedded in patriarchal assumptions presents in the comparison of polygyny and polyandry:

> '[I find] the idea of a woman having several partners horrific, and equally I wouldn't find a male having several partners horrific but

I would struggle to agree with it. … From a religious perspective … I can understand why women aren't allowed, but I think there is gender inequality in that, from a third person point of view, it is unequal that women can't marry several men but men can marry several women.' (Kiara)

Kiara demonstrates how social norms affect personal views towards polyandry as less acceptable than polygyny. It is unequal in a formal sense that polygyny is the main form of polygamy and women are much less likely to have multiple husbands, but we can also see the influence of the patriarchy here in the perception that it is horrific for women to have several partners but not for men. In Kiara's view:

'It's part of the society we've been brought up in Britain that men are portrayed to be … erm … kind of characters who do have several partners and several different girlfriends and they cheat, whereas females have it a lot harder to do that.' (Kiara)

The social stereotyping narrated here by Kiara explains how equality is shaped in the context of polygamy. While from a formal equality approach, polyandry and polygyny should both be permitted and practised, social conventions still ensure that the former is more frowned upon than the latter. This shows the dominance of the patriarchal social structures that relationships are tangled up in. Kiara's last observation is interesting because it is not specifically about polygamy. Her comments are about men having several different girlfriends or partners and cheating, while women find it harder to do the same. We can see therefore that broad stereotypes about the behaviour of men and women are at play in the perception of polygamy. Formal equality is an ideal that is limited by the patriarchy so relying on it to reject polygamy compared to other relationships is also limited.

If formal equality is limited, is there another approach to equality that helps to make sense of polygamy? Marriage is deeply embedded in the social, so it follows that looking for a model which accounts for this might be useful. I now consider what insights Cooper's (2004) equality of power framework can provide for polygamy and equality. Cooper argues that 'we cannot think about equality outside the social processes, forms and claims that structure our lives' (2004: 69–70). Equality needs to be situated within the social, and 'political and social action should engender greater equality in people's capacity to shape the social and physical world … [but] this is denied … by the way organising principles such as gender, age, class, race … skew people's ability to exercise power' (Cooper, 2004: 80). This skewing process is where the problem lies, because 'nobody has an inherent right to impact more on their social and physical environment than anyone else' (Cooper, 2004: 78).

In this model, the skewed exercise of power by certain people compared to others is caused by organising principles of inequality which are

> conceptual/material matrices that articulate norms, relations, institutions, resources, and practices in particular, socially meaningful ways … they structure the ways in which elements of the social combine into distinct formations. Amongst other things, [they] identify the asymmetrical situating of people according to relations of race, gender, class, and so on … they span out to include organizational processes and culture, everyday practice, as well as social norms and values. (Cooper, 2004: 261)

These principles structure hierarchies of difference and the main aim of the equality of power framework is to challenge and undo them. To do this, we look more closely at the norms, values and social relations that underpin them. The key organising principle of inequality for gender is patriarchy which skews the exercise of power in favour of men demonstrating how intertwined harm and inequality are. Power is a creative and productive force which is concentrated in institutions and systems so that it loses its fluidity. The patriarchy is the result of power being concentrated in institutions in ways that allow men to exercise power more than women. It is because of power relations locating people according to their differences from the ideal elite White man that minoritised women are denied equal power.

Undoing these organising principles requires us to challenge the 'norms that anchor, legitimate or sustain the inequality' (Cooper, 2004: 92). We cannot aim our challenge straight at the patriarchy from the outset, but we can start by addressing the norms which set the dominant and idealised standards guiding individuals and institutions. These norms have created the figure of the elite White man as the ideal who then exercises power in ways that everyone else cannot. We therefore work to undo the patriarchy by exposing and trying to undo its normative components. But what are these components? Several of the Muslim women who participated in this study found the concept of 'gender equality' problematic when applied to Islam and to polygamy. To them, this ideal of equality failed to understand how equality between men and women is constructed in Islam, and this then affected mainstream responses to polygamy. From their stories, gender equality emerged as an unexpected normative component of the patriarchy promoting the orientalist understanding of Islam and Islamic polygyny as unequal and subordinating for women. This makes for an interesting case study. If the concept of gender equality itself is upholding the patriarchal and orientalist perceptions of polygamy and Islam, then where does that leave us?

Gender equality and Islam: a case study

For some of the Muslim women who spoke with me, equality in Islam was a given:

> 'For me, we have gender equality, I am saying from Islamic perspective. We are equal in front of God eyes.' (Liyanah)

Men and women are equal *in God's eyes*, and this is the baseline for Muslims as reinforced in the Qur'an. Leila Ahmed notes that 'in comparison with the scriptural texts of other monotheistic traditions … women are explicitly addressed; one passage in which this occurs declares by the very structure of the utterance, as well as in overt statement, the absolute moral and spiritual equality of men and women' (2021: 64–5).

How does Liyanah's view compare to broader understandings of gender equality that influence the law? In a lot of the existing scholarship, there is no clear definition of 'gender equality' and it is often used as a synonym for 'women's equality'.[6] Cornell argues that although 'feminist anthropologists have undertaken to dismantle any simplistic understanding … of the meaning of gender; no known society has been shown to be completely free from the symbolic traces of an ideological masculine and a correspondingly degraded feminine other' (1998: 15). For this reason, gender equality is structured along a masculinity/femininity axis and here we start to experience a tension. If it is defined according to a particular interpretation of masculinity and femininity, social norms decide what this type of equality is and the people it is relevant for. If gender equality is about achieving women's equality, this is reminiscent of the liberal feminists' formal equality mission to ensure women are treated the same as men. However, it only works for women who conform to the ideal standards set by the patriarchy. From this view, gender equality has the potential to sustain inequalities as a component of patriarchy which favours men but also creates a hierarchy of women with minoritised women's views and experiences framed as inferior because of their differences from the liberal feminists' target group: White, middle-class women in the West.

Several of the Muslim women I spoke with challenged understandings of gender and equality between men and women in the West and the relevance of these to their lives and beliefs.

> '[T]o be fair, my view of the male and female gender in Islam is kind of, is that men and women are not equal but that does not mean that

[6] For further discussion, see van der Vleuten (2007), Burns et al (2009), Hoffman Williams (2009), Fredman (2011), Vlasoff (2013) and Conley and Page (2015).

there isn't justice. So, you have this view in Western society that men and women are equal, but if you look at the naked body of a man and a woman, we are biologically and naturally different … and I think Islam takes all these differences into account and gives each man and woman different roles to play in all aspects of life, whether it's work, community, erm, family, relationships, as a mother or father, etc. So, you can't argue gender equality in Islam, because men and women are fundamentally not equal in the first place. What I can say and what I will vouch for is that there is justice between men and women in that men and women can both be successful in this world, in this dunya, in every point of their life, but they can do so in different ways. The reward that a woman gets by being a mother is never attainable by a man, so I can argue gender inequality in that sense. So I would say that I wouldn't say that there is gender inequality but there is justice.' (Maha)

'I think that the way in which we view gender is a very Westernised concept of that – you're either hyper-masculine or hyper-feminine, and the way that is enacted in Muslim spaces is, I find, really alarming. So, erm, it feels very much like this gender constructs that have moved very far away from the way in which we are supposed to think about, erm, gender and sexuality, erm, within Islam. I feel like this in the way that I think that, erm, sort of with the advent of European colonialism – till this point we are still under a process of colonisation and thinking of gender as a colonial project and the way in which our people at that point were subjected to gender norms that were alien to our communities and came from Europe.' (Juweriyah)

As a young Muslim woman living in the UK, Maha associates formal equality with Western society. Equality between men and women is complicated by her religious beliefs, and a tension exists between formal equality and her minoritised faith. As a normative indicator of the good society that shapes organising principles (Cooper, 2004), gender equality dictates that men and women be treated equally. However, there is less consideration given to how gender and equality are constructed. Juweriyah is alarmed by the way gender norms she views as alien to her community are enacted in Muslim spaces. Gender is a colonial project for her, and this then influences the wider framework around gender equality and its place in the good society project. This also affects equality in marriage which is rooted in Western and Christian monogamy as a champion of formal equality between spouses. Islamic polygyny cannot meet the 'equality as sameness' standards that govern gender and marriage equality.

Maha's description of motherhood provides another example of how equality in Islam is incompatible with mainstream formal equality. In

Islam, being a mother is valued far more highly than fatherhood because in general women do more physically in terms of pregnancy and childbirth. To Muslims, God accounts for this and the privilege of that spiritual reward is never available to men. However, we need to note that Maha's critique of equality fits with her world view and religious beliefs, which uphold a certain perspective on the roles and bodies of men and women displaying the patriarchal attitudes that can still present in relation to equality in Islam.

At another point in our conversation, Juweriyah stated:

> 'I think the issue of gender needs to be unpacked a lot more than it is, and it's not a simple fact of, the thing that's often kind of said over and over, Islam gave women rights, but it's a lot more complicated than that. And it's also not good enough to say that, well, Islam came and gave women rights, because how does that look in real life right now in terms of how you are treating women? It's often used to gloss over the fact that women are treated in really appalling ways. And I don't just mean in terms of physical violence or any sort of violence. I just mean in terms of interactions with women.' (Juweriyah)

These remarks offer an important insight into how a lot of the rhetoric around Muslim women's rights and position can fail to reflect their lived realities. So it is important to recognise the Christian imperialist basis for equality and gender, but also the role of patriarchy in how equality plays out in all contexts regardless of what the religious or wider social guidance says about the treatment of women. We can similarly make these arguments around situations outside of Islam and marriage – women still experience mistreatment, oppression and discrimination even though there are enshrined commitments to preventing this in law and policy.

Thinking more about polygamy in Islam, earlier in the chapter I explained that the Qur'an states that a husband must treat his wives in a just manner which indicates the need for equality and fairness. Muslims believe that they are judged according to their intentions and having good intentions can build trust in a polygynous situation. This is seen in Noreen's thoughts about her fiancé's panic about their marriage:

> 'I have more faith in him because of the way that the situation is and the way that he's already panicking that he wants to make sure that he does it justly and everything.' (Noreen)

Even so, there is no real guarantee of wives being treated with justice. Although Noreen's fiancé indicated his sincere intentions to practise polygyny in an acceptable way, in the end the only way to guarantee this is for all parties to be God-fearing and care about the spiritual consequences

(Jawad, 1998: 49). The religion therefore only expects a husband to strive for equality in their treatment of their wives because it is unrealistic to expect more. Women are greatly respected in Islam but treated differently to men because of their social function as explained by Maha earlier. Men are supposed to treat women well and justly, but patriarchal power structures mean that women are by default in a subjugated position. Therefore, it is down to individual men whether they treat women with justice, equality and fairness. Noreen has no guarantee that her fiancé will treat her correctly, but she is hopeful.

This complicates the blanket argument that polygamy promotes gender inequality and should therefore be rejected. Through this argument, it is implied that gender equality and the better treatment of women have been accomplished for women and wives who live in accordance with the norms of the mainstream (Western) society. This false standard of equality is imposed on minoritised women, but it also diminishes the ongoing struggle for women and monogamous wives. For example, monogamous wives in the West suffered inequalities and deprivations in marriage for centuries through the legal doctrine of coverture where a woman's legal personhood was absorbed into her husband's and she was not allowed to own property or enter a contract under her own name while married (Conaghan, 2013). It was down to the individual husband to treat his wife with justice and fairness. With time, the law became stronger at enforcing women's protections through financial remedies which eroded the power structures and coverture. While this has not completely eradicated the potential for unfair and unequal treatment of monogamous wives, legal regulation gives them relief to offset the structural power issues of marriage. We therefore see how inequality is visible in monogamy and that the law attempts to compensate, but the same nuance is not applied to polygamy. This approach to equality prevents a more realistic and progressive engagement with polygamy and the range of experiences that women have within it. I am not diminishing the importance or need for equality in relationships. Instead, I want to go beyond asking whether polygamy upholds gender equality, which is difficult to answer even for monogamy and relationships in general.

By broadening out our explorations of this relationship, the possibilities for understanding and unpacking a greater range of women's experiences increase. For example, Majeed (2015) has collected the only data on African American Islamic polygyny in a contemporary context where she spoke with polygynous husbands and wives. She identified three categories of polygyny in the community: coercion, choice and liberation. Polygyny by coercion was reflected in many of the stories that women told me. For instance, with Jamilah, there was no prior consultation or understanding that her husband would marry again. Polygyny was done to these women. In this context, some, like Jamilah, leave while others remain in the marriage because they feel they have to. This is the type of experience that the law pictures when refusing recognition for polygamy. It is polygyny by choice when women seek polygyny or choose to remain married to their husbands after they marry again. Noreen, as described in Chapter 5, is mostly aligned with this category: she did not seek polygyny as a structure but chose to accept it because of her feelings for a married man. There is some potential for a woman to be helpless even when she chooses polygyny. This might be due to the wider social attitudes towards divorce and single parenthood, that Noreen experienced. These categories are not watertight, reinforcing how complex lived experiences can be. The final category is polygyny of liberation. Here,

> husbands and wives are overwhelmingly content with their experiences and view multiple-wife marriage as a mutually beneficial family affair. Wives describe polygyny as a blessing [and] may seek other wives for their husbands. … Women who live polygyny of liberation do not have stress or jealousy-free marriages, and they may at times consider divorce. But in the end, these women view multiple-wife marriage as a conscious choice that they freely accept. Some assert, as did a woman in Atlanta, that their husbands are not 'right' unless they have multiple wives. (Majeed, 2015: 38)

Majeed's work shows there is a range of experiences we may be missing out on in the UK context. Dismissing polygamy because it is unequal obscures women's voices and ends the discussion before disruptive and counter-narratives like those of polygyny of liberation can be heard. This colonialist approach which cuts the story short needs to be challenged so that we can move to a more progressive engagement with polygamy in women's lives.

Is agency the answer?

I end this chapter by considering whether we have been looking in the wrong place all along in this discussion. Instead of only engaging with the debates around polygyny as a harm and unequal, should we instead be thinking about women's lived experiences in the context of their agency? Campbell who spent time with a Mormon polygynous community in Canada argues that we should not be looking for gender equality in this type of marriage: 'The claim … is not that polygamous life offers full gender equality and parity. Rather, it is that state laws fail to identify and account accurately for the sources of women's authority and command within their familial and cultural settings' (2013: 82). Campbell may be excluding the possibility of polygyny that gives parties equality, but in doing so, she also says that the law is not accounting for women's authority and command. The limiting factor for equality in this small religious community remains the patriarchy. Power relations have become restricted and institutionalised around marriage leading to women's subordination. It is likely that the level of female subordination in this context would be similarly visible even if monogamy was being practised.

Campbell's point around wives' authority and command points us in an interesting direction around choice. In thinking about legal responses to polygyny, we spend a lot of time focussing on marriage equality, while less attention is devoted to religious and marriage-based agency. This is because 'a powerful social narrative presumes [polygynous wives] consent to [being] coerced or to be the product of false consciousness' (Johnson, 2014: 110–11), so they are thought to lack the agency to freely choose such a relationship. We have seen that marriage and polygamy are heavily intertwined with religion and the scholarship looking at the politics of piety explores women's agency as part of their religious observance. Agency is rooted in the old Protestant doctrine of individual responsibility and its liberal nature has generally excluded women and the minoritised. It is concerned with the relationship between the individual and the system through the individual's capacity to act against, or independently of, structural constraints (Mack, 2003; Bilge, 2010).

Based on her time with women in the Egyptian Islamist movement, Mahmood (2005) contests this definition, as it creates a dichotomy in which women are either subordinated or are resisting (and therefore exercising their agency). The conventional view of agency excludes forms that do not fit within this subordination/resistance binary, but Mahmood posits that we should leave the meaning of agency open, seeing it as a 'product of the historically contingent discursive traditions' in which women are located (2005: 32). This makes space for modalities of agency that are not fully captured by resistance or subversion, or those that entail acting or disrupting within oppressive structures like the patriarchy and not completely submitting to them. Mahmood looks at this while exploring women's piety and religious practices. At first glance, the women she spent time with conformed to patriarchal traditions without objection because of their desire to develop their piety, but does this mean that they lack agency? The argument being made here is that we cannot recognise choices as agentic only when they conform to the Western secular liberal values that underpin original theories of agency (Bilge, 2010). There are cases where women's choices are not readily understood within this framing and polygyny is one practice where this applies. Mahmood carefully explains the importance of not giving in to 'culturalist arguments that seem to authorize practices that underwrite women's oppression' (2005: 195). She instead suggests a way of

> encountering the Other which does not assume that in the process of culturally translating other lifeworlds one's own certainty about how the world should proceed can remain stable. This attitude requires the virtue of humility: a sense that one does not always know what one opposes and that a political vision at times has to admit its own finitude in order to even comprehend what it has sought to oppose. (Mahmood, 2005: 199)

To decide that polygyny is harmful and unequal and should be rejected without further examination comes from a particular story told about it (Johnson, 2014). The insights provided by critiques of gender equality, the way that the law accounts for monogamous wives' agency by offsetting their subordination in marriage through relief and remedies, and the lack of an expansive view of agency for polygynous wives tell us that there are more stories to be told here. We should not be dismissing gender equality and supporting the behaviour of those that use polygamy as a harm. These ideas around promoting equality and preventing harm need to be disrupted because of their normative potential to facilitate minoritised women's oppression. The law and its dominant narrative around polygamy hide behind the ideal of equality without accounting for the lived realities of monogamous and polygynous wives. Gender equality has not been fully realised, but legal responses to polygamous marriage are shaped around the false narrative that it has. Moreover, this approach ignores the breadth of women's capacity for action and choices in their relationships and family structures to advance their command and authority. If we want to better understand married women's experiences in this context, it would be beneficial to decentre formal gender equality and start to think about other approaches we can use to improve legal understandings and responses to women's choices and agency. We need to approach polygyny and polygynous wives' stories with humility, accepting that the dominant political vision of marriage is imperfect. It is a constantly evolving process which is a product of historically contingent discourses around where it is located along with those who engage in it.

Concluding thoughts

From being forced into marriage as a child bride to the sustained abuse she suffered throughout her marriage Jamilah's experiences were harrowing. In this chapter, I looked critically at the main charges that polygamy is harmful and unequal. On the surface, it is tempting to accept these claims, but looking a little deeper, we see that the picture is still complicated. As a relationship form, it is not clear enough that polygamy alone is the source of harm, and this led me to conclude that the blame lies with the patriarchy. Looking at the way power is organised and then manifests in real lives and relationships, polygamy is being used as a tool to hurt women. The arguments made about it are also possibly applicable to monogamy, but there is little acknowledgement of this. Monogamy attracts more latitude than polygamy, but this is a problem because it tells an oversimplistic story of marriage. When we blame polygamy as the root of the problem, the awful behaviour of individuals and the structures that facilitate this are being obscured – it is polygamy that is at fault, not the abusers or the systems. The amplification of harms suffered by polygamous wives over those experienced by monogamous wives is due to the dominant political vision that polygamy should not be permitted rather than because of well-supported and balanced critique.

Equality is another concept that is relied on heavily to prohibit polygamy, but the formal equality in law was challenged by the women in this project on the basis that it fails to address them and their lives. Gender equality is an important ideal but when it is framed in terms of formal equality, this perpetuates the simple story that one plus one makes for an equal marriage when this is not guaranteed. Applying a framework of equality as power, I showed that gender equality can also be deployed as a normative component of the patriarchy that shuts out polygynous wives and their choices. I finish with the call for us to take a more sensitive and humble approach to marriage. One that accepts polygamy is not going to disappear any time soon and makes space for multilayered, shifting narratives. One that sees women as agentic and does more to locate their experiences beyond the pursuit of harm and equality. The law opposes polygamy but does not truly know (or care to know) what it is opposing, which is why women's disruptive lived experiences and attitudes are so important. Just because we do not understand or relate to another person's choice, that does not mean we should dismiss it out of hand. Instead, we should try to understand what that choice looks like as part of an everyday lived reality.

7

Religion, Recognition and Marriage Law

Karimah

I came to the UK for marriage on a fiancée visa, and we got married on the same day in Islamic marriage ceremony. The marriage was arranged by my parents, especially my father. He trusted these people – they were from same community in Pakistan and my parents met them. I didn't meet the guy, I didn't see him, I didn't talk to him – just a few messages. So I came over here and I had a few things in the back of my mind, but I kept ignoring them. That was because my parents found out before the marriage that he has a daughter from his previous relationship. When I found out, I found that hard to accept, because I thought 'I didn't do anything wrong so why do I deserve such a person?' My husband talked to my dad all the time. And he said, 'you know, I'm very guilty.' So my dad thought that he's going to respect me even more because I'm willing to ignore this thing. My dad cried in front of me and said, 'don't say no.' He's suffered with depression before because of my sister's divorce.

My family were also concerned because I had a childhood engagement with my cousin. He was super happy, but then he went to Canada and liked someone and he said, 'I fell in love with someone.' That time I was a really simple, shy person – I didn't talk to him and he said, 'because you didn't talk to me, I went to someone else'. In our culture, if you get married and you're good age, you're respectful … if you're not, they might be thinking there's something wrong in your personality, but this doesn't have to do anything with religion.

So I came here, but the marriage didn't work from day one. I was just shocked. He left me at his parents' house and he went to his own house. Sometimes, he would pick me up, and sometimes he would leave me in his parents' house. He would say: 'I'm the eldest son, you're the eldest daughter-in-law – you have to do everything. You have to keep my parents happy. I have only one sister – she's my princess. I have only one daughter – she's my everything. My mother is my queen.' So I was trying really hard, but within like eight or nine weeks I couldn't make it work. And when he said he was going to hurt me physically … I respect myself, I was like 'no'. He was forced into this marriage, because he liked someone else in the past and because his dad was strict and his mother suffered all of her life. I wasn't allowed to talk to my parents alone, and they wouldn't say there was any issue but they would say that 'oh, she's busy with this and that' – I couldn't cry to them. I was not thinking about divorce or leaving the house because I am from the Pashto community in Pakistan and if you even think about leaving the house, everything would be finished: your parents might disown you.

When I was getting married, one of my friends said, 'if there's any problem, this is my sister-in-law, here is her address', and she called me one day and I said, 'I can't talk to you'. She understood and said, 'listen, if they hurt you in any way, just call 999'. I didn't know about 999. I didn't know the road name or anything outside. Then he started to leave the keys in his house, he knew that I didn't know anything outside and I didn't have any rights – I was only his fiancée and my visa was going to expire in October, and he didn't register the marriage and he kept saying: 'I'm not going to register the marriage. I'm not gonna get a stay for you if I'm not satisfied, because you don't seem happy.' And I was thinking 'it's because of you and your family.'

He was in another relationship when I was living there. There was something dodgy going on. He would be out at night with someone else, but I don't know if he was in another Islamic marriage or civil marriage. It couldn't have been a civil marriage, because that's always recognised. I would always try to think the best, but when I left, my in-laws mentioned it. They were like, 'oh, he was not going to that woman'.

When I left, I went outside, I opened the back kitchen door, and I climbed the fence. It was when he was sleeping in the morning. I called the police from outside and I was running on the roads and saying to them 'pick me up – he's going to find me'. I was thinking he's gonna wake up and he's going to look for me and grab me and then I will have no chance. I had nothing with me – just by chance, the visa I had kept hidden and a passport copy. I had no place to go – just to my friend's sister. And she asked me to leave after three days. I was on the road and a police officer he helped me. I was told: 'Your visa's going to expire. You need to sort your immigration problem out with the immigration people and the solicitor will come tomorrow.'

The next day, I spoke to the solicitor, and she said, 'this is your case and no one's going to ask you to leave.' I applied to the shari'a council for my divorce, and my husband came in the sixth or seventh month of the process. He lied, telling the council that I had stolen the gold bangles on my hand, that I had received as a wedding gift. He also said that it was a condition of our Nikah that he would sign the divorce papers only if I left the UK. I didn't know the maulvi who performed our Nikah or where the mosque was, but I had a video that my parents had saved from WhatsApp, so my uncle's friend found the maulvi and I got a copy of the Nikah certificate. The council's shaykh asked about the condition, and as soon as I showed them the certificate and that the condition was not there, they found out the truth. My husband couldn't look at me – he didn't make eye contact. At first, I didn't want to see him, but the shari'a council assistant inside said, 'if you don't come, they won't help you so much, because they don't know who is on the true.' He didn't sign the divorce, but after that final meeting, the shari'a court granted it.

My parents thought my in-laws were good people – that they would do whatever they do for their family, and civil marriage was expected so we didn't ask for it. They asked to do the Islamic marriage here, and we didn't realise that this was their pre-plan. I suffered with this thing: English marriage, English marriage, you're not married. I was married! So, it wasn't English marriage. You're only allowed one and he had this plan that he would only register one English marriage with a person he's happy. So he misused that need for civil marriage. Here you do Islamic marriage and then you don't have recognised. Now we're asking for permission from the upper tribunal, and we are going to challenge their policy on domestic violence. I'm saying that I was married to a British person – they didn't register the marriage purposely, because he had all these plans to legally marry someone else, and he said this to me. He said, 'look, I married to you because of my parents, and I can get second marriage easily.' They have accepted that I am a victim, and the problem is with the policy.

Now my family's priority is my protection, because they got threats from this family. They saw me going through all this by myself, and I didn't ask anyone for help. When I left, I contacted my parents and I said, 'don't tell anyone where I am, what I'm doing, anything', and they're all asking 'oh, where is she?' I didn't let them interfere, because I have seen in my community that if a woman suffers, they don't take a stand. And if they take a stand, they will be bullied, abused and told to go back to their husband's house and told: 'Try! How can you make a decision within two or three months?' Even if they do that for five years, they will be told: 'It's just five years. Try for ten more years.' My point was I am not their slave. I am not a slave of the community.

I met Karimah in a shelter for homeless Muslim women after she had staged a scary and daring escape from her husband's house. From her story, I draw out some important themes around marriage and recognition. Karimah's situation displays the consequences of the law's indifference to non-legally binding marriages[1] discussed in Chapter 3. She was vulnerable during and after her marriage because it was not legally binding meaning that in English law she was seen as a cohabitant rather than recognised as a wife. Her entry into the UK on a fiancée visa was used against her by her husband and when she spoke with me, she was fighting to secure her stay in the country as a spouse who had suffered domestic violence. This immigration battle was happening amid her family being threatened by her ex-husband's family because of her escape. If she returned to her family, it is possible that she would have been endangering herself and them. Clearly, being denied legal recognition for her marriage made her more vulnerable to harm during and after her marriage. Ironically, if Karimah's ceremony had taken place in Pakistan rather than in a mosque in the UK, it would have been recognised in the English courts. However, if its polygamous nature had been confirmed, she would have then been stopped from entering the country on the fiancée visa in the first place. From this, we see the practical consequences of being denied legal recognition for your marriage; these consequences can take the form of safeguards or restrictions according to the structure of the marriage. The negative effects of being without legal recognition have been highlighted in existing scholarship as 'paradigm cases': a wife in a non-legally binding marriage is disadvantaged and left homeless and penniless once her relationship breaks down, and she has no access to judicial remedies (Akhtar, 2018a). These cases have attracted attention in politics, the media and legal practice because they promote the image of the oppressed Brown woman in need of saving (Akhtar, 2018a, 2018b).

In this chapter, I explore the different opinions and experiences of legal recognition for marriage to think about whether it would be desirable for people to be able to enter into a legally binding polygamous marriage in England and Wales. I asked the women who spoke with me whether they saw marriage as a legal institution; whether there were any benefits or disadvantages to marriage when viewed as a legal institution; whether they thought polygamy should be legally recognised in the UK; and whether they would change anything about the current English law on marriage. I start with their answers to the question of whether polygamy should be legally recognised. Views range from wanting to maintain the current situation to wanting polygamy to be recognised as a way to gain tolerance

[1] As mentioned in Chapter 3, Probert et al (2022) argue that this is the best way to describe marriages that have previously been called 'non-marriages', 'unregistered marriages', 'religious-only marriages' or 'non-qualifying ceremonies'. Where I use the terms 'non-legally binding' or 'non-legally recognised', it is with reference to English law only. This description has its limitations, not least because a marriage that is not legally binding in English law may still be legally binding according to another system overseas or in Shari'a, which is an equally legitimate legal system.

and protection. After delving into these attitudes, I argue that recognition is viewed uncritically and its positive implications are taken as a given. This needs to be unpacked further. In existing literature, recognition is viewed broadly as a vital way to achieve social justice and equality, but what does this mean? Karimah's physical and material situation would have been improved by having legal recognition but there are additional consequences to recognition beyond accessing economic and material resources. For example, when Karimah spoke of being "respectful" if you get married, she showed that recognition also has social consequences. Both practical and social consequences of marriage recognition were present in other women's narratives. For some, without recognition there is a risk that the relationship will be dismissed as inferior because it does not conform to mainstream ideals leading to their lives being severely affected. I therefore argue that any conception of recognition must take these broader effects on women's experiences into account. The wider implications and significance of legal recognition for women need to be included in any discussion on this area.

Until now, I have talked about how a lack of legal recognition for polygamous wives can be harmful, but what do we mean by recognition? And it is really desirable for them? Like the marriage equality mission, the pursuit of legal recognition for minoritised groups has a dark past. When examining a practice like polygamy which is subjected to racist and imperialist attitudes, we need to make sure that we have this historical context in mind. I explore the politics of recognition to argue that marital legal recognition in its current form is not the best way to serve the needs of polygamous wives. Picking up the threads on religious agency that I introduced in the previous chapter, I show multiple instances where women who are not paradigm cases exercise their agency to disrupt legal recognition and reject it. In doing so, they open up and inhabit a third space to reimagine legal recognition in a way which is meaningful for them thereby operationalising a disruptive politics of recognition.

How do these disruptive stories solve Karimah's problems? I argue that recognition in law is not desirable for everyone. Ideally it needs to be fundamentally reconfigured to unpick the harmful attitudes towards non-normative marriages; but it could still provide some remedies for women in Karimah's position. I conclude the chapter by thinking about the different options for reform. Even though a review of weddings law in England and Wales has recently concluded, this has not created an opportunity to carry out a sweeping re-evaluation of marital legal recognition (Law Commission, 2022). At this time, the best we can aim for is recognition for non-legally binding marriages for those in need of it, decided on a case-by-case basis. This offers support for women like Karimah while ensuring that women who do not want their marriage recognised in mainstream law can continue to be disruptive and create their own third space.

Attitudes to legal recognition for polygamous marriages

To set the scene for my deeper discussion of legal recognition today, I start by considering the various attitudes towards legal recognition for polygamous marriage. The women I spoke with expressed attitudes that were both for and against recognition but motivations differed. Some opinions were quite strongly against recognition. For example:

> 'I think that's right [that polygamy is not legally recognised] … it's fair, it's more civilised.' (Daisy)

Here, Daisy appears to oppose not just recognition, but also the existence of polygamy. Her use of the word "civilised" suggests she was concerned with the ideological foundations for polygamy. I showed in Chapter 2 how the imperialist civilising mission imposed Christian monogamous ideals of domesticity on colonised peoples to 'save them'. Daisy is reproducing the imperialist civilising narrative of marriage which does not allow for the view that polygamy should be given legal recognition. Daisy further states that polygamy not being formally recognised in English law is fair. It is not clear whether she is saying that polygamy is unfair or that it would be unfair to recognise it, but both interpretations reflect how ingrained the arguments around equality are in attitudes and responses to this relationship form. I addressed this claim in more detail in Chapter 6, but Daisy's statement shows how persuaded people are by the claims of inequality such that there is an uncritical acceptance of it.

As we have seen in earlier chapters these troubling narratives are present in legal and scholarly attitudes towards Muslim marriages whether they are monogamous or polygamous in practice. For instance, Nash (2017) asserts that Muslim marriages are problematic because of their informal structure and supposed predisposal towards inbreeding since cousin marriages are permitted in Islam. Informal and cousin marriages are not unique to Islam. Cousin marriages were legalised in England in the Marriage Act 1540 to facilitate Henry VIII's marriage to Catherine Howard, who was the first cousin of his former wife Anne Boleyn. First cousin marriage has been legally permitted since (Wiebracht, 2015). We therefore need look no further than the British monarchy for examples of cousin marriage and informal ceremonies being performed in a back garden,[2] but the blatant

[2] I talk here of the recent revelation that three days before their 'official' ceremony, (then) Prince Harry and Meghan Markle had a private marriage ceremony in their back garden which was not legally valid.

orientalism displayed when others do it shows the unlevel playing field when it comes to minoritised marriage practices in England and Wales. The roots of people's rejection of a marriage form that has been practised for millennia need to be considered.

In another spin on things staying the same, some of the Muslim women that spoke with me did not expect polygamy to be recognised in English law.

> 'Erm, for me, we're not living in an Islamic country so I don't expect the UK to recognise polygamy. If they did, it would be their goodwill, and I think that a lot of Muslims have forgotten that we don't live in an Islamic country, so, erm, you know, the fact that … I work in a [public institution] and we have a really beautiful prayer room, but it's not the [public institution]'s duty to provide a prayer room for us, you know. Like a university, they have a proper ablution area and they're a secular university. It's not really their duty to provide that, and they do so because there are a lot of Muslims there … I don't particularly expect the country that we're living in to recognise polygamous marriages if they don't want to … I think that if they did recognise polygamous marriages, it would be good for us, but I don't think Muslims should expect it, because we are not living in a country where our religion is making up a huge population … I think we make up less than 5 per cent of the population. I wouldn't expect this country to recognise polygamous marriage … in the same way that they wouldn't recognise a shari'a court, for example, either, or a Nikah as a legal marriage.' (Maha)

> 'We don't have Shari'a law in this country so I can understand why it's not part of the UK law right now … being in a Christian, what is it, country, it makes sense that it's not part of the UK law.' (Imaan)

These were Maha's and Imaan's responses when I asked if they thought polygamous marriages should be legally recognised in the UK. They make some interesting observations. First, because the UK is not an Islamic state, there are no expectations of recognition. Although I did not specify that I was asking about Islamic polygynous marriages, they speak from their own context by limiting their concern to Muslims and their private lives. Maha explains her stance by stating that "a lot of Muslims have forgotten that we don't live in an Islamic country". Her lack of expectations is also displayed when she talks about a "secular university" providing a prayer room for Muslims despite not being duty-bound to do so. In Maha's opinion, her religion and religious practice fall outside state interest and recognition because of secularism, which refers to the formal removal of religion from state governance. She is absorbing and narrating the impact of the dominant culture in the UK on public and legal responses to her religion and marital practices. The 'removal' of religion from public life has caused religious-minority adherents like Maha to dismiss the idea of recognition for their marriages. For Imaan, the lack of legal recognition for polygamous marriages is explained by the UK being a Christian country. She identifies the UK in religious terms, and though she does not refer to secularism the way Maha does, the sentiment is the same.[3]

That these women separate their religious beliefs and practices from the Christian and secularised state could mean one of two things: they have either internalised the orientalist mainstream discourses which are also presented in the law that alienate and marginalise them; or they are manifesting the principles under the Siyar[4] which require obedience to state law (An-Na'im, 2010; Rehman, 2015; Ali, 2016). Muslims living in a non-Muslim majority state must follow the law of the land as long as they continue to fulfil their personal religious obligations (Abdalla, 2012). It is possible that Maha and Imaan are sharing an example of how by living according to the Siyar, they accept that polygamy is not recognised in English law, rather than expecting their minoritised faith to be accommodated by the state. There is still an undertone in these excerpts that the situation is unlikely to change because recognition for polygamy is an orientalist 'us versus them' problem. The state and law that these women live within is not geared towards seeing polygamy in any other way, which is why it is not surprising there is no recognition and no expectation this will change.

For the views in favour of recognition, there are two main motivations: respect for individual choices and protection of women. Respecting individual choices is the more liberal-based perspective that people have the freedom to engage in behaviours which do not directly harm or affect others. This aligns with other recognition struggles, such as the ones for same-sex marriage and civil partnerships. As Lauren shared:

> 'Personally, because I would hope that by the time I get to the point of marrying someone, I would feel confident enough that they only wanna marry me and that wouldn't change … so I think why not? Because to me it would be like saying divorce can't be legally recognised … because I might get married and then they might divorce me, so it's got that it might not last or something. Yeah – it should be a choice and I don't think it's right that the law doesn't recognise something that is recognised in other parts of the world when we profess that we're this

3 Secularism is itself a complex concept that has been the subject of a lot of discussion for its role as the seeming opposite of religion. For further discussion, see Easat-Daas (2020).

4 This refers to aspects of Shari'a (the legal system that Muslims follow) that regulate the conduct of states towards each other – also known as the Islamic law of nations.

> multicultural society that welcomes everybody in and respects their ways of life.' (Lauren)

Accepting recognition for polygamy does not take away her desire to be monogamous, and it should not affect her marriage either. Lauren does not think that recognition should hinge on fears about what will happen to a society where monogamy is the norm. Polygamy is not for her personally, but it is unlikely to endanger her monogamous relationship. This is a counterbalance to arguments that have been made previously against marriage equality movements for both same-sex marriage and polygamy. There is an anxiety about same-sex marriage paving the way for further 'inappropriate' forms of marriage (Chambers, 1997). These relationships are a threat because they are different. Some feel that marriage will change for them if polygamy is included in mainstream understandings of marriage. For Lauren, this is similar to avoiding marriage because you are afraid of divorce. Different forms of relationship, whether traditional or minoritised, are a choice – making these choices available for legal recognition does not take anything away from marriage but rather adds to it.

Many of the women were in favour of recognition because of the protections that it can provide. This emphasises the practical consequences of being married:

> 'I think that, erm, perhaps the recognition of Islamic marriages, so not having to … cos I think I have heard of so many instances where women have been really hard done by because, er, especially women who are not from here but marry someone who is from here and they just do the Nikah and then are treated really badly and divorced and left with nothing. I think that if that Nikah was recognised by the English courts, then that would afford her some rights to her husband's assets if, erm, and sort of wouldn't leave her destitute. I've certainly heard of so many cases like that, erm, so yeah I think the recognition of the Nikah by the law.' (Juweriyah)

As a charity worker, Juweriyah saw many cases where women in religious-only marriages, both polygamous and monogamous, suffered due to lack of legal recognition for their relationships. The scenario she narrates is a paradigm case like Karimah's. Under the Home Office's (2017) immigration rules, a victim of domestic violence can only apply for indefinite leave to remain in the country if they were a partner other than a fiancée or a proposed civil partner of a British citizen settled in the UK. This rule is curiously framed: it allows a person to claim leave to remain if they were not engaged to their partner. This means that a person who entered the country specifically to get married cannot claim leave after domestic abuse;

but if they came to the UK through another route, they can. Such a rule disproportionately affects women like Karimah, who enter the country on a fiancée visa. If Karimah had been legally recognised as a wife or had entered the country on a different visa, she would have been able to claim indefinite leave to remain under this rule. For paradigm cases, legal recognition could mitigate these kinds of disadvantages, but it is not the only experience of women in religious-only marriages. For this reason, we need to think more critically about whether recognition is always a positive thing.

Why is recognition so important? Practical and social consequences

At its core, the process of being legally married is about recognition. Women's attitudes give us an idea of what people think about polygamy in English law. And across these views, recognition emerges as a good thing that should not be awarded and withheld according to whether something is worthy. Recognition and its positive consequences have been touted as an important part of equality struggles, but what does this mean? And what can it lead to? Recognition has emerged as a standard by which to assess, understand and acknowledge individuals and groups, mainly through the lens of difference (Balaton-Chrimes and Stead, 2017). This means that contemporary social justice movements are concerned with whether and how our differences from the mainstream majority are seen and then responded to (that is, recognised) by state processes and institutions. This is identity politics or the demand of disadvantaged groups for recognition of their group identity, which simultaneously challenges the dominant social and cultural patterns of representation that lead to their marginalisation in the first place (Borren, 2013). The idea is to be seen and valued because of differences rather than in spite of them.

Traditionally, recognition has been tied to questions around identity (Hines, 2013). For example, Taylor argues that

> our identity is partly shaped by recognition or its absence, often by the misrecognition of others, and so a person or group of people can suffer real damage, real distortion, if the people or society around them mirror back to them a confining or demeaning or contemptible picture of themselves. Nonrecognition or misrecognition can inflict harm, can be a form of oppression, imprisoning someone in a false, distorted, and reduced mode of being. (1994: 25)

Recognition is framed here as a way for us to be seen and understood. It is interpreted as vital to our identity and sense of self, with severe consequences when it is denied to us. Therefore, the 'need for recognition is pre-rational;

humans are driven not by self-interest but by the desire for understanding and reciprocity' (Hines, 2013: 10). When a marriage is legally recognised, it provides a public status – the status of being married. As we see with Karimah's situation, there are practical implications or safeguards to having this public status. In another example:

> 'I can't remember what I was applying, for but my Nikah is not legally viewed as a marriage as I am not legally viewed as married in this country. But that's the same as Hindu going to a temple and having their marriage there … that's not legally married.' (Maha)

Though in a non-legally binding Muslim marriage, Maha is not explicitly impacted by her lack of legal marital status. She described her factual situation and demonstrated her awareness that other minoritised religious marriages are also potentially not recognised. However, there are processes of non- and mis-recognition at play here. When Maha was applying for something which required her to disclose her marital status, this triggered a reflection on her mainstream recognition as a wife. Under Taylor's (1994) interpretation, she is actively non-recognised because her marriage is not included under legal perceptions of marriage, and she is passively mis-recognised as being unmarried. We do not know what Maha was applying for – the fact she cannot remember herself is also telling about the importance of this public status to her – but it could have been something official or public. When we apply for something like a degree programme, a job or a passport, we are being asked to express our identity within the parameters set by the formal application. Maha had to declare her marital status, but *her* recognition and understanding of marriage did not match what the official application was supposedly willing to recognise. Interestingly, she uses the phrase "I am not legally viewed as married *in this country*" [emphasis added]. To her, the non- and mis-recognition that she is being subjected to are a result of the state's limited view of marriage; the problem is not her marriage which would be recognised outside of the UK.

In some approaches to recognition, the focus is on redistributing resources which is where the practical implications are most visible. For example, the redistribution approach offered by Fraser (1998) talks of recognition as a marker of justice which is enabled when economic resources are redistributed. Social class and economic inequality are what we need to tackle to achieve recognition and therefore justice. By addressing these, we look mainly at the practical benefits to legal marriage recognition. However, recognition cannot really be achieved by simply redistributing economic resources; focussing on the economic means that the cultural and social aspects around identity and difference are sidelined (Young, 1997). In the case of marriage recognition, the material/cultural divide does not exist.

We cannot separate the economic disadvantages from the lack of social and cultural opportunities that women suffer without legal marriage recognition.

The redistribution perspective on recognition has since been interpreted more widely so that social justice is now the 'morally proper distribution of social benefits and burdens among society's members' (Young, 1990: 16). Through this, the politics of recognition has developed as a framework to make sense of identity and difference at the heart of contemporary social struggles. As Busbridge (2018) notes, we become who we are through our relations with others and our larger communities. These relations set out moral expectations and conceptions of the good life. Marriage forms part of these moral expectations and conceptions because it says certain things about who we are and how we live our lives that go beyond the practical advantages. This can only be understood when we take a more expansive view of what recognition is and how we achieve it. Some women shared examples of the social-related functions for mainstream marriage recognition that show how prevalent these considerations are. For example:

> 'I think the reason I would want to get married was maybe more of a social thing. I just quite like the idea of … showing everybody that you're married and you're committed to each other, so you've taken that step. And I quite like the idea of being someone's wife and having a husband.' (Lauren)

Here, marriage is desirable because it is a public display of commitment, and the ceremony is the public declaration of a personal and intimate relationship. Public recognition provides the label and status of being a wife, which then feeds into the individual personally liking the idea of "being someone's wife and having a husband". As a White woman from a Catholic background, Lauren's legal and public recognition as a wife are relatively guaranteed because her identity and personal belief conform to the mononormative ideals that underpin English legal marriage.[5] As a Catholic, her marriage would be required to follow the same procedure as other non-Anglican religions in law,[6] but based on recent figures, it is unlikely that the Catholic Church would struggle to meet the requirements for a valid marriage

[5] By mononormative, I mean a relationship which conforms to mainstream normative ideals based on its monogamous structure. See Ritchie and Barker (2006).

[6] Interestingly, Catholic marriage ceremonies fall under the same category as all "other religions". While Jewish, Quaker and Anglican marriages have their own procedures with fewer steps to achieve a legally binding ceremony, a Catholic ceremony needs to go through the same steps as most minoritised communities. See further Law Commission, 2015a: 30 for a clear infographic which explains the different routes to legally binding marriage in England and Wales.

ceremony. The Law Commission (2015a) found that 22,071 non-Anglican Christian places of worship were registered to solemnise legal opposite-sex marriages in 2015, which can be contrasted against only 270 Muslim places of worship.

For women whose marriages do not fit within the Christian ideal, the social-related functions of marriage recognition are not as easily obtained:

> 'I would like it … if I had the chance, I would be registered, just because it's nice for your marriage to be recognised everywhere. A Nikah is not really recognised in the UK unless you register it, so technically in the eyes of the law, if they haven't registered it, they're not married, which is a sad thing to do. Well, it's not sad, it's just kind of like "oh, OK" kind of thing. For me, it doesn't make a difference, but it doesn't really make me happy either.' (Noreen)

Noreen's forthcoming Muslim marriage was denied legal recognition because it involved an Islamic ceremony and was polygynous in nature. Her personal reflection is more emotive than Maha's: it may not be bad for her, but it does not really make her happy since it is nice for your marriage to be seen and recognised everywhere. She demonstrates again that there is nonrecognition with her "technically" not being married, and mis-recognition with her being seen as unmarried.

At another point in our conversation, Noreen shared the view that denying legal recognition for Islamic polygamous marriages had broader impacts on the faith-based community it is practised within:

> 'I think it's kind of unfair to, you know, just because a law says so, to stop religion, to stop it from being you know, a religion being able to be itself, if that makes sense. I think it's a bit unfair.' (Noreen)

Noreen makes an interesting observation about the role of the law towards minoritised religions and religious marriages. There is a prescriptive and almost controlling dynamic which is disproportionately experienced for minoritised religions and religious practices that fall outside of the state's ideal for how communities should live and marry. By expecting conformity within the existing legal framework, the law is preventing the religion from "being able to be itself". In this way, the religion and its followers are not necessarily able to be themselves or realise their beliefs while accessing the rights and privileges of being married that the majority enjoys. This represents the concern that by mis-recognising the religion and the marriages of its followers, the concerned religious community is not speaking for itself, but is being subjected to outsider interpretation and misrepresentation by the state (Grim, 1996). These kinds of distortions and mis-recognitions then shape the story told in history and law about that faith, its recommended form of marriage and its followers.

At a procedural level, the unfairness that Noreen described has been noted by the Law Commission while exploring how the three categories of Anglican marriage, Jewish and Quaker marriages, and marriages according to the rites of other religions attract different levels of legal regulation.

> The fact that different religious groups are subject to different levels of regulation can also be perceived as unfair. We have heard that some other religious groups wonder why Jews and Quakers alone have the scope to conduct a legally binding marriage in accordance with their own religious beliefs and wherever they wish it to take place (subject to the rules and requirements of those organisations). (Law Commission 2015a: para 2.90)

The Law Commission's assessment of 'perceived' unfairness is evidenced by the disadvantages that Noreen narrates – it does not make a practical difference to her, but it would be nice to be recognised as married everywhere. The social and cultural currency of marriage recognition and therefore being "respectful", as Karimah tells us in her story are what has led to marriage equality movements in the first place (see Chapter 6). These initial views are not surprising or novel, because if recognition is about being seen and therefore valued for our ways of life and being, it follows that there are positive and desirable attributes to marriage recognition. Along this vein, recognition is an innate good and when people are subjected to non- and mis-recognition, they suffer harm or oppression. However, there is a growing branch of literature which raises concerns about the centrality of recognition for achieving justice because traditional theories of recognition lack an account of power (Balaton-Chrimes and Stead, 2017). The view that recognition is the desired result for minoritised communities is being suggested without deeper consideration of what that recognition looks like or its use as a tool for assimilation.

It is not enough to take an expansive approach to legal recognition which encompasses the practical and social implications women narrated around marriage. We must also think about how the legal recognition of marriage in its current form is a regulatory process which has an institutional context, defined by Young as

> any structures or practices, the rules or norms that guide them, and the language and symbols that mediate social interactions within them, in institutions of state, family, and civil society, as well as the workplace. These are relevant to judgments of justice and injustice insofar as they condition people's ability to participate in determining their actions and their ability to develop and exercise their capacities. (1990: 22)

Recognition has not appeared out of nowhere, and we need to look critically at its construction as well as the systemic and structural factors that define it for marginalised groups and their marriages. A lot of time is spent on recognition as beneficial and aspirational because it is a marker of inclusion, but there has been less focus on how recognition can force people into a mainstream paradigm by conditioning people and their ability to participate. Recognition in its institutional role can force or coerce assimilation leaving little room for the differences which shaped the minoritised individual and their relationship in the first place. Recognition may be used by the state to demand that people conform, first by telling them that recognition is the best thing for them and then telling them that to achieve it, they have to become like everyone else (Hines, 2013).

To challenge these assimilationist strategies, scholars like Young (1990) have called for a politics in which recognition highlights and celebrates difference. Young (1990) centres the two social conditions of oppression and domination for conceptualising injustice and therefore framing the struggle for recognition. While oppression is defined as 'institutional constraint on self-development', domination is defined as 'institutional constraint on self-determination' (Young, 1990: 37). The institutional aspect of these two conditions indicates the importance of considering the structural and systemic factors which give rise to injustice. This could be helpful for women in non-legally binding and polygamous marriages to ensure their relationships are not subjected to non- and mis-recognition. The law provides the civil ceremony so that couples can have a legally recognised marital status outside of religion. However, this entails the performance of another ceremony, placing these women in the orientalised position of being told that their marriage ceremony is inferior because it fails to fulfil the legal formalities for marriage. It is possible to have a legally binding marriage solemnised at the same time as the religious ceremony provided it is conducted in a registered building in the presence of an authorised person and fulfils all the necessary formalities. So for example, if a Nikah ceremony is performed in a registered mosque in the presence of an authorised imam fulfilling all the legal requirements, it would be legally recognised without the need for a second ceremony. This option needs to be considered within the context of how and where Nikah ceremonies are performed, taking into consideration widespread community norms that include the at-home Nikah (Law Commission, 2015a). Moreover, to make the marriage valid in law, it still requires the parties, the imam and the mosque to take additional steps which are modelled on the Anglican Christian ceremony down to the words that need to be said by the parties. If the differences of the minoritised religious ceremony are highlighted and celebrated, it could be possible to target these issues but does this go far enough? To answer this question, we need to delve into some of the context that has been missing in our stories of recognition so far which will require us to do some disrupting.

Recognition: triumph or trial?

In the theories of recognition that emphasise redistributing resources or celebrating difference, it is implied that we work with the current framework. For redistribution, the simplified idea is that we take recognition and redistribute it among groups equally so that everyone has the same recognition. If we choose to celebrate difference, the aim is to challenge oppression and domination, by reworking the existing framework for recognition to account for the differences of those on the margins. However, there is a dark side to recognition and its use by the state against minoritised individuals and communities. Coulthard (2014) observes that a lot of existing literature looks at how recognition shapes state accommodation of cultural differences on one hand and the freedom and autonomy of marginalised people on the other. In Chapter 4, I spoke about how cultural difference has been the foundation for conflict of laws meaning the legitimacy of states and their laws turn on their cultural differences from European colonial ideals. This shows already how recognition may be implicated in the mission of marking out the marginalised based on how and whether the state should 'accommodate' or tolerate them. Critical scholars like Spivak (2003) and Bhabha (2003) are wary of the politics of recognition because it works to 'fix' cultural difference along the lines of Western thought and self/other relations. This all feeds into the assumption that the state's legal and political framework are legitimate and worthy of marginalised communities' respect in the first place. The recognition the state is offering them is portrayed as something worth having but we need to question whether this is true.

In the settler colonial context, where colonisers moved into a territory and settled down, these issues with the politics of recognition are more visible because we can ask what makes the settler state's claim to sovereignty over indigenous people valid in the first place (Coulthard, 2014). For an imperial centre like the UK, the relevance of this question seems less applicable since the state predates the British Empire, yet the lives and behaviour of colonised peoples at odds with colonial Western liberal thought are still being highlighted and othered through recognition (Balaton-Chrimes and Stead, 2017). In this conception of recognition, the state is always in the privileged position. Should minoritised people unquestioningly accept the judgements of the colonial state on their lives which then dictate whether they should be 'recognised'? Bhabha (2003) encourages us to consider whether recognition and the politics of recognition help to reproduce existing colonial power relations and shape the identities of minorities in the neocolonial state (see also Mookherjee, 2005). Once we ask this, we can think about recognition in the context of colonialism as a relation of domination which exists to deny equal dignity and esteem for the colonised where their nonrecognition is enmeshed with their cultural and social inferiority to the colonisers (Busbridge, 2018). The colonial state has a particular agenda: to push an ideal way of life and marriage because it is what they think is best. When minoritised people and their lifestyles are held up against this and then dismissed as unworthy of recognition, they are being told that their lives are not good enough. If they are fortunate enough to get that recognition, it is only because their rights and identities do not interfere with the state's authority and agenda (Coulthard, 2014). This echoes the civilising mission of imposing a particular template of life and behaviour on the colonised because they cannot decide what is best for themselves. The current legal and political system is designed around this narrative, and so is recognition along with more common interpretations of the politics of recognition. This has led to the charge that the politics of recognition does not sufficiently account for existing and dominant power relations (Coulthard, 2014). Recognition is defined and awarded on the state's terms, which then establishes and perpetuates the boundaries of the relationship between the state and the minoritised: it limits rather than opens up possibilities for this relationship (Hinkson, 2017). These more critical approaches are not against recognition itself or the cultural esteem that it can facilitate for the minoritised; rather, they argue that the politics of recognition is missing this crucial context and that the Western liberal version of recognition is not the perfect solution to injustice it is portrayed to be (Bhabha, 2003; Busbridge, 2018).

There are two things to take away here: first, recognition should not necessarily be at the heart of social justice struggles for marginalised communities; and second, obtaining recognition is not the end of that struggle. Scholars like Fanon (2008), who are even more critical of recognition argue that it causes an over-reliance and dependence on the oppressor to achieve self-worth and freedom. This means that we should see the exclusion faced by marginalised communities not in terms of injustice through a lack of recognition, but injustice through a lack of freedom (Borren, 2013). We should therefore be looking elsewhere for our freedom, and instead of celebrating difference or redistributing recognition, Fanon (2008) argues that we should be reconstructing the universal category of humanity to include the marginalised and excluded (see also Busbridge, 2018). It is not recognition that we need to rebuild, but our understanding of humanity itself, and this cannot be done by accepting the way recognition is framed in state processes and institutions. Recognition is not the end of the story; it can sometimes be the start of a new and greater struggle which I now explore in relation to marriage.

The dark side of marriage recognition

There is evidence that certain members of minoritised groups living in non-normative marriages wish to remain in an unrecognised relationship. There is a theme of anti-recognition sentiment in same-sex marriage and civil partnership debates as well as in the discussions on non-legally binding Muslim marriages (see for example, Harding, 2008; Akhtar, 2015). What does this tell us about legal marriage recognition in particular? More generally, Hines (2013) observes that recognition struggles often have a negative impact on the most marginalised members of a minoritised group because they are unable or unwilling to conform to the normalising strategies that are needed to achieve mainstream recognition (see also Young, 1990). These people are doubly marginalised: first by the dominant cultural majority and then by the majority within their own group who find it easier to conform. For example, it is much easier for a woman in a monogamous Muslim marriage to gain legal recognition for her relationship by undergoing an additional civil ceremony than it is for a polygynous wife whose co-wife is legally married to their husband. The use of formal legal recognition to improve the status of a minoritised group therefore hinges on conforming to the norms of the majority (Eskridge, 2001). Recognition is never accessible for everyone anyway.

Legal recognition for marriage is interesting because of the specific aims attached to it. Herring (2015) suggests that family law, including marriage law, is designed to support and promote *certain* forms of intimate life, protect individuals from abuse in their family lives, and remedy the advantages and disadvantages caused by being in a relationship. I have emphasised the word 'certain' here because formal recognition for relationships is limited to those which are state approved. The test for this approval leads to a boundary between acceptable relationships in law and society and those which are not, based on the parties' sex lives which are ideally structured around Christian monogamous values. The focus on sex feeds into wider issues around hierarchies of sexual shame. Warner (1999) tells us that these hierarchies develop when sexual practices are labelled 'good' or 'bad' and then relationship privileges like recognition are distributed according to the labels. Those associated with 'bad' (non-monogamous) sexual practices are then denied full access to civic belonging which includes legal recognition for their marriages (Bailey, 2015). If this is the way that legal recognition for marriage is organised, it may not be helpful or desirable for every woman who lives outside of this framework.

There is an even darker side to this framework where it has explicitly been used as a colonial state tool of control and oppression against minoritised communities. Franke (1999, 2015) shares the disturbing experiences of legal marriage recognition in her work on newly emancipated enslaved people in the US during the 19th century. To begin with, marriages between enslaved people were not recognised. They were property, and as objects, they could not be in human relationships. Even if they had celebrated an informal marriage, the parties could be split up and sold to different owners at any time along with their children. When abolition movements started to gain pace, it was envisaged that once the enslaved people were freed, things would be better but this was not the case. If an enslaved person was freed, they no longer had any reason to remain on their former enslaver's land, and they would have to leave their unrecognised spouse and children behind unless they all managed to obtain their freedom at the same time which was unlikely. In addition, enslaved people did not just form marriages but also engaged in more fluid relationships, such as trial marriages or taking more than one spouse. Franke (2015) suggests that this could have been a result of the lack of legal recognition for their marriages or the remnant of past customs or even to adapt to the constant threat of being broken up and sold by their owners. So, these were the consequences of not having legal recognition – families were carved up and treated like property even after emancipation became a possibility for them.

Things did not improve. Franke (2015) discovered that after the American Civil War, emancipated enslaved people were granted recognition for their marriages. Although their relationships were finally being recognised the context in which this recognition was given caused violent backlash against the emancipated enslaved people. For example, to fill the dwindling ranks of the Union Army in Kentucky during the war, the authorities started to recruit enslaved Black men in the area by enticing them with money and 'freedom certificates'. The offer was too good to refuse, and these Black men would escape from their owners to enlist. However, the women and children left behind paid the price. As revenge for the men's escape, the women and children were subjected to horrific abuse and violence by enslavers. When word spread of this, enslaved men stopped running away and enlisting. To address this, the federal government offered recognition for the enlisted men's marriages so that their wives and children would also be freed at the same time. This had a positive effect on recruitment again, but the consequences for the wives and children were dire. The state had got what it wanted but with their husbands and fathers gone, the women and children were even more vulnerable. Enslavers refused to recognise their freedom certificates or pay them as labourers, and continued to punish them for the men's departure. For these women, being married was not a protection as Herring (2015) suggested could be the case, but was instead very dangerous. Marriage recognition was not a solution for these women. It just provided a new way for White people to enact racist violence against former enslaved people (Franke,

2015). These former enslaved people were recognised as married, but that does not mean they were recognised as human. We see here the value of Fanon's (2008) assertion that it is not recognition we need to reconsider, but our understanding of humanity.

These emancipated enslaved people experienced other consequences which display the dangers of recognition for minoritised communities. With their marriages now legally recognised, the state prescribed the way that their intimate relationships had to be structured. State recognition had no tolerance for the fluid relationships that they had previously lived in, and recognition became a method of imposing normative conceptions of sexual fidelity and monogamy on this marginalised community (Franke, 1999). Marriage and its recognition are a tool for a society to accept a previously marginalised group, but while giving that group the freedom to marry, it takes away their freedom to decide what their marriage should look like (Franke, 2015). Here, recognition was actively used against the marriages of enslaved people to suit the colonialist agenda of imposing state-approved marital norms. Emancipated enslaved people did not have any of the benefits that Herring (2015) refers to such as protection from abuse and remedying of disadvantages. We might argue that this is all in the past and with the institution of slavery abolished this situation is not relevant to the present day, but the same logic of using marriage recognition to secure state interests regardless of the consequences for women and children persists today. In Chapter 4, I showed numerous instances where polygamous marriages were recognised to deny women and children welfare assistance and entry into the state. The recognition of these marriages was used to disadvantage them. Marriage recognition can carry a heavy price because the law and the state are not centring humanity and making sure that everyone is included but are protecting the state's interests. With this racist history and legacy, we need to approach marriage recognition with caution otherwise we risk giving the state too much power over those it has typically oppressed.

Towards a disruptive politics of recognition

If legal recognition for marriage is so risky, where does that leave us? For Fanon, a violent break with the colonial regime and its system of recognition is needed with the underlying message of 'accommodate me as I am; I'm not accommodating anyone' (2008: 110). Through this, the native can develop self-respect and self-worth and redefine recognition for themselves, making sure that they are fully included in the definition of humanity. Building on this, Coulthard argues for a shift away from rights- and social justice-based views of recognition which have dominated scholarship for the past few decades, towards a 'resurgent politics of recognition that seeks to practice decolonial, gender-emancipatory and economically nonexploitative alternative structures of law and sovereign authority grounded on a critical refashioning of the best of Indigenous legal and political traditions' (2014: 179). A resurgent politics does not look at recognition to reconcile the 'other' with state sovereignty but requires the marginalised to privilege and centre themselves when thinking about recognition and how it should look for them. We should not immediately look to the state for recognition; rather, we should look within ourselves and our communities.

Part of this resurgence is to engage in disruptive action that upsets the dominant majority. Resurgence is not about being nostalgic for the past, but looking critically at the past to transform today's colonial power relations. These perspectives are powerful but the real inspiration for challenging the issues with recognition comes from the actions of the women that spoke with me. Based on their narratives and the scholarship that has come before me, I argue that women are already engaging in a disruptive politics of recognition around their relationships which embodies the reimagining of the category of humanity for themselves. It also entails them asserting their 'right to narrate' by challenging and transforming the myths around belonging and exclusion that shape marriage recognition (Bhabha, 1994: xx; see also Busbridge, 2018). By disruptive politics, I mean one which is grounded in resurgent approaches but takes the different colonial context of the UK into account. Coulthard's (2014) resurgent politics is designed for the settler colonial context and is for indigenous communities in their own lands. The UK does not have the same history at a domestic level, and so instead of engaging in resurgence or reclaiming, I argue that marginalised women can, and are, undertaking a disruption of modern-day British imperial sovereignty and its effects on their relationships.

The paradigm case of a woman dispossessed and destabilised when her marriage breaks down leaving her without vital resources shows us that some kind of public recognition can make a difference. However, there are disruptive experiences that show that being in a non-legally binding marriage can promote women's agency and that they do not always feel disadvantaged without legal recognition:

> 'My husband is ... he's quite anti-secular, so he's not too keen on getting a civil marriage done if it's not necessary. And at the moment it's not been necessary, so we just haven't. It's not something that's high on the priority right now for us ... the civil marriage, as I mentioned, is just a piece of paper for me and my husband, and the religious marriage is what is ... is the reason why we got married.' (Maha)

For Maha, the legal ceremony for her marriage is a formality – a "piece of paper" – that she would only do when necessary for practical rather than symbolic reasons. It is not something she and her "anti-secular" husband need to worry about right now, and if they need to in the future, they will do what they must. The civil marriage is therefore a just a chore. This perception also cropped up in Akhtar's (2018a) research on women in non-legally binding Muslim marriages in England. Couples seem to be more led by convenience and are conscious of the extra hoops they must jump through to gain legal recognition, but the religious ceremony is the one that really meets their needs. In this study, the theme of the religious ceremony being the 'real deal' while the legal one is a formality was expressed repeatedly by women from minoritised faith backgrounds, showing how important it is to see marriage recognition as more than practical and official. The sense of being disadvantaged by lack of recognition is not always felt by wives in non-legally binding marriages, and in some ways, the opposite is true:

> 'The issue of polygamy has arisen as a topic to speak about, but actually part of our marriage contract … for me, I would not personally want to be in a polygamous marriage, I would not want my husband to have, erm, another wife. And I know that is something that is permissible but is not obligatory or necessary in Islam, and part of my marriage contract is that my husband will not take another wife while he is married to me. … We, erm, introduced that fairly recently. It wasn't something that we had discussed when we first got married because, at the time, we weren't clued up about polygamous marriages. Actually we only added that to the marriage contract a couple of months ago when we moved in together and I did some research on it. To be honest, at the time that we did our Nikah, I did not know that … I could have conditions in a marriage contract. I thought it was just receiving a mahr. And the thing that happened with the mahr was because at the time a lot of culture was intertwined with my marriage … at that time, the mahr that was stipulated was very high … so that he wasn't able to pay it to me, even after two years. So what we had decided between ourselves with research done beforehand, as in I asked Islamic scholars, is that I can waive the mahr or reduce it and introduce a marriage contract with conditions of what I wanted and he wanted, and we both agreed to and signed it. So that's what we did a couple of months ago, and with that contract, we introduced that he would not take another wife and he would let me continue studying … I waived the mahr because, for me, those clauses were more important than getting the mahr.' (Maha)

As the wife in a non-legally binding marriage, Maha's experience shows us how the minoritised Nikah ceremony can be used to uplift women and facilitate their agency. Maha contracted a Nikah because she wanted to be recognised as married in her religion. The price of her mahr was extremely high, and this was unaffordable for her husband. The mahr is a gift from the groom to the bride which is meant to be individually set by each bride with guidance from her family and community (Mehdi and Nielsen, 2011). This flexibility allows again for a woman to exercise her agency by choosing a gift which can be anything that works for her, from cash to a house. In most cases, the mahr is an asset that the bride can take with her if the marriage ends, so it could almost be seen as a bespoke marriage insurance policy. After the wedding, Maha was able to waive her mahr when she discovered she had the right to renegotiate the terms of her Nikah agreement. For her, money was less important than the guarantee of her further education and a monogamous marriage. She did not dismiss polygamy, but had decided it was not for her, and she knew it is "not obligatory or necessary in Islam".[7]

Noreen provides a connected view of the Nikah when discussing its Islamic legal status:

> 'When I read about, erm, negative things, the one thing that always pops up is [that] the wife would have no rights if he was to leave or he was to die. And like I said, Islamically, if he's doing everything by the book Islamically, then a woman has the same rights as if it was registered in the UK.' (Noreen)

Here, Noreen is disrupting dominant understandings of 'legal marriage'. In Islam, the Nikah is a legally recognised marriage: it is recognised in Shari'a and should therefore be seen as such. For Muslim women, and for other women practising minoritised marriage practices, their relationships are recognised by the authority which is important to them: their faith, their family, their community. If the state chooses not to recognise the marriage, that does not take away the significance or value of the marriage – they have the same rights regardless. In fact, for many, the legal ceremony is not even the one that makes them feel married – the religious one is the one that matters in this sense (Malik, 2014; Akhtar, 2018a).

[7] While there are prenuptial and postnuptial agreements in English law that allow parties to set out terms and conditions for their relationships, these are not widespread and are not legally binding – they are merely taken into consideration and given weight if the court thinks it appropriate to do this.

I situate these deeper engagements with the Nikah contract as a disruption of marriage recognition whereby women exercise their agency to disrupt the colonial-linked power relations between the state and minoritised communities which dictate what a marriage should look like and do for the parties (Parker, 2018). These women narrate the story of their marriage and ceremony as an agreement that can be shaped and negotiated according to their priorities, thus transforming the myth that they are excluded from recognition and therefore from belonging. There is nothing passive or restrictive about their religious marriages, and through their belief system and the personal worth they derive from it, they disrupt the concept of humanity as one that excludes them because their marriages are different. When they act in this way, they are opening up a third space for themselves which lies between the self and the other (Bhabha, 1994; Zubair and Zubair, 2017). The third space is a theoretical construct which refers to a symbolic space between competing cultural collectives like the colonised–coloniser or the traditional gender roles of man–woman (Bhatt, 2008). It is a place where women can negotiate their identities so that they become their own, and define themselves instead of being defined by the state or others (see also English, 2004). They decide what marriage is according to their location as marginalised women in the UK, thus emphasising a different way of seeing recognition. Women are already undertaking disruptive and reconstructive work around marriage recognition for themselves. They expose the limitations of formal state marriage recognition and reimagine it for themselves so that they are engaging in a disruptive politics of recognition – asserting their humanity, their narratives and their lived realities. This confirms that we need to reconsider the universal application of recognition where non-normative marriages are concerned because there is more to it than we think.

Concluding thoughts

So far, I have highlighted that legal marriage recognition is not the perfect solution and may not lead to the consequences women want. How do we address the obvious suffering of women like Karimah in a way that maintains a space for women who want to use their non-normative marriages to be disruptive? By way of conclusion to this chapter, I offer some thoughts on legal and policy reforms to polygamous and non-legally binding marriages. Suggestions for reform in English law fall into two broad camps: change the validity requirements for marriage so that it is easier for marriages celebrated according to other rites and religions to obtain recognition; or provide legal recognition and rights to cohabitants, which is how non-legally binding and polygamous wives are currently seen. I argue that neither of these proposed changes are suitable, because they only expand or make amendments to the existing framework when what we need is the fundamentals of the system to change.[8] So there is no perfect solution to the issues I present in this book but there is value in thinking through some of the main options for change that have been suggested.

In the largest survey in the UK of Muslim marriages to date, 60 per cent of the 903 women surveyed had only celebrated a religious ceremony and around 11 per cent were in polygynous marriages (Akhtar, 2017). More recently, a large project has been conducted with 170 people on non-legally binding ceremonies in England and Wales. In the findings, it is stated that the current law is restrictive, and reform is needed to reflect the diverse beliefs and practices of contemporary society. Further, many participants particularly felt that the law prevented them from marrying in a form that was meaningful for them and their beliefs (Probert et al, 2022). Despite this, overall there is still limited empirical research and evidence around the needs and experiences of non-legally recognised and polygamous wives in the UK, so it is difficult to make detailed recommendations on a legal approach that centres a disruptive politics of recognition. This is further underpinned by the continuing lack of attention given to polygamous marriages in law reform programmes such as the review of the Offences Against the Person Act 1861 (Law Commission, 2015b) and the recent weddings law review (Law Commission, 2020; 2022).[9]

It is worth summarising the practical effects of being with and without legal marital recognition in England for women because they show us the advantages and pitfalls of expanding marriage formalities or providing rights for cohabitants.[10] The benefits of being legally married are demonstrated in Karimah's story: had she been recognised as a wife in English law, she would have had access to remedies in the courts, including divorce so she would not have needed to go to a shari'a council. In addition, her immigration status would have been less precarious, and she would have fallen under the definition of a victim of domestic violence and could claim leave to remain. A legally recognised wife is automatically recognised in property,

[8] Ironically, in *Hyde*, Lord Penzance made a similar argument against extending the remedies, adjudication or relief of English matrimonial law to polygamous marriages. In his judgment, he decided that English marriage law is only adapted to Christian marriage and cannot apply to polygamy, so it is unhelpful to try and do this. However, the judgment is more a reflection of colonial indifference and hostility along with the lack of desire to engage with polygamy than due to an understanding of the problematic foundations of legal recognition for marriage.

[9] The terms of reference for the review of wedding law indicated that the Law Commission would recommend limited reforms of the law in this area (Parveen, 2020).

[10] I have discussed these in detail previously (see Naqvi, 2020), so I just explain them briefly here.

inheritance and welfare aid matters which contribute to financial security. Finally, if a woman gives birth to a child, her husband is automatically given parental responsibility for the child under the Children Act 1989: this is not the case if they are unmarried.

These benefits of legal recognition can be contrasted against those of being in a non-legally binding relationship. By being in polygamous and non-legally binding marriages, wives can maintain a distinction between the religious marriage and the official marriage. State-recognised marriages can be onerous to enter into and to dissolve as there are a lot of official steps that need to be taken. Religious ceremonies like the Nikah are more flexible and have fewer requirements for validity and dissolution. This can give women the freedom to have a religious marriage easily while being seen as unmarried for official purposes so that they are cohabiting. For example, even after her terrible experiences, Karimah was able to seek a divorce at the shari'a council and scholars like Malik (2014) note that women are engaging with religious forums to legitimise their marriages and divorces (see, for example, Bano, 2008; Parveen, 2018; Uddin, 2018). They can therefore experiment with cohabitation and be in a marriage that has fewer strings attached. These informal marriages also provide space for women to be in a relationship that can be shaped by them and which also disrupts state defined boundaries. As with Noreen's situation (see Chapter 5), non-legally binding marriages and polygamy can be used by women to disrupt stigmas around divorce, cohabitation and polygamy because they give women more options to be in relationships that are not limited to the mainstream Christian ideal of monogamous marriage. Finally, women can benefit from much more flexibility and freedom to negotiate the terms of their relationship. Like Maha, they may want to have clauses in their marriage contract, and this is not something a civil ceremony can provide. Further, in some cases it may be the woman who has built up her own assets and wants to protect her financial security if she separates from her husband (Law Commission, 2020).

With limited evidence about women's experiences, it is not possible at this time to set out what a critical postcolonial feminist legal response to polygamous marriage in English law should look like, but something needs to be done to support women like Karimah in the meantime. The change in legal and policy responses that I propose as a stop gap is concerned with non-legally binding marriages that are currently labelled 'non-qualifying ceremonies' in law (*Her Majesty's Attorney General (Appellant) v Nasreen Akhter and Mohammed Shabaz Khan (Respondents) and Fatima Mohammed Hussain and Southall Black Sisters (Interveners)* [2020] EWCA Civ 122). Sandberg (2021) observes that multiple calls for reform have been made on the basis that non-legally binding religious marriages are always problematic and lead to discrimination, disadvantage and suffering. This assumption is orientalist because it only looks at the paradigm cases that fit within the state's chosen narrative of marriage. If a marriage does not look the way the state wants it to look, it must be a problem. We know that this is not universally the case, so it would be wrong to provide legal recognition on this basis. It would also be irresponsible for me to argue in favour of wholescale recognition for non-legally binding marriages that would cover forms of polygamy when we do not know enough about what would happen to polygynous wives in the UK if they were legally recognised and given the same rights and obligations as monogamous wives. This is taking into consideration the lack of appetite for further consideration of legal responses to polygamy that we have seen through the indifference I demonstrated in Chapter 3.

As a limited measure, I have argued previously that it would be helpful to have a mutual opt-out mechanism in religious and other non-normative ceremonies like the Nikah ceremony (Naqvi, 2020). Legal formalities for a valid marriage could be expanded to include these ceremonies, but as part of the preliminaries, the couple would both be asked to opt out of having legal recognition. The opt-out would only be valid if both parties choose to stay unrecognised. This would require couples to come to a joint decision which would be an active choice for them. The opt-out would further entail a discussion with the celebrant on the ways that the couple can protect their assets and other interests if they choose to not be 'legally' married. As with most agreements and contracts, there is the potential for loopholes and abuse as there are power dynamics at play that could lead to one person being pressured into opting out of recognition. However, this mechanism should at a basic level, raise questions for the parties and their support networks and start a conversation about the rights and implications of legal recognition. A test can be developed to be applied if a dispute arises later to decide whether the consent to the opt-out was given without duress. The opt-out would be triggered automatically for polygamous marriages because it is not possible to make space within the current framework for legal recognition in a way that is sensitive and nuanced for them at this time. It would also require reforms to the offence of bigamy which applies when a person contracts two marriages that would individually be legally valid. Reforms to the offence of bigamy were dismissed by the Law Commission in 2015 (see Law Commission 2015b) and are unlikely to be considered in the future.

If the conversation before the opt-out doesn't happen and the power relations between the parties leads to it being triggered without a party's knowledge or consent, a procedure to seek retrospective legal recognition should be available in limited circumstances for both monogamous and polygamous marriages. In such cases, a party would have to show for example, that they did not provide informed consent, that their religious-only status is being used to harm or disadvantage them, or that they suffered abuse during the marriage which falls under the definition in the Domestic Abuse Act 2021. Through this, we could start to promote a nuanced approach to legal recognition that respects the agency and choices of women in their relationships.

This chapter focussed on how recognition can support but also fail women in non-normative marriages because the law is geared towards a specific ideal of what their relationships should look like. Recognition has a dark history and has been used before in the context of marriage to enact colonial violence on minoritised and oppressed communities. Being aware of this legacy is important for when we think about ways to move forward with legal responses to polygamous and non-legally binding marriages. For a woman like Karimah though, despite its flaws, legal recognition would have completely transformed her position. It would be naïve to say that legal recognition is undesirable for any woman in an informal or unrecognised marriage. In trying to address the spectrum of needs expressed by the women here, we have to work with what we have until English law and policy are more open to doing the vital disruptive work that ensures women are not placed in a position that makes them practically or symbolically inferior.

8

Final Thoughts and Reflections

> For the West to maintain its traditional stance against polygamy does not mean that it needs to trade in all the ugly rhetoric that sometimes historically attended this stance. … We do not have to repeat the haughty and xenophobic arguments used by Graeco-Roman writers against their imperial subjects, by early Christians against Jews and Muslims, by early modern Europeans against New World natives, by nineteenth-century Americans against emancipated slaves, Native Americans, Asian workers, or traditional Mormons who practiced polygamy. The West can now simply and politely say to the polygamist who bangs on its door seeking admission or permission to practice polygamy: 'No thank you; we don't do that here', and close the door firmly. (Witte, 2015: 465)

These closing remarks in Witte's (2015) detailed study of polygamy and law in the West fall into the exact trap of trading in ugly rhetoric, despite claiming otherwise. As I have shown repeatedly, polygamy has been practised in the West and in England in various forms for thousands of years. Therefore, stating that the polygamist is banging on the door to seek admission and permission fails to reflect reality. Polygamists already live in the West, and they do not seek permission to be there – we only need to think about the Mormon Christian communities in North America that practise polygamy to confirm this. Even with this knowledge, polygamy is easily orientalised and racialised; it is something that only other people outside of the West do. In this book, I disrupted the misguided narratives around polygamy by providing the first contextualised account of English legal and judicial responses to this relationship using critical postcolonial feminist approaches. I demonstrated how outdated the law in this area is with the last significant legislative development happening nearly three decades ago in 1995. Marriage as we know it has been increasingly scrutinised by policymakers, scholars and laypeople and this has translated into seismic shifts in our definitions and conceptions of this institution. Still, polygamy remains on the margins both in law and in scholarship (Davis, 2010).

I undertook a closer critical and contextually driven excavation of the current legal framework which has been neglected for too long. The approach of English law to minoritised people and their ways of life needs to be examined considering the colonial context. Feminist scholars have already exposed the influence of coloniality on legal responses to polygamy in North America (for example, Kaganas and Murray, 1991; Denike, 2010), but the same has not happened for the UK. Law is written, enforced, interpreted and applied by people who live in the world and are affected by external factors like time, place, environment and atmosphere. Lawmakers are people, and so are judges. I therefore centred the reality that the British Empire and colonisation shaped the conditions in which we heard the first legal definition of marriage in *Hyde*. These conditions and this context did not vanish after *Hyde*, but have remained influential, so I highlighted the operation and manifestations of coloniality along with its ideological foundations of orientalism and imperialism throughout my analysis.

From my original analysis of the legal sources and the stories shared by the women who spoke with me, I argued that English legal responses to polygamous marriages are archaic and underpinned by racist, imperialist, orientalist and sexist attitudes. These attitudes are also visible in wider cultural and social responses to this form of relationship. The legal arguments in favour of denying recognition to polygamy because it causes harm and inequality are accepted uncritically and have changed very little over the centuries. Legal responses and arguments need to be situated in their wider context to see how much they cohere with the experiences and needs of the people affected by them in everyday life.

Key conclusions

In this book I analysed the English legal and judicial responses to polygamous marriages to better understand their effects on the women who live in these relationships. I drew from the insights of critical postcolonial feminist work that underlines the need for an awareness of the context surrounding the law and women's lives. This approach emphasises the importance of voices, especially the ones that are ignored and dismissed by the mainstream. For this reason, I have ensured that the women behind the stories shared in this book were foregrounded throughout. My critical approach was also founded on the need to disrupt dominant stories in law, institutions and society. I showed how contemporary iterations of imperialism and orientalism operate to tell certain stories about polygamy which we accept without question. We need to start asking where these stories came from and why we accept them so that we can then disrupt them.

Chapters 3 and 4 were dedicated to exploring how real stories are missing from the law, which has led to us being fed a singular narrative about polygamy. I identified two main strands of legal responses to polygamy which tell us different stories about this relationship. In Chapter 3, I tackled the story the law narrates about polygamy celebrated in England at a domestic level. I argued that two interwoven forces shape the law in this area: Christian dominance and colonial indifference. These forces combined have led to the law's lack of interest in even acknowledging that polygamy has and continues to be practised in the UK today. Times changed, marriage changed, the authorities changed, but for centuries, there has been very little change in the legal approach to domestic polygamy and there are no signs of this developing in the future. I further demonstrated how the law's indifference reaches beyond polygamy to other non-normative forms of marriage, such as non-legally binding ceremonies. They are termed 'non-marriages' or 'non-qualifying ceremonies' and are even more void than void marriages which can at least attract some legal remedies.

Following this, in Chapter 4 I explored English legal and judicial responses to polygamy celebrated overseas in places which legally recognise it. The area of law that governs overseas polygamy in England is private international law, or conflict of laws which was developed as a response to colonial encounters. There is a little more legislative and policy engagement with overseas polygamy, but this is still limited. This led me to look at another primary legal source: case law. Building on existing arguments around judicial agency and the ways that judges actively produce and reproduce problematic discourses (Herman, 2011), I carried out the first critical discourse analysis of the English case law on polygamous marriages. I uncovered three discursive strategies that judges employ to respond to overseas polygamy: denigration, mutation and differentiation. The lack of legal recognition for polygamy in earlier cases was based on polygamy being denigrated and not considered marriage. Along with polygamous wives, who were designated concubines or 'slaves', the relationship was rooted in explicit racist and imperialist tropes. The courts even struggled to recognise monogamous marriages celebrated in polygamy-permitting places because they had the potential to be polygamous.

As the courts started to face more overseas marriage cases, this stance on potentially polygamous marriages became unsustainable. To address this, the courts started to mutate, or convert, non-Christian monogamous marriages into the imperialist-approved structure of Christian marriage but this was not a perfect solution. The final strategy involves the courts taking the more subtle approach of differentiating between English marriage and polygamy rather than denigrating the latter. In doing so, polygamous marriages are recognised in English law but only if it suits the state or protects public resources. For example, overseas polygamy has been recognised to refuse women and children from these marriages financial aid or entry into the country. Their marriages are used against them, and the women have all the responsibilities and disadvantages of marriage with none of the rights or benefits. The state denies them a space in contemporary understandings of marriage and the family because their relationships do not fit with public policy ideals.

With this picture of the law in mind, the current legal approach and attitudes need to be reconsidered and updated to meet the needs of women today. To better understand what women need from the law, it was important to ask them. Chapters 5, 6 and 7 share the disruptive voices and stories narrated to me for the first time by women around their experiences and attitudes concerning polygamy. I interviewed 26 women, hearing their stories and views of marriage and polygamy in religion, culture, society and law in the UK. Starting with disruption in religion and culture, Noreen's story in Chapter 5 showcased her disruption of the cultural disdain towards divorce and polygamy by choosing to become a polygamous wife in accordance with her religious beliefs. Noreen's setting up of religion and culture as opposing forces in her life was also noted by other minoritised women. This disrupts legal approaches towards minoritised faiths where they are simply seen as another form of culture. Religions other than Christianity are not seen as religions but as cultures, which has also led to the idea of minoritised people having a singular religio-cultural identity. This does not match women's experiences and creates a hierarchy of religions with Christianity at the top and all other faiths either beneath it or not featured at all because they are seen as cultures instead. To counter this dominant narrative, I argued that religion and culture in this context should be seen as dual and alternative identity markers. They are linked but sometimes they exist in tension with one another so any analysis of minoritised marriage practices must make space for them to conflict. The separation between religion and culture that women expressed portrayed faith as empowering, whereas culture was the opposite and a source of oppression. I argued that things are more complicated. Should we only blame culture for women's suffering? I argued that the source of oppression is not culture itself, but gendered double standards stemming from the patriarchy leading to women's negative experiences.

In Chapter 6, Jamilah's harrowing story of child marriage and prolonged domestic violence which ended after she discovered her husband had married again provided the opportunity to pick up on the arguments that polygamy harms women and promotes gender inequality. My intention was not to defend or rehabilitate polygamy, because this is not constructive. Instead, I set out to disrupt the foundations of these arguments which are disproportionately deployed against polygamy despite being equally relevant for women in monogamous marriages. Harms and inequalities can arise in all situations, so why is it only polygamy which is banned as a result? I argued that these justifications are used to dismiss polygamy and feed into a wider othering of minoritised people and practices which stems from colonial attitudes to them. Coercive polygamy, like that experienced by Jamilah, is a symptom of the patriarchy in the same way negative experiences of monogamy are. There are two assumptions that underpin my engagement here: first, women have different experiences in their relationships and make different choices, so it makes more sense to move away from the default position of seeing them as victims and instead see them as agentic to avoid the colonial saviour narrative; second, polygamy has been practised for a very long time and is not going to disappear anytime soon. By dismissing polygamy because of harms and inequalities and ending our engagement there, we end up silencing women's voices and the potential for learning about the range of experiences they have of polygamy. The stories shared here show us how the current approach limits our understandings and awareness of this relationship and women's experiences. We need to move towards a more developed and nuanced engagement with the harm and equality arguments around polygamy that is not stuck in patriarchal, colonial understandings and renders women invisible.

Karimah's story as a suspected polygamous wife and the insecurity she endured because she was not recognised as married in English law introduced my interrogation of legal recognition for wives in Chapter 7. Beginning with the views of the women who spoke with me, it was clear that women were unequivocal about recognition – they were either in favour of it or against it. It was further implied that recognition is something you should want if you do not have it, and it was always viewed positively as a way to achieve social justice for marginalised groups. There were practical consequences to having marriage recognition as we saw with Karimah, but there were broader social consequences beyond this. Marriage recognition was seen as attracting greater benefits than legal rights for women, and it was also tied to their personal perceptions and identities. However, the uncritical acceptance of recognition as something good is worrying. Marriage equality movements have a dark past for minoritised groups and we must bear this in mind, especially as responses to polygamous marriages are enmeshed in racist, imperialist attitudes. State recognition is not always empowering, and I showed that in some instances women choose to disrupt and reject legal recognition, thereby opening up a third space for themselves. This all led me to conclude that arguing for full recognition of polygamous marriages in English law is not appropriate at this time. The law needs to change on a fundamental level so that marriage is no longer tangled up with colonialist racist and sexist understandings of how it should be structured. To address the immediate needs and concerns of women like Karimah, I suggested a limited reform whereby non-legally binding marriages are recognised in law unless the parties both decide to opt out of recognition. In certain situations, those marriages where the opt-out was used could be recognised retrospectively. This is not a permanent or ideal solution but provides support for women like Karimah while also preserving the third space for women who do not want to be recognised by the state as married.

Lingering questions and future directions

In this book, I started a conversation about polygamy, policy and law in the UK – one that has thrown up further questions and lingering thoughts about the issues introduced here. There is still so much we do not know about how polygamy is lived and practised in the UK and this is also true on an international scale. The conversation started here will help shed light on further directions for research in other systems around the world and their approach to polygamy. The discussions I had with women around their attitudes and experiences were limited in several ways. Polygamy is a sensitive topic and a practice that has been demonised over the years, so it is unsurprising that it is difficult to find people willing to talk about it. Another limitation was the time it takes to build trust with people. Some people became worried about the implications of talking with me and pulled out of interviews. The trust issue was driven home for me after I had completed this project when I discovered that a woman I had been friends with for several years was a polygamous wife. She was aware of my research and showed an interest in it, but she never felt comfortable revealing this information about her life until I was no longer recruiting people to speak with me for the study. Polygamy is highly personal, and its participants are less likely to openly share their experiences and lives because of the exhaustion and anxiety that comes from being forced to defend their relationship choices and even their humanity.

Among the women who spoke with me, only Noreen, Jamilah and Karimah had direct experiences of polygamy, which is why their narratives were foregrounded at the start of Chapters 5, 6 and 7. However, I was unable to find a woman for this project who was openly and actively living in a polygamous marriage. Even so, many of the women in this study had secondary experiences, and it is interesting that they all had some story to share about a friend, relative, acquaintance or member of their community who was living polygamously. Nevertheless, my hope of speaking directly with active polygamous wives remained unfulfilled and it would be hugely beneficial to undertake a much larger study with the time and space to find and develop the trust needed to find out what these women need from the law today.

Another limitation is that I only chose to speak with women and did not include men's narratives. This was deliberate since it was easier to find women willing to speak with me and I wanted to address the ways women are silenced and spoken for. I also prioritised women's voices because responses to polygamy are rooted in problematic perceptions of polygamous wives – whether it is telling us that they are 'slaves' or that they are a burden on the state. Men's experiences and attitudes might provide insight on these areas as well and conducting a narrative-based study with people from a variety of age groups and backgrounds that centres their voices could add further colour and depth to the picture I have drawn of polygamy in the UK in this book.

For the legal analysis, I was limited in several places, including my evaluation of domestic polygamy in Chapter 3. Due to time and resource constraints, I was unable to spend as much time as I would have liked searching for and scrutinising the primary legal materials for domestic polygamy. For example, although the case law around bigamy in the later years is more accessible, it was not possible within the scope of this book to delve into this and undertake a more forensic analysis. In addition, I still have many questions about the legal status and approaches towards non-legally binding marriages like the Islamic Nikah. This project gave some insight into the different concerns and considerations of women in these marriages, and the first larger empirical project on this has recently been concluded which provided many important findings (see Probert et al, 2022) but there is more to do. It would be fascinating for example to look at legal responses to non-legally binding marriages from a critical postcolonial feminist perspective. This would feed into wider discussions relevant to the Law Commission's (2020; 2022) weddings law review around how the law approaches minoritised marriage ceremonies and relationships.

Finally, I wish that this project had shown a clearer path towards reform. I was unable to provide a solid model for legal and policy reform and there are more questions than answers at this stage. However, it would be irresponsible of me to suggest reforms to the current system when I have repeatedly shown how racist, imperialist, orientalist and sexist it is. In the future, it may be possible to make progress towards developing an anti-colonialist approach to polygamy in law, but this would require the engagement of law and policy makers on a grander scale. So, I am in favour of being cautious and careful by highlighting that current law does not hold the answers or the solutions and we need to learn more about polygamous households in the UK before we start thinking about changes to the framework.

This book is made up of stories about polygamy – a relationship that has been celebrated and practised for thousands of years. I have shared historical stories, legal and judicial stories, and religious, cultural and social stories. I have shared stories of indifference and hostility, of oppression and civility, all bound up with the question of whether polygamy should even exist. I have shared the stories of women talking about how religion and culture interact and conflict, how they suffer from harm, inequalities and violence, and how they experience recognition. Throughout this journey, I have felt the impact of these stories on me, my experiences and my attitudes. This project, the women I spoke with and their narratives have transformed me in ways that I could never have imagined. In solidarity with them and their bravery in sharing their lives with me, I end this book the way I started it: with my story.

Negotiating my closeness

In the opening lines of this book, I shared the childhood memory which triggered my journey and the person at the heart of it – Bari Amma, my personal counter-narrative to disrupt the dominant discourses. I never met her, but along with my dad's mum Granny, she has a special place in my family tree. However, the way that polygamous wives like my two grandmothers are portrayed is sensationalised and negative reducing them to their marriage structure. The courts have told us that they are little more than concubines or 'slaves', that they want a free living from the state and that they are always victims. In the beginning, I wanted to think more about whether polygamy was as harmful and unequal as it is portrayed, because if my grandparents chose to live it, could it really be that bad? The law seems to think so. When I first started looking at the law, my knee-jerk reaction to the explicit racism and sexism in the older cases on polygamy was to find it comedic and a relic of the past, but as time went on and I realised how little has changed, it became painful. It was painful because people were being dehumanised and vilified for failing to meet White supremacist standards. It remains painful because, as I have since discovered, this is not localised to one area or issue, but is embedded throughout the legal system. Minoritised people are constantly apologising for things that are not their fault; they are constantly being forced to defend their status as humans. As a Muslim woman of colour, I have been made to feel responsible for proving my humanity, and the humanity of practices or behaviours associated with my identities are included in this. This has always placed me in a defensive position around Islam and, by extension, polygamy. When I went into this project and the interviews, I was conscious of this, and it has been so difficult for me to detach myself from the stories of harm and abuse women recounted, especially since many of their experiences intersected with the way that religion and polygamy are used against them.

The internal conflict that this has created has not been fully resolved and is part of a lifelong struggle that started a long time ago but has intensified with my work on polygamy. Over the years, my commitment to Islam has compelled me to look for an explanation for all the harm and abuse Muslim women live through, and as discussed in Chapter 5, the culprit of choice for me was culture. It has always been easy to slip into the binary thinking of good religion/bad culture, but as earnestly as I tried to hold on to this, something did not add up. When I think about my culture, it involves so many things: languages, clothing, etiquette, food that I have been raised with and that I am immensely proud of. I have always loved the fact that I grew up (mostly!) understanding three languages, so how can I say that my culture is wholly bad? It took me a long time over the course of this project to unpick this and look deeply enough to see the patriarchy inside. To see that women suffer regardless of their religious and cultural backgrounds. In addition, there is a pattern to this religion versus culture mindset which only seems apply to minoritised cultures and communities. The dramatic separation between the two is arguably a response to the way mainstream dominant perspectives tend to collapse them into each other to diminish them and make them inferior. However, this further strikes me as possibly manifesting a form of self-objectification in which the oppressed person starts to see themselves through the colonialist gaze and internalise what the coloniser says about them until they can no longer recognise themselves and their lives (Fanon, 2008). In my desperate attempts to defend my religion, did I internalise the colonialist interpretation of my culture? It is a convenient culprit but also achieves one of the insidious aims of the colonialist agenda – to direct us away from the real cause of minoritised oppressions and blame ourselves. We are told that our cultural and religious communities are the problem, that Brown women need saving from the Brown men that uphold and impose this bad culture on them. It is an effective deflection tactic to stop us from blaming the racist, Eurocentric and patriarchal systems that construct this narrative. This has been an important lesson for me, but it does not end there. I may see that there is more going on beneath the surface, but that does not mean culture and religion and the ways they are practised should be let off the hook and viewed uncritically. There needs to be more careful and thoughtful work done around religion, culture, gender and power which neither others nor indulges in a singular depiction of them. This requires more of the critical yet committed scholarship that we are seeing around Islam and women that has helped me on this journey (for example, Ali, 2006; Abu-Lughod, 2013; Ahmed, 2021).

Another flashpoint for me during this time has been the question of equality in Islam. Yet another thing for Muslim women to defend is that their faith does not expect them to be oppressed or treated as inferior. However, this is difficult to address when faced with the mounting evidence which tells us that women are not treated equally despite being told that they should be. In this project, I struggled with the lack of uplifting and positive experiences of polygyny because of my personal history and because polygamy is so heavily associated with Islam. My concerns then expanded out towards gender roles in Islam more generally and based on my conversations and interactions with other Muslim women, I see it is something that is thought about and discussed a lot. We tell ourselves and others that we are equal, but then we see women being abused, harassed, dismissed and insulted in front of us. We hear talks given in mosques (as I once did) that on average women are not as smart as men – unsurprisingly, a man was saying this to a congregation of other men. Where does this leave us? As I talked with the women in this project and learned and read more, I came across the following explanation of the disconnect between equality and women's lived realities in Islam:

> Even as Islam instituted marriage as a sexual hierarchy in its ethical voice – a voice virtually unheard by rulers and lawmakers – it insistently stressed the importance of the spiritual and ethical dimensions of being and the equality of all individuals. While the first voice has been extensively elaborated into a body of political and legal thought, which constitutes the technical understanding of Islam, the second – the voice to which ordinary believing Muslims, who are essentially ignorant of the details of Islam's technical legacy, give their assent – has left little trace on the legal and political heritage of Islam. The unmistakable presence of an ethical egalitarianism explains why Muslim women frequently insist, often inexplicably to non-Muslims, that Islam is not sexist. They hear and read in its sacred text, justly and legitimately, a different message from that heard by the makers and enforces of orthodox, androcentric Islam. (Ahmed, 2021: 66)

Ahmed's comments emphasise how vital it is that we see law, religion, culture and society as part of a bigger picture. Context is everything – being conscious of how things have become what they are today matters. The faith tells us without a doubt that all humans are equal, but the patriarchal human imprint has completely distorted this. My faith has not failed me and other women; the discriminatory systems that have structured its practice and operation have. And this is not limited to Muslim women. So we speak out and we challenge it all. We challenge the law and the ways that religion and culture operate and are used against women. We challenge ourselves and our communities. We cannot take responsibility for proving our worth or humanity because of the decisions and choices we make about our lives and relationships. This realisation means I am no longer defensive or apologetic about polygamy. I am not personally invested in the practice, but the women who practise it – I am protective over Granny's and Bari Amma's stories. And, inspired by them and all the women who shared their lives in this project, I have one thing left to say: take us as we are; we are not accommodating or apologising anymore.

References

Abbas, T. (2003) 'The Impact of Religio-Cultural Norms and Values on the Education of Young South Asian Women', *British Journal of Sociology of Education*, 24(4): 411–28.

Abbas, T. (2010) 'Muslim-on-Muslim Social Research: Knowledge, Power and Religio-Cultural Identities', *Social Epistemology*, 24(2): 123–36.

Abdalla, M. (2012) 'Sacred Law in a Secular Land: To What Extent Should Shari'a Law Be Followed in Australia?', *Griffith Law Review*, 21(3): 657–76.

Abduh, M. (1979) *al-Mar'a Fi al-Islam*, Kitab-al-Hilal No 347, Riyadh: Dar al-Hilal.

Abu-Lughod, L. (2013) *Do Muslim Women Need Saving?* Cambridge, MA: Harvard University Press.

Ahmed, L. (2021) *Women and Gender in Islam: Historical Roots of a Modern Debate*, New Haven, CT: Yale University Press.

Ahmed, S. (1996) 'Moving Spaces: Black Feminism and Post-Colonial Theory', *Theory, Culture and Society*, 13(1): 139–46.

Ahmed, S. (2000) *Strange Encounters: Embodied Others in Post-Coloniality*, London: Routledge.

Akhtar, R.C. (2015) 'Unregistered Muslim Marriages: An Emerging Culture of Celebrating Rites and Compromising Rights', in J. Miles, P. Mody and R. Probert (eds) *Marriage Rites and Rights*, London: Hart Publishing, pp 167–92.

Akhtar, R.C. (2017) '"The Truth About Muslim Marriages": 60% of Muslim Women Surveyed Are in Marriages Not Recognised by Law', *True Vision*, [online] 21 November, Available from: https://www.truevisiontv.com/films/the-truth-about-muslim-marriages [Accessed 23 January 2022].

Akhtar, R.C. (2018a) 'Modern Traditions in Muslim Marriage Practices, Exploring English Narratives', *Oxford Journal of Law and Religion*, 7(3): 427–54.

Akhtar, R.C. (2018b) 'Unregistered Muslim Marriages in the UK: Examining Normative Influences Shaping Choice of Legal Protection', in M.-C. Foblets, M. Graziadei and A.D. Renteln (eds) *Personal Autonomy in Plural Societies*, London: Routledge, pp 140–55.

Akhtar, R.C. (2020) 'From "Non-Marriage" to "Non-Qualifying Ceremony"', *Journal of Social Welfare and Family Law*, 42(3): 384–7.

Ali, K. (2006) *Sexual Ethics and Islam: Feminist Reflections on Qur'an, Hadith, and Jurisprudence*, London: Oneworld Publications.

Ali, S.S. (2016) *Modern Challenges to Islamic Law*, Cambridge: Cambridge University Press.

Ali, Y. (1992) 'Muslim Women and the Politics of Ethnicity and Culture in Northern England', in G. Sahgal and N. Yuval-Davis (eds) *Refusing Holy Orders: Women and Fundamentalism in Britain*, London: Virago, pp 101–23.

Allen, R.E. (ed) (1990) *The Concise Oxford Dictionary* (8th edn), Oxford: Oxford University Press.

Al-Saji, A. (2016) 'Too Late: Racialized Time and the Closure of the Past', *Insights*, 6(5): 2–13.

Alsunaid, O. and Almofadda, B. (2014) 'Women's Rights in Islamic Perspective', *European Journal of Law Reform*, 16(2): 303–16.

Anghie, A. (2005) *Imperialism, Sovereignty and the Making of International Law*, Cambridge: Cambridge University Press.

Anghie, A. (2006) 'The Evolution of International Law: Colonial and Postcolonial Realities', *Third World Quarterly*, 27(5): 739–53.

An-Na'im, A.A. (2010) 'The Compatibility Dialectic: Mediating the Legitimate Coexistence of Islamic Law and State Law', *Modern Law Review*, 73(1): 1–29.

Archer, M. (1996) *Culture and Agency: The Place of Culture in Social Theory*, Cambridge: Cambridge University Press.

Arendt, H. (1970) *On Violence*, San Diego, CA: Harcourt Brace Jovanovich Publishers.

Aristides, P.A. (1981) 'Oration 26, 101-2', in *The Complete Works: Volume II, Orations XVII–LIII* (trans C. Behr), Leiden: Brill Academic Publishers.

Aristotle (1925) *Ethica Nichomachea*, Oxford: Oxford University Press.

Asad, T. (1993) *Genealogies of Religion*, Baltimore, MD: Johns Hopkins University Press.

Ash, A., Jun, A. and Jones Jolivet, T. (2018) *White Jesus: The Architecture of Racism in Religion and Education*, New York: Peter Lang.

Asher, K. (2017) 'Spivak and Rivera Cusicanqui on the Dilemmas of Representation in Postcolonial and Decolonial Feminisms', *Feminist Studies*, 43(3): 512–24.

Bailey, C. (2015) 'Love Multiplied: Sister Wives, Polygamy and Queering Heterosexuality', *Quarterly Review of Film and Video*, 32(1): 38–57.

Bailey, M. and Kaufman, A. (2010) *Polygamy in the Monogamous World: Multicultural Challenges for Western Law and Policy*, Santa Barbara, CA: ABC-CLIO.

Baker, J., Lynch, K., Cantillon, S. and Walsh, J. (2009) *Equality: From Theory to Action* (2nd edn), Basingstoke: Palgrave Macmillan.

Balaton-Chrimes, S. and Stead, V. (2017) 'Recognition, Power and Coloniality', *Postcolonial Studies*, 20(1): 1–17.

Balibar, E. (1991) *Race, Nation, Class: Ambiguous Identities*, London: Verso Books.

Bano, S. (2008) 'In Pursuit of Religious and Legal Diversity: A Response to the Archbishop of Canterbury and the "Shari'a Debate" in Britain', *Ecclesiastical Law Journal*, 10(3): 283–309.

Barker, N. (2012) *Not the Marrying Kind: A Feminist Critique of Same-Sex Marriage*, Basingstoke: Palgrave Macmillan.

Barlow, A. (2004) 'Regulation of Cohabitation, Changing Family Policies and Social Attitudes: A Discussion of Britain within Europe', *Law and Policy*, 26(1): 57–86.

Barlow, A. (2020) 'Modern Marriage Myths: The Dichotomy Between Expectations of Legal Rationality and Lived Law', in R.C. Akhtar, P. Nash and R. Probert (eds) *Cohabitation and Religious Marriage: Status, Similarities and Solutions*, Bristol: Bristol University Press, pp 39–52.

Barratt, A. (2019) '"I Also Am a Barolong": Re *Bethell* and Shaping of Marriage Law and Conflict of Laws Doctrine', *Fundamina*, 25(1): 1–25.

Bartholomew, S.W. (1958) 'The Origin and Development of the Law of Bigamy', *Law Quarterly Review*, 74(2): 259–71.

Bartlett, K. (2012) 'Feminist Legal Scholarship: A History through the Lens of the *California Law Review*', *California Law Review*, 100(2): 381–429.

Basit, T.N. (1997) '"I Want More Freedom but Not Too Much": British Muslim Girls and the Dynamism of Family Values', *Gender and Education*, 9(4): 425–40.

Batool, S.S. and de Vissec, R.O. (2016) 'Experiences of Infertility in British and Pakistani Women: A Cross-Cultural Qualitative Analysis', *Healthcare Women International*, 37(2): 180–96.

Beaman, L.G. (2014) 'Introduction: Is Polygamy Inherently Harmful?', in G. Calder and L.G. Beaman (eds) *Polygamy's Rights and Wrongs: Perspectives on Harm, Family and Law*, Vancouver: University of British Columbia Press, pp 1–20.

Bell, V. (1993) *Interrogating Incest: Feminism, Foucault and the Law*, London: Routledge.

Bennion, J. (1998) *Women of Principle: Female Networking in Contemporary Mormon Polygyny*, Oxford: Oxford University Press.

Bennion, J. and Fishbayn Joffe, L. (eds) (2016) *The Polygamy Question*, Logan, UT: Utah State University Press.

Benton, L. and Ford, L. (2016) *Rage for Order: The British Empire and the Origins of International Law 1800–1850*, Cambridge, MA: Harvard University Press.

Berry, T.R. (2010) 'Engaged Pedagogy and Critical Race Feminism', *Educational Foundations*, 24(3–4): 19–26.

Beyers, J. (2017) 'Religion and Culture: Revisiting a Close Relative', *HTS Teologiese Studies/Theological Studies*, 73(1): 1–9.
Bhabha, H.K. (1983) 'The Other Question … Homi K. Bhabha Reconsiders the Stereotype and Colonial Discourse', *Screen*, 24(6): 18–36.
Bhabha, H.K. (1986) 'Foreword: Remembering Fanon', in F. Fanon, *Black Skin, White Masks* (trans C.L. Markmann), London: Pluto Press.
Bhabha, H.K. (1994) *The Location of Culture*, London: Routledge.
Bhabha, H.K. (1998) 'Culture's in Between', in D. Bennett (ed) *Multicultural States: Rethinking Difference and Identity*, London: Routledge, pp 29–36.
Bhabha, H.K. (2003) 'On Writing Rights', in M.J. Gibney (ed), *Globalizing Rights: The Oxford Amnesty Lectures 1999*, Oxford: Oxford University Press, pp 162–83.
Bhatt, R.M. (2008) 'In Other Words: Language Mixing, Identity, Representations, and Third Space', *Journal of Sociolinguistics*, 12(2): 177–200.
Bilge, S. (2010) 'Beyond Subordination vs Resistance: An Intersectional Approach to the Agency of Veiled Muslim Women', *Journal of Intercultural Studies*, 31(1): 9–28.
Bolognani, M. (2009) *Crime and Muslim Britain: Culture and the Politics of Criminology among British Pakistanis*, London: IB Taurus.
Bolognani, M. and Mellor, J. (2012) 'British Pakistani Women's Use of the "Religion Versus Culture" Contrast: A Critical Analysis', *Culture and Religion*, 13(2): 211–26.
Bomhoff, J. (2008) 'The Reach of Rights: "The Foreign" and "The Private" in Conflict-of-Laws, State-Action, and Fundamental-Rights Cases with Foreign Elements', *Law and Contemporary Problems*, 71(3): 39–72.
Bonnett, A. (2004) *The Idea of the West: Culture, Politics and History*, Basingstoke: Palgrave Macmillan.
Borren, M. (2013) 'Feminism as Revolutionary Practice: From Justice and the Politics of Recognition to Freedom', *Hypatia*, 28(1): 197–214.
Bourdieu, P. (1977) *Outline of a Theory of Practice*, Cambridge: Cambridge University Press.
Boyd, S. (2015) 'Equality: An Uncomfortable Fit in Parenting Law', in R. Leckey (ed) *After Formal Equality: Family, Sex, Kinship*, London: Routledge, pp 42–58.
Brake, E. (2012) *Minimizing Marriage: Marriage, Morality and the Law*, Oxford: Oxford University Press.
Braun, V. and Clarke, V. (2013) *Successful Qualitative Research: A Practical Guide for Beginners*, London: Sage.
Bretschneider, C.A. (ed) (1963) 'Letter of August 1531 to Henry VIII', in *Corpus Reformatorium*, Vol 2, Col 536, New York: Johnson Reprint Corporation.
Brooke, C. (1989) *The Medieval Idea of Marriage*, Oxford: Clarendon Press.

Brooks, A. (2007) 'Feminist Standpoint Epistemology: Building Knowledge and Empowerment through Women's Lived Experience', in S. Nagy Hesse-Biber and P. Lina Leavy (eds) *Feminist Research Practice*, London: Sage, pp 53–82.

Brooks, T. (2009) 'The Problem with Polygamy', *Philosophical Topics*, 37(2): 109–22.

Brown, J. (2014) 'Factors Related to Domestic Violence in Asia: The Conflict Between Culture and Patriarchy', *Journal of Human Behaviour in the Social Environment*, 24(7): 828–37.

Brown, N. (2012) 'Negotiating the Insider/Outsider Status: Black Feminist Ethnography and Legislative Studies', *Journal of Feminist Scholarship*, 3: 19–34.

Brown, W. (2008) *Regulating Aversion: Tolerance in the Age of Identity and Empire*, Princeton, NJ: Princeton University Press.

Bryce, J. (1914) *The Ancient Roman Empire and the British Empire in India; The Diffusion of Roman and English Law throughout the World: Two Historical Studies*, Oxford: Humphrey Milford Oxford University Press.

Burns, N., Schlozman, K.L. and Verba, S. (2009) *The Private Roots of Public Action: Gender, Equality and Political Participation*, Cambridge, MA: Harvard University Press.

Burrington, G. (1757) *An Answer to Dr William Brakenridge's Letter Concerning the Number of Inhabitants within the London Bills of Mortality. Wherein the Doctor's Letter Is Inserted at Large, his Arguments Proved Inclusive, and the Number of Inhabitants Increasing*, London: J. Scott.

Burton, A. (ed) (1999) *Gender, Sexuality and Colonial Modernities*, London: Routledge.

Busbridge, R. (2018) *Multicultural Politics of Recognition and Postcolonial Citizenship: Rethinking the Nation*, London: Routledge.

Bush, B. (2004) 'Gender and Empire: The Twentieth Century', in P. Levine (ed) *Gender and Empire*, Oxford: Oxford University Press, pp 77–111.

Cain, P. (1990) 'Feminism and the Limits of Equality', *Georgia Law Review*, 24: 803–47.

Calder, G. (2009) 'Penguins and Polyamory: Using Law and Film to Explore the Essence of Marriage in Canadian Family Law', *Canadian Journal of Women and the Law*, 21(1): 55–89.

Calder, G. and Beaman, L.G. (eds) (2014) *Polygamy's Rights and Wrongs: Perspectives on Harm, Family and Law*, Vancouver: University of British Columbia Press.

Campbell, A. (2013) *Sister Wives, Surrogates and Sex Workers: Outlaws by Choice?* London: Routledge.

Cannadine, D. (2002) *Ornamentalism: How the British Saw their Empire*, London: Penguin.

Capp, B. (2009) 'Bigamous Marriage in Early Modern England', 52(3): 537–56.

Carling, J., Erdal, M.B. and Ezzati, R. (2014) 'Beyond the Insider–Outsider Divide in Migration Research', *Migration Studies*, 2(1): 36–54.

Casey, L. (2016) *The Casey Review: A Review into Opportunity and Integration*, London: Department for Communities and Local Government.

Castelli, E. (2001) 'Women, Gender and Religion: Troubling Categories and Transforming Knowledge', in E. Castelli and R. Rodman (eds) *Women, Gender and Religion: A Reader*, Basingstoke: Palgrave Macmillan, pp 3–25.

Chambers, D. (1997) 'Polygamy and Same-Sex Marriage', *Hofstra Law Review*, 26(1): 53–84.

Chan, M. (2011) 'Beyond Bountiful: Toward an Intersectional and Postcolonial Feminist Intervention in the British Columbia Polygamy Reference', *Appeal: Review of Current Law and Law Reform*, 16(1): 15–30.

Chapman, S. (2001) *Polygamy, Bigamy and Human Rights Law*, Philadelphia, PA: Xlibris.

Chatterjee, N. (2010) 'English Law, Brahmo Marriage, and the Problem of Religious Difference: Civil Marriage Laws in Britain and India', *Comparative Studies in Society and History*, 52(3): 524–52.

Chrisman, L. (2003) *Postcolonial Contraventions: Cultural Readings of Race, Imperialism and Transnationalism*, Manchester: Manchester University Press.

Chung, H.K. (1996) 'Asian Christologies and People's Religions', *Voices from the Third World*, 19(1): 214–27.

Cohen, M. (2009) 'Jews and Muslims in France: Changing Responses to Cultural and Religious Diversity', in R. Grillo, R. Ballard, A. Ferrari, A. Hoekema, M. Maussen and P. Shah (eds) *Legal Practice and Cultural Diversity*, London: Ashgate, pp 219–36.

Conaghan, J. (2013) *Law and Gender*, Oxford: Oxford University Press.

Conley, H. and Page, M. (2015) *Gender Equality in Public Services: Chasing the Dream*, London: Routledge.

Connell, R. (2014) 'Rethinking Gender from the South', *Feminist Studies*, 40(3): 518–39.

Cooper, D. (1995) *Power in Struggle: Feminism, Sexuality and the State*, Maidenhead: Open University Press.

Cooper, D. (2004) *Challenging Diversity: Rethinking Equality and the Value of Difference*, Cambridge: Cambridge University Press.

Cornell, D. (1998) *At the Heart of Freedom: Feminism, Sex and* Equality, Princeton, NJ: Princeton University Press.

Coughlin, A. (1995) 'Regulating the Self: Autobiographical Performances in Outsider Scholarship', *Virginia Law Review*, 81(5): 1229–340.

Coulthard, G.S. (2014) *Red Skin, White Masks: Rejecting the Colonial Politics of Recognition*, Minneapolis: University of Minnesota Press.

Cretney, S. (2005) *Family Law in the Twentieth Century: A History*, Oxford: Oxford University Press.

Curtin, P. (1972) 'Introduction: Imperialism as Intellectual History', in P. Curtin (ed) *Imperialism*, London: Macmillan, pp ix–xxiii.

Das, V. (2007) *Life and Words: Violence and the Descent into the Ordinary*, Oakland: University of California Press.

Davis, A. (2010) 'Regulating Polygamy: Intimacy, Default Rules and Bargaining for Equality', *Columbia Law Review*, 110(8): 1955–2046.

de Beauvoir, S. (1997) *The Second Sex*, London: Vintage Classics.

De Cruz, P. (2010) *Family Law, Sex and Society: A Comparative Study of Family Law*, London: Routledge.

Denike, M. (2010) 'The Racialization of White Man's Polygamy', *Hypatia*, 25(4): 852–74.

de Sousa Santos, B. (2018) *The End of the Cognitive Empire: The Coming of Age of Epistemologies of the South*, Durham, NC: Duke University Press.

Dicey, A.V. (1896) *A Digest of the Law of England with Reference to the Conflict of Laws*, London: Steven and Sons Limited.

Diwan, P. (1957) 'The Hindu Marriage Act, 1955', *The International and Comparative Law Quarterly*, 6(2): 263–72.

Dixon, P. (2009) *We Want for Our Sisters What We Want for Ourselves: African American Women Who Practice Polygyny/Polygamy by Consent*, Baltimore, MD: Black Classic Press.

Doĝan, R. (2013) 'Honour Killings in the UK Communities: Adherence to Tradition and Resistance to Change', *Journal of Muslim Minority Affairs*, 33(3): 410–17.

Donaldson, L.E. and Kwok, P. (2002) 'Introduction', in L.E. Donaldson and Kwok Pui-lan (eds) *Postcolonialism, Feminism and Religious Discourse*, London: Routledge, pp 1–40.

Dube, M.W. (2002) 'Postcoloniality, Feminist Spaces, and Religion', in L.E. Donaldson and Kwok Pui-lan (eds) *Postcolonialism, Feminism and Religious Discourse*, London: Routledge, pp 100–20.

Dubuisson, D. (2003) *The Western Construction of Religion: Myths, Knowledge, and Ideology*, Baltimore, MD: Johns Hopkins University Press.

Duidam, J., Harries, J., Humfress, C. and Hurvitz, N. (2013) 'Introduction', in J. Duidam, J. Harries, C. Humfress and N. Hurvitz (eds) *Law and Empire: Ideas, Practices, Actors*, Leiden: Brill Academic Publishers, pp i–xi.

Durkheim, E. (1915) *The Elementary Forms of Religious Life*, London: Allen and Unwin.

Dvornik, F. (1961) *The Ecumenical Councils*, London: Hawthorn Books.

Dworkin, R. (2000) *Sovereign Virtue*, Cambridge, MA: Harvard University Press.

Easat-Daas, A. (2020) *Muslim Women's Political Participation in France and* Belgium, Basingstoke: Palgrave Macmillan.

Ehrenzweig, A.A. (1960) 'The Lex Fori – Basic Rule in the Conflict of Laws', *Michigan Law Review*, 58(5): 637–88.
El-Enany, N. (2020) *(B)ordering Britain: Law, Race and Empire*, Manchester: Manchester University Press.
Elmarsafy, Z. and Bernard, A. (2013) 'Orientalism: Legacies of Performance', in Z. Elmarsafy, A. Bernard and D. Atwell (eds) *Debating Orientalism*, Basingstoke: Palgrave Macmillan, pp 1–17.
English, L.M. (2004) 'Feminist Identities: Negotiations in the Third Space', *Feminist Theology*, 13(1): 97–125.
Erickson, A.B. and McCarthy, J.R. (1971) 'The Yelverton Case: Civil Legislation and Marriage', *Victorian Studies*, 14(3): 275–91.
Ertman, M.M. (2010) 'Race Treason: The Untold Story of America's Ban on Polygamy', *Columbia Journal of Gender and Law*, 19(2): 287–366.
Eskridge, W., Jr (2001) 'The Ideological Structure of the Same-Sex Marriage Debate (and Some Postmodern Arguments for Same-Sex Marriage)', in R. Wintermute and M. Andenaes (eds) *Legal Recognition of Same-Sex Partnerships: A Study of National, European and International Law*, London: Hart Publishing, pp 113–29.
Fanon, F. (1961) *Les Damnes de la Terre*, Paris: Maspero.
Fanon, F. (1994) *A Dying Colonialism*, New York: Grove Press.
Fanon, F. (2008) *Black Skin, White Masks*, London: Pluto Press.
Featherstone, M. (1995) *Undoing Culture: Globalization, Postmodernism and Identity*, London: Sage Publications.
Fenn, R. (ed) (2003) *The Blackwell Companion to Sociology of Religion*, London: Blackwell Publishing.
Festa, L. and Carey, D. (2013) 'Introduction: Some Answers to the Question: "What is Postcolonial Enlightenment?"', in D. Carey and L. Festa (eds) *The Postcolonial Enlightenment: Eighteenth-Century Colonialism and Postcolonial Theory*, Oxford: Oxford University Press, pp 1–33.
Fitzpatrick, P. (2001) 'Terminal Legality: Imperialism and the (De) composition of Law', in D. Kirby and C. Colebane (eds) *Law, History, Colonialism: The Reach of Empire*, Manchester: Manchester University Press, pp 9–25.
Foucault, M. (1978) *The History of Sexuality, Volume 1: An Introduction*, London: Penguin.
Foucault, M. (1980) *Power/Knowledge*, New York: Pantheon.
Foucault, M. (1997) *Ethics, Subjectivity and Truth: Essential World of Foucault 1954–1984, Volume 1*, New York: New Press.
Franke, K. (1999) 'Becoming a Citizen: Reconstruction Era Regulation of African American Marriages', *Yale Journal of Law and Humanities*, 11: 251–310.
Franke, K. (2015) *Wedlocked: The Perils of Marriage Equality*, New York: New York University Press.

Fraser, N. (1998) 'From Redistribution to Recognition? Dilemmas of Justice in a "Postsocialist" Age', in A. Phillips (ed) *Feminism and Politics*, Oxford: Oxford University Press, pp 430–60.

Fredman, S. (2011) *Discrimination Law*, Oxford: Oxford University Press.

Friedan, B. (1963) *The Feminine Mystique*, New York: W.W. Norton.

Frost, G.S. (2019) '"Not Always Logical": Binational/Biracial Marriages in Britain, 1900–1940', *The History of the Family*, 24(3): 585–607.

Fryer, P. (1984) *Staying Power: The History of Black People in Britain*, London: Pluto Press.

Gathii, J.T. (2007) 'Imperialism, Colonialism and International Law', *Buffalo Law Review*, 54(4): 1013–66.

Gill, A. and Brah, A. (2014) 'Interrogating Cultural Narratives about "Honour"-Based Violence', *European Journal of Women's Studies*, 21(1): 72–86.

Gill, R. (2004) 'The Imperial Anxieties of a Nineteenth-Century Bigamy Case', *History Workshop Journal*, 57(1): 58–75.

Gleditsch, K., Wucherpfennig, J., Hug, S. and Reigstad, K.G. (2011) 'Polygyny or Misogyny? Reexamining the "First Law of Intergroup Conflict"', *The Journal of Politics*, 73(1): 265–70.

Goldfeder, M. (2017) *Legalizing Plural Marriage: The Next Frontier in Family Law*, Waltham: Brandeis University Press.

Gopal, P. (2019) *Insurgent Empire: Anticolonial Resistance and British Dissent*, London: Verso Books.

Grabham, E. (2006) 'Taxonomies of Inequality: Lawyers, Maps, and the Challenge of Hybridity', *Social & Legal Studies*, 15(1): 5–23.

Granzow, K. (2020) *Invested Indifference: How Violence Persists in Settler Colonial Society*, Chicago: University of Chicago Press.

Greenfield, D.E. (1958) 'Marriage by Chinese Law and Custom in Hong Kong', *International and Comparative Law Quarterly*, 7(3): 437–51.

Grewal, I. (2013) 'Outsourcing Patriarchy', *International Feminist Journal of Politics*, 15(1): 1–19.

Grim, J.A. (1996) 'Cultural Identity, Authenticity, and Community Survival: The Politics of Recognition in the Study of Native American Religions', *American Indian Quarterly*, 20(3/4): 353–76.

Grosfoguel, R. (2007) 'The Epistemic Decolonial Turn', *Cultural Studies*, 21(2–3): 211–23.

Guzman, A.T. (2002) 'Choice of Law: New Foundations', *Georgetown Law Journal*, 90(4): 883–940.

Haggis, J. (2003) 'White Women and Colonialism: Towards a Non-Recuperative History', in R. Lewis and S. Mills (eds) *Feminist Postcolonial Theory: A Reader*, Edinburgh: Edinburgh University Press, pp 161–89.

Hall, C. (2004) 'Of Gender and Empire: Reflections on the Nineteenth Century', in P. Levine (ed) *Gender and Empire*, Oxford: Oxford University Press, pp 46–76.

Hall, J., Neitz, M.J. and Battani, M. (2003) *Sociology on Culture*, London: Routledge.

Hallaq, W.B. (2011) 'On Orientalism, Self-Consciousness and History', *Islamic Law & Society*, 18(3–4): 387–439.

Han, S. (2017) 'The Culture-Religion Nexus: (Neo-)Durkheimianism and Mediatized Confucianism in Korean "Piety Travel"', *Journal of Korean Religions*, 8(2): 91–116.

Hansard (1862) [HC] vol 168, col 1201, [online] Available at: https://api.parliament.uk/historic-hansard/commons/1862/aug/04/question-3#column_1201 [Accessed 28 August 2022].

Harding, R. (2008) 'Recognizing (and Resisting) Regulation: Attitudes to the Introduction of Civil Partnership', *Sexualities*, 11(6): 740–60.

Harding, R. (2012) 'Legal Constructions of Dementia: Discourses of Autonomy at the Margins of Capacity', *Journal of Social Welfare and Family Law*, 34(4): 425–42.

Hassig, R. (2016) *Polygamy and the Rise and Demise of the Aztec Empire*, Albuquerque: University of New Mexico Press.

Hegel, G. (1976) *The Phenomenology of the Spirit*, Oxford: Oxford University Press.

Henriques, H.S.Q. (1908) 'Jewish Marriages and the English Law', *The Jewish Quarterly Review*, 20(3): 391–449.

Herman, D. (2011) *An Unfortunate Coincidence: Jews, Jewishness, and English Law*, Oxford: Oxford University Press.

Herring, J. (2015) 'Making Family Law Less Sexy … and More Careful', in R. Leckey (ed) *After Legal Equality: Family, Sex and Kinship*, London: Routledge, pp 25–41.

Hillman, E. (1975) *Polygamy Reconsidered: African Plural Marriage and the Christian Churches*, Ossining: Orbis Books.

Hines, S. (2013) *Gender, Diversity, Recognition and Citizenship: Towards a Politics of Difference*, Basingstoke: Palgrave Macmillan.

Hinkson, M. (2017) 'Beyond Assimilation and Refusal: A Warlpiri Perspective on the Politics of Recognition', *Postcolonial* Studies, 20(1): 86–100.

Hiraide, L.A. (2021) 'Postcolonial, Decolonial, Anticolonial: Does It Matter?', *New Voices in Postcolonial Studies Magazine*, Summer: 10–15.

Hoffman Williams, S. (ed) (2009) *Constituting Equality: Gender Equality and Constitutional Comparative Law*, Cambridge: Cambridge University Press.

Hollander, R. (2019) 'Indifference as Resistance: Virginia Woolf's Feminist Ethics in *Three Guineas*', *Feminist Modernist Studies*, 2(1): 81–103.

Home Office (2017) 'Immigration Rules Appendix FM: Family Members', *GOV.UK*, [online] 2 May, Available from: https://www.gov.uk/guidance/immigration-rules/updates [Accessed 25 January 2022].

Home Office (2018) *The Independent Review into the Application of Sharia Law in England and Wales*, Cm 9560, London: TSO.

hooks, b. (1986) 'Sisterhood: Political Solidarity Between Women', *Feminist Review*, 23: 125–38.

Hopkins, L. and McAuliffe, C. (2010) 'Split Allegiances: Cultural Muslims and the Tension between Religious and National Identity in Multicultural Societies', *Studies in Ethnicity and Nationalism*, 10(1): 35–58.

Huntington, S. (1996) *The Clash of Civilization and the Remaking of World Order*, New York: Simon and Schuster.

Husni, R. and Newman, D. (2007) *Muslim Women in Law and Society: Annotated Translation of al-Tāhir al-Haddād's* Imra'tunā fi 'l-shari'a wa 'l-mujtama' *with an Introduction*, London: Routledge.

İbiloğlu, A., Atlı, A. and Özkan, M. (2018) 'Negative Effects of Polygamy on Family Members in the Province of Diyarbakir, Turkey', *Cukurova Medical Journal*, 43(4): 982–8.

Igenoza, A.O. (2003) *Polygamy and the African Churches: A Biblical Appraisal of an African Marriage System*, Ibadan: African Association for the Study of Religion.

Isar, Y.R. (2006) 'Cultural Diversity', *Theory, Culture and Society*, 23(2–3): 372–5.

Jacobson, C. and Burton, L. (eds) (2011) *Modern Polygamy in the United States: Historical, Cultural, and Legal Issues*, Oxford: Oxford University Press.

Jacobson, J. (1997) 'Religion and Ethnicity: Dual and Alternative Sources of Identity among Young British Pakistanis', *Ethnic and Racial Studies*, 20(2): 238–56.

Jacobson, J. (1998) *Islam in Transition: Religion and Identity among British Pakistani Youth*, London: Routledge.

Jawad, H. (1998) *The Rights of Women in Islam: An Authentic Approach*, Basingstoke: Palgrave.

Jenks, C. (2005) *Culture* (2nd edn), London: Routledge.

Jivraj, S. and Herman, D. (2009) '"It Is Difficult for a White Judge to Understand": Orientalism, Racialisation and Christianity in English Child Welfare Cases', *Child and Family Law Quarterly*, 21(3): 283–308.

Joffe, L.F. (2016) 'What's the Harm in Polygamy: Multicultural Toleration and Women's Experience of Plural Marriage', *Journal of Law and Religion*, 31(3): 336–53.

John, M. (1996) *Discrepant Dislocations: Feminism, Theory and Postcolonial Histories*, Oakland: University of California Press.

Johnson, R. (2014) 'Reflecting on Polygamy: What's the Harm?', in G. Calder and L.G. Beaman (eds) *Polygamy's Rights and Wrongs: Perspectives on Harm, Family and Law*, Vancouver: University of British Columbia Press, pp 97–119.

Jones, R. and Gnanapala, W. (2000) *Ethnic Minorities and English Law*, London: Trentham Books Ltd.

Kaganas, F. and Murray, C. (1991) 'Law, Women and the Family: The Question of Polygyny in a new South Africa', *Acta Juridica*, 116–34.

Kang'ara, S.W. (2012) 'Beyond Bed and Bread: Making the African State through Marriage Law Reform – Constitutive and Transformative Influences of Anglo-American Legal Thought', *Hastings Race and Poverty Journal*, 9: 353–96.

Kapur, R. (2019) 'On Gender, Alterity and Human Rights: Freedom in a Fishbowl', *Feminist Review*, 122: 167–71.

Kaye, H. (1995) 'Introduction: Imperialism and its Legacies', in V.G. Kiernan, *Imperialism and its Contradictions* (ed H. Kaye), London: Routledge, pp 1–22.

Kennedy, D. (1996) 'Imperial History and Post-Colonial Theory', *The Journal of Imperial and Commonwealth History*, 24(3): 345–63.

Khan, Q. (1988) *The Status of Women in Islam*, Lahore: Islamic Book Foundation.

Khan, S. (2005) 'Reconfiguring the Native Informant: Positionality in the Global Age', *Signs*, 30(4): 2017–37.

Kindregan, C., Jr (2007) 'Religion, Polygamy and Non-Traditional Families: Disparate Views on the Evolution of Marriage in History and in the Debate Over Same-Sex Unions', *Suffolk Law Review*, 41(1): 19–48.

King, U. (2004) 'General Introduction: Gender-Critical Turns in the Study of Religion' in U. King and T. Beattie (eds) *Gender, Religion and Diversity*, London: Continuum, pp 1–31.

Klerman, D., Mahoney, P.G., Spamann, H. and Weinstein, M.I. (2011) 'Legal Origin or Colonial History?', *Journal of Legal Analysis*, 3(2): 379–409.

Knop, K. (2008) 'Citizenship, Public and Private', *Law and Contemporary Problems*, 71(3): 309–42.

Kolsky, E. (2010) 'The Rule of Colonial Indifference: Rape on Trial in Early Colonial India, 1805–57', *The Journal of Asian Studies*, 69(4): 1093–117.

Koskenniemi, M. (2011) 'Empire and International Law: The Real Spanish Contribution', *University of Toronto Law Journal*, 61(1): 1–36.

Kusow, A. (2003) 'Beyond Indigenous Authenticity: Reflections on the Insider/Outsider Debate in Immigration Research', *Symbolic Interaction*, 26(4): 591–9.

Kwok, P. (1991) 'Gospel and Culture', *Christianity and Crisis*, 51(10–11): 223–4.

Kwok, P. (2012) '2011 Presidential Address: Empire and the Study of Religion', *Journal of the American Academy of Religion*, 80(2): 285–303.

Landry, D. and MacLean, G. (1996) 'Introduction', in D. Landry and G. MacLean (eds) *The Spivak Reader: Selected Works*, London: Routledge, pp 1–14.

Law Commission (1971) *Family Law: Polygamous Marriages*, Law Com No 42, London: HMSO.

Law Commission (2015a) *Getting Married: A Scoping Paper*, London: HMSO.

Law Commission (2015b) *Reform of Offences Against the Person*, Law Com No 361, London: HMSO.

Law Commission (2020) *Getting Married: A Consultation Paper on Weddings Law*, Consultation Paper No 247, London: HMSO.

Law Commission (2022) *Celebrating Marriage: A New Weddings Law*, HC 557 Law Com No 408, London: TSO.

Law Commission and Scottish Law Commission (1985) *Private International Law. Polygamous Marriages: Capacity to Contract a Polygamous Marriage and Related Issues*, Law Com No 146, Scot Law Com No 96, Cmnd 9595, London: HMSO.

Lee, K.-W. (1997) 'Is the Glass Half-Empty or Half-Full? Rethinking the Problems of Postcolonial Revisionism', *Cultural Critique*, 36: 89–117.

Lee, W.A. (2013) 'A Case for Hard-Heartedness: *Clarissa*, Indifferency, Impersonality', *Eighteenth-Century Fiction*, 26(1): 33–65.

Lemmings, D. (1996) 'Marriage and the Law in the Eighteenth Century: Hardwicke's Marriage Act of 1753', *The Historical Journal*, 39(2): 339–60.

Leo, J. (2001) 'The History and Description of Africa', in A. Hatfield (ed) *Amazons, Savages and Machiavels: Travel and Colonial Writing in English, 1550–1630*, Oxford: Oxford University Press, pp 139–51.

Lewis, B. (1982) 'The Question of Orientalism', *The New York Review*, [online] 24 June, Available from: https://www.nybooks.com/articles/1982/06/24/the-question-of-orientalism/ [Accessed 23 January 2022].

Lewis, R. (2003) 'On Veiling, Vision and Voyage: Cross-Cultural Dressing and Narratives of Identity', in in R. Lewis and S. Mills (eds) *Feminist Postcolonial Theory: A Reader*, Edinburgh: Edinburgh University Press, pp 520–41.

Lewis, R. and Mills, S. (2003) 'Introduction', in R. Lewis and S. Mills (eds) *Feminist Postcolonial Theory: A Reader*, Edinburgh: Edinburgh University Press, pp 1–24.

Lichtheim, G. (1971) *Imperialism*, London: Allen Lane.

Lilith, R. (2000–01) 'Buying a Wife but Saving a Child: A Deconstruction of Popular Rhetoric and Legal Analysis of Mail-Order Brides and Inter-Country Adoptions', *Buffalo Women's Law Journal*, 9: 225–62.

Lim, B.S., Hashim, A. and Buttny, R. (2014) 'Accounts of Religio-Cultural Identity in Singapore and Malaysia', *International Journal of the Sociology of Language*, 229: 9–28.

Lincoln, M. (2021) *London and the Seventeenth Century: The Making of the World's Greatest City*, New Haven, CT: Yale University Press.

Little, D. (1979) 'Three Arab Critiques of Orientalism', *Muslim World*, 69(2): 118–21.

Liversage, A. (2014) 'Secrets and Lies: When Ethnic Minority Youth have a *Nikah*', in P. Shah, M.-C. Foblets and M. Rohe (eds) *Family, Religion and Law: Cultural Encounters in Europe*, London: Ashgate, pp 165–80.

Locke, J. (1706) 'Of the Conduct of Understanding', in P. King (ed) *Posthumous Works of Mr John Locke*, London: WB, pp 1–137.

Lord Collins of Mapesbury, Morse, C.G.J., McClean, D., Briggs, A., Harris, J., McLachlan, C., Dickinson, A. and McEleavy, P. (2012) *Dicey, Morris and Collins on the Conflict of Laws* (15th edn), London: Sweet & Maxwell.

Lyons, K., Parreñas, J. and Tamarkin, N. (2017) 'Engagements with Decolonization and Decoloniality in and at the Interfaces of STS', *Catalyst: Feminism, Theory and Technoscience*, 3(1): 1–47.

Macedo, S. (2015) *Just Married: Same-Sex Couples, Monogamy & The Future of Marriage*, Princeton, NJ: Princeton University Press.

Mack, P. (2003) 'Religion, Feminism, and the Problem of Agency: Reflections on Eighteenth-Century Quakerism', *Signs*, 29(1): 149–77.

MacKenzie, J. (1994) 'Edward Said and the Historians', *Nineteenth-Century Contexts*, 18(1): 9–25.

Mahmood, S. (2005) *Politics of Piety: The Islamic Revival and the Feminist Subject*, Princeton, NJ: Princeton University Press.

Malik, M. (2007) 'Modernising Discrimination Law: Proposals for a Single Equality Act for Great Britain', *International Journal of Discrimination and the Law*, 9(2): 73–94.

Malik, M. (2014) 'Minorities and Law: Past and Present', *Current Legal Problems*, 67(1): 67–98.

Majeed, D. (2015) *Polygyny: What It Means when African American Muslim Women Share their Husbands*, Gainesville: University Press of Florida.

Mama, A. (1995) *Beyond the Masks: Race, Gender and Subjectivity*, London: Routledge.

Marasinghe, M.L. (1978) 'Polygamous Marriages and the Principle of Mutation in the Conflict of Laws', *McGill Law Journal*, 24(3): 395–421.

March, A. (2011) 'Is there a Right to Polygamy? Marriage, Equality and Subsidizing Families in Liberal Public Justification', *Journal of Moral Philosophy*, 8(2): 246–72.

McClintock, A. (1995) *Imperial Leather: Race, Gender and Sexuality in the Colonial Contest*, London: Routledge.

McDermott, R. and Monroe, K.R. (2018) *The Evils of Polygyny: Evidence of Its Harm to Women, Men, and Society*, Ithaca, NY: Cornell University Press.

McDougall, S. (2010) 'Bigamy: A Male Crime in Medieval Europe?', *Gender & History*, 22(2): 430–46.

McGrath, B. and McGarry, O. (2014) 'The Religio-Cultural Dimensions of Life for Young Muslim Women in a Small Irish Town', *Journal of Youth Studies*, 17(7): 948–64.

Mehdi, R. and Nielsen, J. (eds) (2011) *Embedding Mahr (Islamic Dowry) in the European Legal System*, Copenhagen: DJØF Publishing.

Midgley, C. (1998) 'Gender and Imperialism: Mapping the Connections', in C. Midgley (ed) *Gender and Imperialism*, Manchester: Manchester University Press, pp 1–20.

Mills, A. (2006) 'The Private History of International Law', *International and Comparative Law Quarterly*, 55(1): 1–50.

Mohanty, C.T. (1984) 'Under Western Eyes: Feminist Scholarship and Colonial Discourses', *Boundary*, 2(12/13): 333–58.

Mojab, S. (2012) 'The Politics of Culture, Racism and Nationalism in Honour Killing', *Canadian Criminal Law Review*, 16(2): 115–34.

Mommsen, W. (1981) *Theories of Imperialism*, London: Weidenfeld and Nicolson.

Mookherjee, M. (2005) 'Affective Citizenship: Feminism, Postcolonialism and the Politics of Recognition', *Critical Review of International Social and Political Philosophy*, 8(1): 31–50.

Moore-Gilbert, B. (2000) 'Spivak and Bhabha', in H. Schwarz and S. Ray (eds) *A Companion to Postcolonial Studies*, Malden, MA: Blackwell, pp 451–66.

Morris, J.H.C. (1953) 'The Recognition of Polygamous Marriages in English Law', *Harvard Law Review*, 66(6): 961–1012.

Muir Watt, H. (2011) 'Private International Law beyond the Schism', *Transnational Legal Theory*, 2(3): 347–427.

Muir Watt, H. (2017) 'Hospitality, Tolerance, and Exclusion in Legal Form: Private International Law and the Politics of Difference', *Current Legal Problems*, 70(1): 111–47.

Naber, N. (2005) 'Muslim First, Arab Second: A Strategic Politics of Race and Gender', *The Muslim World*, 95(4): 479–95.

Nair, R.B. (1999) 'Postcoloniality and the Matrix of Indifference', *India International Centre Quarterly*, 26(2): 7–24.

Nair, R.B. (2002) *Lying on the Postcolonial Couch: The Idea of Indifference*, Minneapolis: University of Minnesota Press.

Naqvi, Z. (2020) 'Nikah Ceremonies in the UK – A Tool for Empowerment?', in R.C. Akhtar, P. Nash and R. Probert (eds) *Cohabitation and Religious Marriage: Status, Similarities and Solutions*, Bristol: Bristol University Press, pp 103–18.

Narayan, U. (1997) *Dislocating Culture: Identities, Traditions, and Third World Feminism*, London: Routledge.

Narayan, U. (1998) 'Essence of Culture and a Sense of History: A Feminist Critique of Cultural Essentialism', *Hypatia*, 13(2): 86–106.

Narayan, U. (2019) 'Sisterhood and "Doing Good": Asymmetries of Western Feminist Location, Access and Orbits of Concern', *Feminist Philosophy Quarterly*, 5(2): Article 7, [online] Available from: https://doi.org/10.5206/fpq/2019.2.7299 [Accessed 28 August 2022].

Nash, P.S. (2017) 'Sharia in England: The Marriage Law Solution', *Oxford Journal of Law and Religion*, 6(3): 523–43.

Nussbaum, M. (2000) *Women and Human Development: The Capabilities Approach*, Cambridge: Cambridge University Press.

Okoli, C. (2019) 'Private International Law in Africa: Comparative Lessons', *Conflict of Laws*, [online] 26 November, Available from: https://conflictoflaws.net/2019/private-international-law-in-africa-comparative-lessons/?print=print:%20Private%20International%20Law%20in%20Africa:%20Comparative%20Lessons%20%E2%80%93%20Chukwuma%20Okoli [Accessed 24 January 2022].

Oksala, J. (2017) 'Feminism and Power', in A. Garry, S. Khader and A. Stone (eds) *The Routledge Companion to Feminist Philosophy*, London: Routledge, pp 678–88.

Olds, G. (2010) *Religio-Cultural Integration among Muslim-Americans*, College Station: Texas A & M University.

Onalaja, T. and Onalaja, K. (2004) *Polygamists' Wives and the Chamber of Secrets: How Polygamists' Wives Affect our World*, Milton Keynes: TK-One Ventures UK.

O'Sullivan, K. and Jackson, L. (2017) 'Muslim Marriage (Non) recognition: Implications and Possible Solutions', *Journal of Social Welfare and Family Law*, 39(1): 22–41.

Otter, R. (2015) *In Defense of Plural Marriage*, Cambridge: Cambridge University Press.

Pande, R. (2015) '"I Arranged My Own Marriage": Arranged Marriages and Post-Colonial Feminism', *Gender, Place and Culture*, 22(2): 172–87.

Parekh, B. (2010) *Rethinking Multiculturalism: Cultural Diversity and Political Theory*, Basingstoke: Palgrave Macmillan.

Parker, J. (2018) 'Questioning Appropriation: Agency and Complicity in a Transnational Feminist Location Politics', *Journal of Feminist Scholarship*, 3(3): Article 2, [online] Available from: https://digitalcommons.uri.edu/jfs/vol3/iss3/2 [Accessed 25 August 2022].

Parveen, R. (2018) 'Religious-Only Marriages in the UK: Legal Positionings and Muslim Women's Experiences', *Sociology of Islam*, 6(3): 1–24.

Parveen, R. (2020) 'From Regulating Marriage Ceremonies to Recognizing Marriage Ceremonies', in R.C. Akhtar, P. Nash and R. Probert (eds) *Cohabitation and Religious Marriage: Status, Similarities and Solutions*, Bristol: Bristol University Press, pp 85–102.

Pathak, Z. and Rajan, R.S. (1992) 'Shahbano', in J. Butler and J. Scott (eds) *Feminists Theorize the Political*, London: Routledge, pp 257–79.

Patterson, F.A. (1931–38) *History of Great Britain*, in *The Works of John Milton*, 18 vols, New York: Columbia University Press.

Pearsall, S.M.S. (2019) *Polygamy: An Early American History*, New Haven, CT: Yale University Press.

Perez, B.E. (2003) 'Woman Warrior Meets Mail-Order Bride: Finding an Asian American Voice in the Women's Movement', *Berkeley Women's Law Journal*, 18(1): 2110–36.

Phillips, A. (2007) *Multiculturalism without Culture*, Princeton, NJ: Princeton University Press.

Phillips, A. (2010) *Gender and Culture*, Cambridge: Polity Press.

Poulter, S. (1976) '*Hyde v. Hyde*: A Reappraisal', *The International and Comparative Law Quarterly*, 25(3): 475–508.

Poulter, S. (1979) 'The Definition of Marriage in English Law', *Modern Law Review*, 42(4): 409–29.

Poulter, S. (1986) *English Law and Ethnic Minority Customs*, London: Butterworths.

Probert, R. (2007) '*Hyde v Hyde*: Defining or Defending Marriage?', *Child and Family Law Quarterly*, 19(3): 322–36.

Probert, R. (2008) 'R v Millis Reconsidered: Binding Contracts and Bigamous Marriages', *Legal Studies*, 28(3): 337–55.

Probert, R. (2009) *Marriage, Law and Practice in the Long Eighteenth Century: A Reassessment*, Cambridge: Cambridge University Press.

Probert, R. (2012) *The Changing Legal Regulation of Cohabitation: From Fornicators to Family, 1600–2010*, Cambridge: Cambridge University Press.

Probert, R. (2013) 'The Evolving Concept of "Non-Marriage"', *Child and Family Law Quarterly*, 25(3): 314–35.

Probert, R. (2017) 'English Exports: Invoking the Common Law of Marriage across the Empire in the Nineteenth Century', in J. Moses (ed) *Marriage, Law and Modernity: Global Histories*, London: Bloomsbury, pp 168–80.

Probert, R. (2019) '*R v Hall* and the Changing Perceptions of the Crime of Bigamy', *Legal Studies*, 39(1): 1–17.

Probert, R. (2021) *Tying the Knot: The Formation of Marriage, 1836–2020*, Cambridge: Cambridge University Press.

Probert, R. (2022) 'Secular or Sacred? The Ambiguity of "Civil" Marriage in the Marriage Act 1836', *The Journal of Legal History*, 43(2): 136–60.

Probert, R. and D'Arcy-Brown, L. (2019) 'The Transportation of Bigamists in Early Nineteenth-Century England and Wales', *The Journal of Legal History*, 40(3): 223–52.

Probert, R., Harding, M. and Dempsey, B. (2013) 'A Uniform Law of Marriage? The 1868 Royal Commission Reconsidered', *Child and Family Law Quarterly*, 30: 217–35.

Probert, R., Akhtar, R. and Blake, S. (2022) *When Is a Wedding Not a Marriage? Exploring Non-Legally Binding Ceremonies – Final Report*, London: Nuffield Foundation.

Quijano, A. (1992) 'Colonialidad y Modernidad/Racionalidad', *Perú Indígena*, 13(29): 11–20.

Rackley, E. (2013) *Women, Judging and the Judiciary: From Difference to Diversity*, London: Routledge.

Rajan, R.S. (1993) *Real and Imagined Women: Gender, Culture and Postcolonialism*, London: Routledge.

Reddy, R. (2008) 'Gender, Culture and the Law: Approaches to "Honour Crimes" in the UK', *Feminist Legal Studies*, 16: 305–21.

Rehman, J. (2015) *Islamic State Practices, International Law and the Threat from Terrorism: A Critique of the "Clash of Civilizations" in the New World Order*, London: Hart Publishing.

Reid, K. (1998) *A Practitioner's Guide to the European Convention on Human Rights*, London: Sweet & Maxwell.

Riles, A. (2008) 'Cultural Conflicts', *Law and Contemporary Problems*, 71(3): 273–308.

Rivers, J. (2012) 'Is English Law Christian?', in N. Spencer (ed) *Religion and Law*, London: Theos, pp 143–50.

Rivers, J. (2017) 'Could Marriage Be Disestablished?', *Tyndale Bulletin*, 68(1): 121–51.

Ritchie, A. and Barker, M. (2006) '"There Aren't Words for What We Do or How We Feel So We Have to Make Them Up": Constructing Polyamorous Languages in a Culture of Compulsory Monogamy', *Sexualities*, 9(5): 584–601.

Roald, A.S. (2004) 'Who Are the Muslims? Questions of Identity, Gender and Culture in Research Methodologies', in U. King and T. Beattie (eds) *Gender, Religion and Diversity*, London: Continuum, pp 179–89.

Roy, A. (2008) 'Postcolonial Theory and Law: A Critical Introduction', *Adelaide Law Review*, 29(1/2): 315–57.

Ruskola, T. (2013) *Legal Orientalism: China, the United States, and Modern Law*, Cambridge, MA: Harvard University Press.

Sahgal, G. and Yuval-Davis, N. (1992) 'Introduction', in G. Sahgal and N. Yuval-Davis (eds) *Refusing Holy Orders: Women and Fundamentalism in Britain*, London: Virago, pp 7–31.

Said, E. (1978) *Orientalism*, New York: Pantheon Books.

Said, E. (1994) *Culture and Imperialism*, London: Vintage.

Sanasarian, E. (1986) 'Political Activism and Islamic Identity in Iran', in L. Iglitzin and R. Ross, *Women in the World 1975–1985* (2nd edn), Santa Barbara, CA: ABC-Clio, pp 207–24.

Sandberg, R. (2021) 'Marital Problems: The Law Commission's "Getting Married" Consultation Paper and Non-Qualifying Wedding Ceremonies', *Ecclesiastical Law Journal*, 23(2): 140–59.

Sankin Speech Improvement (nd) 'What Is the Difference Between Voice and Speech?', [online] Available from: http://www.sankinspeechimprovement.com/speech-pathologist-voice-vs-speech/ [Accessed 23 January 2022].

Sartre, J.-P. (1968) *Anti-Semite and Jew*, New York: Grove Press Inc.

Schmidhauser, J.R. (1992) 'Legal Imperialism: Its Enduring Impact on Colonial and Post-Colonial Judicial Systems', *International Political Science Review*, 13(3): 321–34.

Schutte, O. (1998) 'Cultural Alterity: Cross-Cultural Communication and Feminist Theory in North-South Contexts', *Hypatia*, 13(2): 53–72.

Scott, J.W. (1999) *Gender and the Politics of History*, New York: Columbia University Press.

Selfe, P. and Starbuck, M. (1998) *Religion*, London: Hodder and Stoughton.

Sen, A. (2009) *The Idea of Justice*, Cambridge, MA: Harvard University Press.

Seth, S. (2013) 'Postcolonial Theory and the Critique of International Relations', in S. Seth (ed) *Postcolonial Theory and International Relations: A Critical Introduction*, London: Routledge, pp 15–31.

Shah, P. (2003) 'Attitudes to Polygamy in English law', *International Comparative Law Quarterly*, 52(2): 369–400.

Shah, P. and Menski, W. (eds) (2006) *Migration, Diasporas and Legal Systems in Europe*, London: Routledge-Cavendish.

Shanley, M.L. (1989) *Feminism, Marriage, and the Law in Victorian England, 1850–1895*, Princeton, NJ: Princeton University Press.

Shrage, L. (2016) 'Polygamy, Privacy and Equality', in E. Brake (ed) *After Marriage: Rethinking Marital Relationships*, Oxford: Oxford University Press, pp 160–79.

Shifman, P. (1978) 'The English Law of Bigamy in a Multi-Confessional Society: The Israel Experience', *American Journal of Comparative Law*, 26(1): 79–90.

Sinclair, I.M. (1954) 'Polygamous Marriages in English Law', *British Yearbook of International Law*, 31: 248–72.

Sinha, M. (2004) 'Nations in an Imperial Crucible', in P. Levine (ed) *Gender and Empire*, Oxford: Oxford University Press, pp 181–202.

Slonim-Nevo, V., Al-Krenawi, A. and Yuval-Shani, B. (2008) 'Polygynous Marriage in the Middle East: Stories of Success and Failures', *Ethnology*, 47(3): 195–208.

Smart, C. (1989) *Feminism and the Power of Law*, London: Routledge.

Smith, J.A.C. (1952) 'Eastern Marriages in English Law', *International and Comparative Law Quarterly*, 1(3): 301–12.

Snow, S. and Jones, E. (2011) 'Immigration and the National Health Service: Putting History to the Forefront', *History & Policy*, [online] 8 March, Available from: https://www.historyandpolicy.org/policy-papers/papers/immigration-and-the-national-health-service-putting-history-to-the-forefron [Accessed 24 January 2022].

Sokol, M. (2009) 'Jeremy Bentham on Love and Marriage: A Utilitarian Proposal for Short-Term Marriage', *Journal of Legal History*, 30(1): 1–21.

Song, S. (2016) 'Polygamy in Nineteenth-Century America', in J. Bennion and L. Fishbayn Joffe (eds) *The Polygamy Question*, Logan: Utah State University Press, pp 25–41.

Soothill, K., Ackerley, E., Sanderson, B. and Peelo, M. (1999) 'The Place of Bigamy in the Pantheon of Crime?', *Medicine, Science and the Law*, 39(1): 65–71.

Southern, R.W. (1962) *Western Views of Islam in the Middle Ages*, Cambridge, MA: Harvard University Press.

Spivak, G.C. (1988) *In Other Worlds: Essays in Cultural Politics*, London: Routledge.

Spivak, G.C. (1989) 'Who Claims Alterity?', in B. Kruger and P. Mariani (eds) *Remaking History*, Seattle, WA: Bay Press, pp 57–72.

Spivak, G.C. (1999) *A Critique of Postcolonial Reason*, Cambridge, MA: Harvard University Press.

Spivak, G.C. (2003) *Death of a Discipline*, New York: Columbia University Press.

Stybnarova, N. (2020) 'Teleology Behind the Prohibition of Recognition of Polygamous Marriages Under the EU Family Reunification Directive: A Critique of Rule Effectiveness', *Journal of Muslim Minority Affairs*, 40(1): 104–16.

Sweet, J. (2013) 'Equality, Democracy and Monogamy: Discourses of Canadian Nation Building in the 2010–2011 British Columbia Polygamy Reference', *Canadian Journal of Law and Society*, 28(1): 1–19.

Talbot, C.H. (1954) *The Anglo-Saxon Missionaries in Germany, Being the Lives of SS Willibrord, Boniface, Leoba and Lebuin together with the Hodoepericon of St Willibald and a Selection from the Correspondence of St Boniface*, London and New York: Sheed and Ward.

Taras, R. (2013) '"Islamophobia Never Stands Still": Race, Religion, and Culture', *Ethnic and Racial Studies*, 36(3): 417–33.

Taylor, C. (1994) 'The Politics of Recognition', in A. Gutmann (ed) *Multiculturalism: Examining the Politics of Recognition*, Princeton, NJ: Princeton University Press, pp 25–73.

Thornton, A.P. (1961–62) 'Colonialism', *International Journal*, 17(4): 335–57.

Turner, J. (2020) *Bordering Intimacy: Postcolonial Governance and the Policing of Family*, Manchester: Manchester University Press.

Uddin, I. (2018) '*Nikah*-Only Marriages: Causes, Motivations, and their Impact on Dispute Resolution and Islamic Divorce Proceedings in England and Wales', *Oxford Journal of Law and Religion*, 7(3): 401–26.

van der Vleuten, A. (2007) *The Price of Gender Equality: Member States and Governance in the European Union*, London: Ashgate.

Van Herck, W. and Drigo, A. (2019) 'The Plausibility of Pure Religion: Olivier Roy's Thesis about the Separation between Religion and Culture', *Toronto Journal of Theology*, 35(2): 150–60.

Vanner, C. (2015) 'Positionality at the Center: Constructing an Epistemological and Methodological Approach for a Western Feminist Doctoral Candidate Conducting Research in the Postcolonial', *International Journal of Qualitative Methods*, [online], Available from: https://doi.org/10.1177/1609406915618094 [Accessed 26 August 2022].

Vasallo, B. (2019) 'Monogamous Mind, Polyamorous Terror', *Sociological Research*, 24(4): 680–90.

Verma, R.R. (1995) 'Femininity, Equality and Personhood', in M. Nussbaum and J. Glover (eds) *Women, Culture and Development: A Study of Human Capabilities*, London: Clarendon Press, pp 433–43.

Vlasoff, C. (2013) *Gender Equality and Inequality in Rural India: Blessed with a Son*, Basingstoke: Palgrave Macmillan.

Vogel, U. (1991) 'Political Philosophers and the Trouble with Polygamy: Patriarchal Reasoning in Modern Natural Law', *History of Political Thought*, 12(2): 229–51.

Volpp, L. (2001) 'Feminism Versus Multiculturalism', *Columbia Law Review*, 101(5): 1181–218.

Vora, V. (2016) 'Unregistered Muslim Marriages in England and Wales: The Issue of Discrimination through "Non-Marriage Declarations"', in Y. Suleiman and P. Anderson (eds) *Muslims in the UK and Europe II*, Cambridge: Centre of Islamic Studies, 129–41.

Warner, M. (1999) *The Trouble with Normal: Sex, Politics, and the Ethics of Queer Life*, Cambridge, MA: Harvard University Press.

Weber, M. (1965) *The Sociology of Religion*, London: Methuen.

West, T.C. (2010) 'Extending Black Feminist Sisterhood in the Face of Violence: Fanon, White Women, and Veiled Muslim Women', in M. del Guadalupe Davidson, K.T. Gines and D.L. Marcano (eds) *Convergences: Black Feminism and Continental Philosophy*, Albany: State University of New York Press, pp 157–81.

Whitehead, P. and Crawshaw P. (2012) 'Markets, Privatisation and Justice: Some Critical Reflections', in P. Whitehead and P. Crawshaw (eds) *Organising Neoliberalism: Markets, Privatisation and Justice*, London: Anthem Press, pp 229–41.

Wiebracht, B. (2015) 'First-Cousin Marriage in Tudor and Stuart England: 1540–1688', *Journal of Family History*, 40(1): 24–38.

Williams, G.L. (1950) 'Bigamy and the Third Marriage', *Modern Law Review*, 13(4): 417–27.

Williams, P. (1991) *The Alchemy of Race and Rights*, Cambridge, MA: Harvard University Press.

Williams, W. (1982) 'The Equality Crisis: Some Reflections on Culture, Courts and Feminism', *Women's Rights Law Reporter*, 14(2/3): 151–74.

Wilson, K. (2004) 'Empire, Gender, and Modernity in the Eighteenth Century', in P. Levine (ed) *Gender and Empire*, Oxford: Oxford University Press, pp 14–45.

Wing, A.K. (ed) (2000) *Global Critical Race Feminism: An International Reader*, New York: New York University Press.

Wing, A.K. (2001) 'Polygamy from Southern Africa to Black Britannia to Black America: Global Critical Race Feminism as Legal Reform for the Twenty-First Century', *Journal of Contemporary Legal Issues*, 11(2): 811–80.

Winkel, H. (2019) 'Religious Cultures and Gender Cultures: Tracing Gender Differences across Religious Cultures', *Journal of Contemporary Religion*, 34(2): 241–51.

Witte, J., Jr (2015) *The Western Case for Monogamy Over Polygamy*, Cambridge: Cambridge University Press.

Woodhull, W. (2003) 'Unveiling Algeria', in R. Lewis and S. Mills (eds) *Feminist Postcolonial Theory: A Reader*, Edinburgh: Edinburgh University Press, pp 567–85.

Yeatman, A. (1993) 'Voice and Representation in the Politics of Difference', in S. Gunew and A. Yeatman (eds) *Feminism and the Politics of Difference*, London: Allen and Unwin, pp 228–45.

Yeğenoğlu, M. (1998) *Colonial Fantasies: Towards a Feminist Reading of Orientalism*, Cambridge: Cambridge University Press.

Young, I.M. (1990) *Justice and the Politics of Difference*, Princeton, NJ: Princeton University Press.

Young, I.M. (1997) *Intersecting Voices: Dilemmas of Gender, Political Philosophy and Policy*, Princeton, NJ: Princeton University Press.

Young, R. (1995) *Colonial Desire: Hybridity in Theory, Culture and Race*, London: Routledge.

Zalesne, D. and Dexter, A. (2018) 'From Marriage to Households: Towards Equal Treatment of Intimate Forms of Life', *Buffalo Law Review*, 66(4): 909–77.

Zayid, M. (1980) *The Quran: An English Translation of the Meaning of the Quran*, Beirut: Dar Al-Coura.

Zeitzen, M.K. (2018) *Elite Malay Polygamy: Wives, Wealth and Woes in Malaysia*, New York: Berghahn Books.

Zubair, S. and Zubair, M. (2017) 'Situating Islamic Feminism(s): Lived Religion, Negotiation of Identity and Assertion of Third Space by Muslim Women in Pakistan', *Women's Studies International Forum*, 63: 17–26.

Index

References to footnotes show both the page number and the note number (231n3)